COLLEGE FINDER

THE COLLEGE FINDER

Steven R. Antonoff, Ph.D.

FAWCETT BOOKS
THE RANDOM HOUSE PUBLISHING GROUP • NEW YORK

A Fawcett Book
Published by The Random House Publishing Group

www.ballantinebooks.com

Library of Congress Cataloging-in-Publication Data
Antonoff, Steven R.
The college finder / Steven R. Antonoff.—Rev. ed.
p. cm.
Includes indexes.
ISBN 0-449-00389-2 (alk. paper)
1. College choice—United States. 2. Universities and colleges—
United States. I. Title
LB2350.5.A58 1999
378.73—dc21 98-45525

Text design by Holly Johnson
Cover design by Kristine Mills-Noble

Manufactured in the United States of America

First Edition: September 1993
Revised Edition: April 1999

8 10 9 7

To Joshua, Jacob, Lauren, Rebekah,
Kate, Rachel, Elizabeth, and Benjamin:

Stand for something of value, be who you are, and make humor a part of every day.

CONTENTS

ACKNOWLEDGMENTS

I want to extend my gratitude to my students over the years who, often unknowingly, gave me ideas and inspired the compilation of many of the lists in this book. Several people provided research time to this project. Margaret Palmer Van De Mark researched lists with passion, coordinated reprint permission efforts, and laughed at my jokes as if she thought they were funny. Special thanks to Anjenette Cooper, who was tireless in her pursuit of accurate information, and to Paul Gerdes, who was particularly helpful with the tabulation of the Experts' Choice surveys. I am also indebted to Mitch Robinson, Cheryl Clark, Ruth Perotin, and Rebecca Clark. Particular thanks to Marie A. Friedemann: tangibly, she provided good ideas, critiqued the book at various stages, and helped me think through issues I confronted; intangibly, she gave me assurance and friendship.

For this second edition, I thank Mark Guenther, my assistant at Antonoff Associates, for providing research coordination, a strong right arm, and many laughs throughout the process of revising. Most of all, I thank Mark for giving me the confidence to relax a bit during the months of manuscript preparation and enjoy the world outside of the office. Thanks also to Jackie Howard, typist extraordinaire, and, once again, to Ruth Perotin, my trusted associate. I dedicate this edition to the memory of Paul Gerdes. Paul was a senior at Macalester College in Minnesota when he died in March of 1998. Paul's work remains on these pages. I will miss him.

My thanks go to the educational consultants and high school counselors who responded to my surveys. These professionals are often underappreciated for their long hours and for the wealth of expertise they bring to help students and families through the difficult months preceding college entry. I am grateful for the assistance of the people on college campuses, among them faculty members, admission personnel, and other administrators, who offered answers and insights. In addition to thanking those who support and are knowledgeable about higher education, I extend my gratitude to the writers and publishers who granted me permission to cite their work on these pages. Finally, I recognize those who shared my vision about this book and agreed that the more information available to a student as the college choice is being made, the better that choice will be.

Steven R. Antonoff, Ph.D.
Denver, Colorado
April 1999

INTRODUCTION

Incredible options exist in higher education today. You have so many choices and possibilities as you think about where to spend your college years. Since there are over 3,000 colleges and universities in this country alone, you should never feel that you won't be able to find the right place to go to school.

For over a quarter of a century, I have had the privilege of not only aiding students in their college choices, but also sharing in their development as they experience the college years. I've seen the excitement on students' faces when they realize that colleges really do want them. I've consulted with parents who, after a little research, find a college for their teenager that is both appropriate and affordable. Most important, I've celebrated with students who have grown by going to the right college. Students who have found the right school often find themselves feeling enthusiastic about learning and about relating to their new peers, professors, and environment. They can see themselves reaching their true potential intellectually, socially, and emotionally.

No college, however, can guarantee you a successful experience. The "perfect" college likely does not exist. There are both good and bad aspects to any college. Yet your college years are filled with opportunity—opportunity to test your limits, to challenge, to discover. Some of that opportunity is available automatically because of your youth and the overall advantage of the collegiate experience. But much more of an opportunity exists because you have chosen a college that fits your personality, intellectual readiness, and interests. The right college can provide opportunities for growth.

Colleges are neither equal nor identical. Besides obvious differences of size, academic offerings, location, and the like, each school has a unique ethic, culture, and feel, all of which can be either growth producing or growth inhibiting. And success in college really counts. A strong college grade point average, good recommendations, and personal experiences that make you informed, caring, and value-centered matter much more than the name of the college in terms of admission to graduate schools and, more important, employment opportunities and life satisfaction.

The time spent on finding a college that matches your interests, aptitudes, and feelings pays off handsomely. The levels of preparation, interest, and motivation for college vary from student to student. And colleges vary in countless ways. It is the match between you and the school that ultimately determines your academic and social comfort. But the search takes time and effort. You should use the best resources available—the most knowledgeable people and the most thorough literature—to help in your transition from high school to college. There are few easy answers. Picking a college requires commitment, dedication, intensity, and passion. But it can be done. And the results, I'm convinced, are worth the effort.

I've written this book to help you and your parents find a good college match. In 1970, I started working on a college campus. Through the next eleven years, I worked in several administrative positions, including dean of students, at the University of Denver. I listened to students talk about what they got out of their college years, I saw how admission offices operate, and I learned about how families grapple with college costs. In 1981, I left my administrative position, then dean of admission and financial aid, to begin work as an educational consultant because I wanted to work directly with students who were choosing colleges. I have worked with over 2,500 students in the last seventeen years. Many of my clients are top students; many are not. Some can afford any college; most cannot. Some attend public high schools; some private. Some will be first-generation college students; others have college-educated parents. Some will be first-year college students; others are transfers. Whatever their background, each shares the belief that taking some extra time and exploring colleges thoroughly is worth it.

The college search has its share of myth and mystique, which can often hinder a full exploration of your options. Contrary to popular opinion, you don't need all A's (or even all B's) to be admitted to a "good" college. While there are about forty colleges that accept fewer than half of their applicants, the vast majority accept well over 80 percent of those who apply. Families don't need the wealth of Bill Gates to afford the cost of college today. Of course, there are colleges that are very expensive, but many others provide a high-quality academic experience at a reasonable price. Bigger colleges are not always impersonal, small colleges are not without a social life, more expensive colleges don't necessarily provide a better education, Eastern colleges (or private colleges) are not inherently better, and Western colleges are neither laid-back nor fundamentally bizarre. Hopefully, this book will help you and your parents to get beyond these and other misconceptions and really explore.

Over the last two decades, I have also had the opportunity to listen as students struggle to understand the distinctions between colleges and to make sense of college planning resources. I'm troubled by the lack of good materials available. I'm concerned by the perception that only a handful of colleges in the country are worth the price. It bothers me that one of every two undergraduate students transfers from one four-year college to another. Commonly, on my travels, students tell me they have no idea why they selected their college in the first place. Few investments as costly or as important are made on so inaccurate data. After talking to students, I realized that many of them had the same complaints about the resources that are available:

- *Materials from colleges are often the same.* Students frequently complain about the slickness and the generality of college brochures, catalogs, and Web sites. Beautiful pictures, coupled with exaggerated descriptions of the virtues of the school, can hardly help you discern differences. Although your mailbox may be crammed with the products of a multimillion-dollar higher education marketing industry, you may remain disillusioned and confused.
- *Many of the guidebooks available include too much information and have too little subjective content.* These thick college guides don't really allow readers to differentiate among colleges. A state-by-state listing of over 3,000 colleges and their features might be helpful if you knew where to begin and how to compare.
- *Many of the narrative-type guidebooks include too much subjective information regarding too few colleges.* Guidebooks that provide "up close and personal" reviews about individual colleges are fun to read, but they may provide only two- or three-page subjective narratives on fewer than 10 percent of the colleges in the nation. Many schools that may be appropriate for you are missing.
- *Other materials are too limited in scope.* Magazines that offer

"best college" issues provide sufficient information about the academic side of campus life and perceptions of quality but don't give the great, diverse majority of college-bound students information about social, financial, or athletic aspects of a particular campus. The cost guides are good but, again, deal with only one aspect of choosing a college. Web sites can be helpful but, again, make differentiating one college from another difficult.

These facts and frustrations led to the evolution of *The College Finder*. I'm concerned that students are choosing colleges without adequate information and that some may have made a different, and likely better, college decision had they had sufficient information with which to work. Of course, no single source should be used in selecting a college. You and your family should use at least a couple of guidebooks as well as consult with a well-informed college counselor. *The College Finder* is the place to start this search; other books and people will round out the facts you need to make an informed choice.

You and your parents may have many questions as you explore your options. Which colleges have strengths in the humanities? Which ones offer the best opportunities for getting academic scholarships? Which schools are strong in track? Which have well-developed academic-year-abroad programs? Years ago, I began to write down such questions and my responses to them. A couple of lists developed. Then a couple more. As I visited campuses, spoke with colleagues, talked with college representatives, and read educational journals, I found myself with more lists and more schools on each list. This book is the culmination of those efforts. What started as a group of lists used for my own reference, and to help my clients, is now in your hands.

The primary goal of *The College Finder* is to expand the pool of schools that you should consider. Too often, families think only of the Ivy League colleges when considering "top" colleges, or they think only of engineering schools when they think of colleges with good science departments. More than anything, it is my hope that this book extends the possibilities and magnifies the sense of power you feel as you begin shopping for a college. No one factor—overall prestige, an academic program of interest, athletic strength, a fact about the social environment of the school—is all-important; college choice is best done when several factors are considered. Hopefully, you will use the unique format of the book for cross-reference and analysis of multiple considerations.

Lists, as opposed to alphabetical or geographical groupings, provide the best vehicle to accomplish my various goals. These lists enable me to present a multitude of issues, perspectives, and possibilities. The format allows me to come at certain topics in multiple ways. The academic and quality chapters, for example, identify hundreds of schools that rank highly in terms of various definitions of academic excellence. Although there is no solitary list of the "best" colleges academically, I feel that many lists conveying some feature or aspect of the quality of the academic experience can be helpful. It is then up to you and your family to pick and choose among the more salient lists in each section to arrive at a group of colleges for exploration.

The topics that the lists cover evolved from many sources. Students with whom I spoke wanted information on such matters as admission, religious life, costs, location, campus facilities, career opportunities, athletics, acceptance of minority concerns, and so forth. These concerns led to several identifying lists in each of these categories. Once I determined what the lists were, I set to researching the inclusions for the lists.

I sent surveys to over 300 high school counselors and educational consultants in the early and mid 1990s. High schools were selected on the basis of such factors as size, public or private status, geographic diversity, and the nature of the student population. Educational consultants were selected on the basis of membership in the Independent Educational Consultants Association, a professional organization of experienced consultants, and on breadth of knowledge and geographic diversity. Counselors and consultants were asked to make recommendations of schools that fit into over thirty categories. Fifty-four percent of those who responded to the survey were consultants; 46 percent were high school counselors. Respondents represented a wide range of high schools and geographical regions. Results of this survey are included in separate lists labeled "Experts' Choice." The results were also used for adding to or verifying inclusion of colleges on other lists.

The following are among the research methods used:

- About thirty colleges were visited each year and discussions were held with faculty, administrators, and students.
- Students were queried about their present school. My past students were solicited for their comments on various aspects of their college experiences, and I have conducted a written survey of their impressions of their college for each of the last fifteen years.

• College personnel were asked for additions, updates, and suggestions. In the academic section, faculty members and heads of departments were queried as to their judgment of best programs in their field. In the athletic section, coaches, sports information directors, and representatives of national sports organizing groups provided input. On other lists, admission counselors or heads of student organizations were asked for advice and perspectives.

• Routine discussions with educational consultants were used to determine the contents of several lists.

• My college counseling files were searched for useful data. For example, the data on admission selectivity comes from actual decisions the colleges made, not claims made by the colleges.

• College guidebooks, data books, and other materials written by or about colleges were analyzed.

• Articles and other materials on higher education were consulted and have been referred to here where helpful.

Although this book primarily covers undergraduate schools, I included some graduate-oriented lists if I felt that such information was useful in understanding a particular aspect of collegiate life. Several community college lists are also included. As millions of students opt for a two-year education, these lists should prove valuable. Although this book emphasizes colleges in the United States, I have included some foreign schools.

I firmly believe that the social environment of a college is critical to academic success. I developed the social chapter of the book with the help of my students and thus with real concerns about the social fit in mind. These lists have helped me identify colleges that might be right for a particular student; I trust they will be helpful to you as well.

Some generalizing was necessary in order to make the lists in the social section useful. While I am aware that you may have more than one criterion, I have nonetheless listed schools according to their appeal to given groups of students. Again, what I sought was data that would allow you to begin the search process, not necessarily to arrive at the final list of colleges to which to apply.

Many lists are ranked by fairly objective data—size of endowment, longest football winning streak, college enrollment, and so on. A list based on subjective data ("Most Overrated Colleges" and "Hidden Treasures" are two examples) reflects the results of my research. It is not my intention to suggest that college 1 is quantifiably different from college 2. You should look at each list broadly, sizing up the data against other lists in a particular section, and other information available, when comparing schools expansively.

A drawback of any book that uses words like *top*, *great*, *beautiful*, *interesting*, *best*, and *fine* is that such adjectives are inherently subjective and imprecise. I feel, though, that subjectivity is what has often been missing in guidebooks for the college-bound. You need to know what research and the perceptions of others suggest about given features of college life. Some subjectivity is necessary in order to provide the kind of guidebook that is most helpful.

As often as lists have been checked and rechecked, *The College Finder* will always be a work in progress. As an industry, higher education is inherently changeable. Researching the lists in this book was like shooting at a moving target. Colleges regularly add and drop majors or programs, switch calendars, revise admission requirements, add special facilities, change fees, add or drop scholarship programs, add or eliminate athletic teams, or change directions in countless other ways. Indeed, the lists of "strong" colleges in various sports are particularly open to change. You should be mindful of these changes and check directly with the school for the most current information.

Picking a college today is different and far more difficult than it was twenty years ago. You are exposed to more college choices today. You may have traveled more widely than students did just a few years ago. You will find that colleges are more diverse and more specialized; thus, finding one that is right for you may seem more difficult. College is no longer a four-year escape from reality. Indeed, the costs and the ramifications have made these next years integral to the realization of your goals. Significantly, as college costs have risen, the need to make an informed choice is even more important. And, with the average student able to gain admission to most colleges, the spotlight has shifted from, "Where can I get in?" to "Where will I fit in?" The latter question is the one I have sought to illuminate through these pages.

Because *The College Finder* is based on actual questions I have received over the years, on knowledge of students and their parents and what they look for in a college, and on familiarity with the colleges themselves, I feel that it will be a useful guide. I hope that it liberates and provides a good start to your quest for schools that fit your academic background, interests, and talents.

Because colleges are clustered not only by characteristics such as geography, size, and admission competitiveness, but by more subtle, more important, characteristics in which my experience suggests that students are interested, I hope it raises new questions and highlights new directions from which you can launch your college search.

Because of the range of topics covered, I hope it realistically and credibly guides you and your parents to appropriate schools and that it will counter the charge that "all colleges sound the same."

Because it includes over 425 different lists, I hope it provides you with places to begin looking for suitable college choices and questions to ask. If the book gives you a sense of possibility, if it identifies one new college you should consider, then it will have been a success in my eyes.

USER'S GUIDE

The College Finder provides a comprehensive approach to college hunting by itemizing many features about schools. The lists here give you several hundred ways that colleges are ranked and viewed by experts. They can help you make choices if you use them wisely and systematically. Before you begin, two features of the book deserve your attention: the table of contents and the index by subject.

First, look at the table of contents. It is organized around the major topics considered by students who select colleges. As you scan the section heads and chapter titles, consider those factors, issues, and needs that are most important to you. The table of contents will lead you to relevant chapters. For instance, if academics are important and you want to learn more about colleges with strong science departments, take a look at the science sections in the Academics chapter. Similarly, if college cost is important, you may look at all the lists in the Cost chapter, or you may only want to know "Where the Money Is."

Next, examine the subject index, an alphabetical listing of specific topics covered in the book. It will direct you to all the lists under relevant categories. If you know what specific qualities you are seeking in a college, then the subject index will give you the pages of the relevant lists. Suppose you are a student with average grades who desires a Catholic college with a good tennis team; you will probably find several lists related to these topics in the index. You will discover colleges for a student with average grades in the Admission chapter, Catholic colleges in the religious life section of the Social chapter, and strong tennis teams in the Athletics chapter. When you see the same colleges mentioned on different lists, you can begin to identify those schools that fit you.

Further, as you read through a section or examine the subject index, you may think of additional college-planning factors or topics that concern you. This book gives you an ample number of topics that you may not have considered, as well as the names of colleges that respond to these newly identified interests.

This book can also be helpful if you already have a particular college in mind. Use the college index to locate the school and flip to any lists on which the college appears. This will help you learn a wide range of characteristics about that school. In addition, you can use the index to help you verify claims made by the school, as well as learn additional facts about it.

Here are some specific recommendations to make *The College Finder* more useful:

- Don't be too quick to dismiss a section as insignificant, even if it does not immediately seem appealing. For instance, a religious college will have a particular "feel" that may be significant even if your plans are not to attend a religious college. Similarly, while you may not want to play on a sports team, going to a school where you can watch a winning team may be important.
- Since many facts about a college change, you will want to check with the current college catalog, the admission office, or the Web site of a school to determine degrees offered, new majors, tuition costs, and other up-to-the-minute facts.
- Pay particular attention to the Social chapter. The atmosphere of a college and the types of students who attend are important considerations.
- Remember, there are many ways to measure the academic quality and the social characteristics of a college, so read many lists in many chapters. Only by looking carefully at the colleges included on a wide range of lists in this book will you be able to determine the colleges that are best for *you*.
- Simply browsing through the book can be eye-opening and useful. You may find an interesting college that you've never heard about. Finding unique colleges in the Academic chapter, colleges that students rave about in the Quality chapter, or intriguing collegiate traditions in the Morsels chapter can increase your understanding of the opportunities available to you.
- You should take note of colleges that appear often on those lists you consider important. If a school appears on several lists, you should seriously consider that school as a viable possibility.

The College Finder is best used in combination with other college reference guides. Use this book as a source of leads, then follow up with other books for complete information about particular colleges. The Resources for College Planning (at the end of this book) identifies college-planning books that can help you. Some of the books are general and will give you facts and figures about each college; others are focused on a particular topic like cost; and some provide advice on how to plan for your college education.

Finally, you will want to discuss your college choices, and colleges of which this book made you aware, with your college counselor, parents, and other knowledgeable advisers. These people can help determine the colleges that will have the highest likelihood of fitting your academic and social needs.

AUTHOR'S NOTE

The asterisks that appear on several of the ranked lists in this book indicate that the college(s) share(s) the same rank position as the schools above them, either because they tie on the criteria for a certain list or because they received the same number of mentions in the Experts' Choice Survey. If more than two schools share a rank, they have been alphabetized for fairness.

This book contains many judgments about the world of higher education, based both on my own perceptions and on views of knowledgeable observers. No claims to precision or infallibility are made here. I do state that this book is my best effort to be fair, reasoned, and responsible. I have worked to provide judgments based both on careful and sustained observation and on facts and figures that are as accurate and current as possible. I encourage you to notify me of mistakes, omissions, or differences of opinion. Your suggestions on ways this book can be made more helpful will be useful to me and, more important, beneficial to future readers.

I would welcome your correspondence at the address below:

Steven R. Antonoff, Ph.D.
875 South Colorado Boulevard
Suite 707
Denver, CO 80246

ADMISSION

GETTING IN

Colleges with the Highest Admission Standards

These colleges accept only a small percentage (usually less than 30 percent) of the students who apply. Admission standards for grades, test scores, extracurricular activities, and personal attributes are exceptionally high and rigorous.

Amherst C (MA)
Brown U (RI)
California Institute of Technology
Columbia U (NY)
Dartmouth C (NH)
Duke U (NC)
Georgetown U (DC)
Harvard U (MA)
Massachusetts Institute of Technology
Princeton U (NJ)
Rice U (TX)
Stanford U (CA)
Williams C (MA)
Yale U (CT)

The Very Selective Colleges

Admission standards at these colleges are very high; often, less than 50 percent of those who apply are admitted.

Bates C (ME)
Boston C (MA)
Bowdoin C (ME)
Bryn Mawr C (PA)
Bucknell U (PA)
California, U of, Berkeley (for out-of-state students)
California, U of, Los Angeles (for out-of-state students)
California, U of, San Diego (for out-of-state students)
Carleton C (MN)
Carnegie-Mellon U (PA)
Chicago, U of (IL)
Claremont McKenna C (CA)
Colby C (ME)
Colgate U (NY)
Cooper Union (NY)
Connecticut C
Cornell U (NY)
Emory U (GA)
Hamilton C (NY)
Harvey Mudd C (CA)
Haverford C (PA)
Johns Hopkins U (MD)
Juilliard School (NY)
Lafayette C (PA)
Michigan, U of, Ann Arbor (for out-of-state students)
Middlebury C (VT)
New C (FL)
North Carolina, U of, Chapel Hill (for out-of-state students)
Northwestern U (IL)
Notre Dame, U of (IN)
Oberlin C (OH)
Pennsylvania, U of
Pomona C (CA)
Richmond, U of (VA)
Swarthmore C (PA)
Tufts U (MA)
Vanderbilt U (TN)
Vassar C (NY)
Virginia, U of (for out-of-state students)
Wake Forest U (NC)
Washington U (MO)
Washington and Lee U (VA)
Wellesley C (MA)
Wesleyan U (CT)
William and Mary, C of (VA) (for out-of-state students)

The Experts' Choice: Great State Schools for the Student with Average Grades and Drive for College Success

Counselors most often mentioned the following colleges for a student with a C average, strong high school courses, and a combined verbal and mathematics score of 900 (out of 1,600) on the SAT.

Alabama, U of, Tuscaloosa
Alaska, U of, Fairbanks
Appalachian State U (NC)
Arizona, U of
Arkansas, U of, Fayetteville
Auburn U (AL)
Bowling Green State U (OH)
California State U, Sonoma
Castleton State C (VT)
Central Michigan U
Charleston, C of (SC)
Colorado State U
Delaware, U of
East Carolina U (NC)
Fort Lewis C (CO)
Georgia Southern U
Georgia, U of
Idaho, U of
Illinois State U
Iowa State U
Kansas State U
Kansas, U of
Keene State C (NH)
Longwood C (VA)
Louisiana State U, Baton Rouge
Louisville, U of (KY)
Maine, U of, Orono
Midwestern State U (TX)
Mississippi, U of
Missouri, U of, Columbia
Montana State U
Montana, U of
Nevada, U of, Las Vegas
Nevada, U of, Reno
New Mexico, U of, Albuquerque
New York, State U of, C at New Paltz
North Carolina, U of (all campuses except Chapel Hill)
Northern Arizona U
Northern Colorado, U of
Ohio U, Athens
Oklahoma State U
Old Dominion U (VA)
Oregon State U
Pennsylvania State U (all campuses except University Park)
Plymouth State C (NH)
Purdue U (IN)
Radford U (VA)
Ramapo C (NJ)
Rhode Island, U of
Sam Houston State U (TX)
Shippensburg U (PA)
South Carolina, U of, Columbia
Southern Illinois U, Carbondale
Stephen F. Austin State U (TX)

The Experts' Choice: Great State Schools for the Student with Average Grades and Drive for College Success (continued)

Tennessee, U of, Knoxville
Texas, U of, El Paso
Towson State U (MD)
Washington State U
Weber State U (UT)
West Virginia U
Wisconsin, U of (all campuses except Madison)
Wyoming, U of

The Experts' Choice: Great Private Schools for the Student with Average Grades and Drive for College Success

Counselors most often mentioned the following colleges for a student with a C average, college preparatory high school courses, and a combined verbal and mathematics score of 1,000 (out of 1,600) on the SAT.

THE TOP CHOICES

Beloit C (WI)
Bethany C (WV)
Catholic U (DC)
Elmira C (NY)
Elon C (NC)
Franklin Pierce C (NH)
Gettysburg C (PA)
Guilford C (NC)
Hartwick C (NY)
Juniata C (PA)
Lynchburg C (VA)
Marietta C (OH)
Miami, U of (FL)
Ohio Wesleyan U
Pacific, U of the (CA)
Randolph-Macon C (VA)
Ripon C (WI)
Roanoke C (VA)
Roger Williams C (RI)
St. John's U (MN)
Western Maryland C
Whittier C (CA)
Wittenberg U (OH)
Wooster, C of (OH)

OTHER COLLEGES MENTIONED

Adelphi U (NY)
Agnes Scott C (GA)
Albion C (MI)
Baker U (KS)
Bard C (NY)
Bryant C (RI)
Buena Vista C (IA)
Calvin C (MI)
Cornell C (IA)
Creighton U (NE)
Defiance C (OH)
Drake U (IA)

Eckerd C (FL)
Evansville, U of (IN)
Fisk U (TN)
Gonzaga U (WA)
Hamline U (MN)
Jacksonville U (FL)
Linfield C (OR)
Manhattan C (NY)
Manhattanville C (NY)
Marietta C (OH)
Mary Baldwin C (VA)
Millikin U (IL)
Misericordia C (PA)
Moravian C (PA)
Morningside C (IA)
Muskingum C (OH)
Oglethorpe U (GA)
Otterbein C (OH)
Oxford C/Emory U (GA)
Portland, U of (OR)
St. Mary's C (CA)
Santa Fe, C of (NM)
Transylvania U (KY)
Washington C (MD)
Wells C (NY)
Western New England C (MA)
Westminster C (MO)
Westminster C (UT)
William Jewell C (MO)

Top Colleges for the Late Bloomer

At these colleges, lower-than-average students with energy and determination are considered for admission.

Albertson C (ID)
Anderson C (SC)
Austin C (TX)
Barat C (IL)
Boise State U (ID)
Bradford C (MA)
Bradley U (IL)
Cardinal Stritch C (WI)
Carroll C (MT)
Cedar Crest C (PA)
Charleston, U of (WV)
Coe C (IA)
Cottey C (MO)
Curry C (MA)
Davis and Elkins C (WV)
Dean C (MA)
Erskine C (SC)
Findlay, U of (OH)
Flagler C (FL)
Florida Southern C
Franklin C (IN)
Green Mountain C (VT)
Hartford, U of (CT)
High Point U (NC)
Idaho State U
Iowa Wesleyan C
Kansas State U
Kendall C (IL)
La Verne, U of (CA)
Lesley C (MA)
Luther C (IA)
Lynn U (FL)
Marymount C (CA)
Menlo C (CA)
Mitchell C (CT)
Montevallo, U of (AL)
New England C (NH)
New Haven, U of (CT)
Niagara U (NY)
Oklahoma City U
Pine Manor C (MA)
Quinnipiac C (CT)
Rocky Mountain C (MT)
St. Ambrose U (IA)
St. Mary's C (MN)
Stephens C (MO)
Tampa, U of (FL)
Teikyo Post U (CT)
Thiel C (PA)
Waldorf C (IA)
Wesley C (DE)
West Virginia Wesleyan C
Western State C (CO)
Woodbury U (CA)

Colleges with Open Admission Policies and Campus Housing

Colleges with open admission policies admit almost all applicants. Historically, many such colleges were commuter colleges. The following schools have open or less selective admission and provide housing for students. Most are two-year colleges.

Akron, U of, Community and Technical C (OH)
Angelina C (TX)
Bakersfield C (CA)
Brevard C (NC)
Briarwood C (CT)
Colby C (KS)
Colorado Mountain C
Colorado Northwestern Community C
Columbia C (CA)
Commonwealth C (VA)
Connors State C (OK)
Cottey C (MO)
Delta C (MI)
Dixie C (UT)
Eastern Arizona C
Eastern New Mexico U, Roswell
Eastern Utah, C of
Fort Hays State U (KS)
Harcum C (PA)
Hilbert C (NY)
Indian Hills Community C (IA)
Iowa Central Community C
Jacksonville C (TX)
Keystone Junior C (PA)
Laramie County Community C (WY)
Lincoln C (IL)
Maui Community C (HI)
Mesa State C (CO)
Minnesota, U of, Crookston
Minnesota, U of, Waseca
Mt. Ida C (MA)
North Iowa Area Community C
Northeastern Christian Junior C (PA)
Northeastern Junior C (CO)
Northwestern Michigan C
Odessa C (TX)
Otero Junior C (CO)
Paul Smith's C (NY)
Peninsula C (WA)
Redwoods, C of the (CA)
Ricks C (ID)
Sage Junior C of Albany (NY)
St. Catharine C (KY)
St. Mary's C (NC)
Santa Rosa Junior C (CA)
Sierra C (CA)
Sierra Nevada C (NV)
Siskiyous, C of the (CA)
Snow C (UT)
Southeastern Louisiana U
Southern Idaho, C of
Southwestern Louisiana, U of
Trinidad State Junior C (CO)
Truckee Meadows Community C (NV)
Vincennes U (IN)
Waldorf C (IA)
Western Nebraska Community C
Yavapai C (AZ)

Don't-Count-Yourself-Out Colleges

These colleges are less difficult to be admitted to than might be expected on the basis of their high academic quality and excellent reputation.

Antioch C (OH)
Bennington C (VT)
Boston U (MA)
Catholic U (DC)
Colorado School of Mines
Creighton U (NE)
Denison U (OH)
Denver, U of (CO)
Dickinson C (PA)
Drake U (IA)
Drexel U (PA)
Fairleigh Dickinson U (NJ)
Franklin and Marshall C (PA)
Goucher C (MD)
Hampshire C (MA)
Hobart C/William Smith C (NY)
Ithaca C (NY)
Kent State U (OH)
Knox C (IL)
Lake Forest C (IL)
Miami, U of (FL)
Mills C (CA)
New York U
Occidental C (CA)
Ohio Wesleyan U
Purdue U (IN)
Rochester, U of (NY)
Rollins C (FL)
St. Lawrence U (NY)
San Diego, U of (CA)
Sarah Lawrence C (NY)
Scripps C (CA)
Simmons C (MA)
Skidmore C (NY)
Southern California, U of
Southern Methodist U (TX)
Stetson U (FL)
Sweet Briar C (VA)
Syracuse U (NY)
Temple U (PA)
Tulane U (LA)
Tulsa, U of (OK)
Vermont, U of
Wisconsin, U of (except for Madison campus)

Pope's Best Admissions Bargains

According to Loren Pope, educational consultant, these colleges were "selected because they are open to students of a wide range of abilities. Their student bodies include top-notch as well as C+ students, and occasionally some of the just plain C variety. Their facilities not only are as first-rate as any, but what is more important, they care about their students."

Allegheny C (PA)
Austin C (TX)
Beloit C (WI)
Birmingham Southern C (AL)
Centre C (KY)
Clark U (MA)
Cornell C (IA)
Denison U (OH)
Earlham C (IN)
Eckerd C (FL)
Emory and Henry C (VA)
Franklin and Marshall C (PA)
Goucher C (MD)
Grinnell C (IA)
Guilford C (NC)
Hampden-Sydney C (VA)
Hendrix C (AR)
Hiram C (OH)
Hope C (MI)
Juniata C (PA)
Kalamazoo C (MI)
Knox C (IL)
Lawrence U (WI)
Lynchburg C (VA)
Millsaps C (MS)
Ohio Wesleyan U
Rhodes C (TN)
Ripon C (WI)
St. Andrews C (NC)
St. Olaf C (MN)
Southwestern U (TX)
Wabash C (IN)
Western Maryland C
Whitman C (WA)
Wooster, C of (OH)

Source: Loren Pope, *Looking Beyond the Ivy League* (New York: Penguin Books, 1995), 154.

What Colleges Seek in Applicants

This is the rank order of factors rated as "of considerable importance" by college admission officers when they make their admission decisions.

1. Grades in college preparatory courses
2. Admission test scores
3. Grades in all subjects
4. Class rank
5. Counselor recommendations
6. Teacher recommendations
7. Essay/writing sample
8. Interview
9. Work/extracurricular experiences
10. Personal recognition programs
11. Ability to pay

Source: *NACAC Bulletin,* National Association for College Admission Counseling (October 1997).

Colleges That Don't Require SAT Scores for Admission

Not all colleges use test scores as a part of the admission process. These schools have eliminated or deemphasized SAT scores; they use grades, strength of classes, and activities to predict academic success in college.

Antioch C (OH)
Bard C (NY)
Bates C (ME)
Bowdoin C (ME)
Bradford C (MA)
Connecticut C
Dickinson C (PA)
Hampshire C (MA)
Hartwick C (NY)
Lafayette C (PA)
Lewis and Clark C (OR)
Maine, U of, Farmington
Muhlenberg C (PA)
New C (CA)
New England C (NH)
St. John's C (MD) and (NM)
Union C (NY)
Wheaton C (MA)

Average Scores on the SAT and ACT

These are the national averages on the Scholastic Assessment Test (SAT) and the American College Test (ACT) for the year 1997.

SAT Verbal	505 (out of a possible 800 points)
SAT Mathematics	508 (out of a possible 800 points)
ACT Composite	21 (out of a possible 36 points)

Source: The College Board, New York, NY, and American College Testing Program, Iowa City, IA.

CHOOSING A COLLEGE

The Experts' Choice: The Five Most Useful Guidebooks

This is the ranking of college admission guidebooks most often recommended to students and parents.

1. College Entrance Examination Board, *The College Handbook* (New York: College Board, published annually).
2. Edward B. Fiske, *The Fiske Guide to Colleges* (New York: Times Books/Random House, published annually).
3. Cass-Liepmann, Julia, *Cass and Birnbaum's Guide to American Colleges* (New York: Harper Perennial, published annually).
4. *Barron's Profiles of American Colleges* (Hauppauge, NY: Barron's Educational Series, Inc., published annually).
5. *Peterson's Guide to Four-Year Colleges* (Princeton, NJ: Peterson's Guides, published annually).

Best Internet Sites for College Planning

http://collegenet.com
http://jerome.signet.com/collegemoney/toc1.html (financial aid)
http://www.uwaterloo.ca/canu
http://www.collegeboard.org
http://www.collegeview.com
http://www.cpnet.com (campus life)
http://www.fastweb.com (financial aid)
http://www.finaid.org (financial aid)
http://www.jayi.com/ACG/search.html
http://www.mit.edu:8001/people/cdemello/univ.html
http://www.review.com
http://www.petersons.com
http://www.sourcepath.com
http://www.usnews.com
http://www.yahoo.com/education/higher_education

Factors That Influence College Choice

This is a ranking of students' reasons for selecting a particular college.

1. Academic quality in major
2. School's overall reputation
3. Scholarships/financial aid
4. Graduate program in major
5. Career placement aid
6. Tuition

Source: *USA Today,* July 18, 1997.

Influence of Family and Friends in Choosing a College

Students often choose a college that friends or family members attended. The following (from a study by Sevier in *Case Currents*) shows how often friends or family members are cited as being significant to students in choosing a school.

	PERCENT
Good friend	36.8
Other relative	12.6
Sibling	11.5
Parent	8.4

ADMISSION POTPOURRI

Colleges That Admit Many Students Early

While many schools have early decision/early action programs, these colleges admit a significant percentage of students through these options. Early decision programs enable students to apply for admission in the fall of their senior year and receive an answer on their application by January (instead of April, which is the typical notification month for selective colleges). At some colleges, the decision is binding; that is, the student must attend if accepted.

Amherst C (MA)
Bates C (ME)
Boston C (MA)
Bowdoin C (ME)
Brown U (RI)
Bucknell U (PA)
California Institute of Technology
Carleton C (MN)
Chicago, U of (IL)
Cornell U (NY)
Dartmouth C (NH)
Davidson C (NC)
DePauw U (IN)
Dickinson C (PA)
Duke U (NC)
Furman U (SC)
Georgetown U (DC)
Grinnell C (IA)
Hamilton C (NY)
Hampshire C (MA)
Harvard U (MA)
Hobart C (NY)
Johns Hopkins U (MD)
Kenyon C (OH)
Macalester C (MN)
Massachusetts Institute of Technology
Middlebury C (VT)
North Carolina, U of, Chapel Hill
Northwestern U (IL)
Notre Dame, U of (IN)
Oberlin C (OH)
Pennsylvania, U of
Pitzer C (CA)
Princeton U (NJ)
Providence C (RI)

Colleges that Admit Many Students Early (continued)

Rice U (TX)
Sarah Lawrence C (NY)
Skidmore C (NY)
Swarthmore C (PA)
Virginia, U of
Wesleyan U (CT)
Williams C (MA)
Yale U (CT)

Outstanding Private Junior Colleges

While most junior (or two-year) colleges are state supported, the following are private, independent schools with well-earned reputations for academic excellence. These colleges also have residence halls.

Becker C (MA)
Brevard C (NC)
Cottey C (MO)
Dean C (MA)
Deep Springs C (CA)
Fisher C (MA)
Keystone C (PA)
Lincoln C (IL)
Marymount C (CA)
Mitchell C (CT)
Newbury C (MA)
Paul Smith's C (NY)
Ricks C (ID)
Sage Junior C of Albany (NY)
Waldorf C (IA)

Four-Year Colleges Offering Two-Year Programs

These four-year colleges offer two-year degree programs. Two-year programs are normally less selective in admissions than four-year programs and typically provide academic support for students.

Adrian C (MI)
Akron U of (OH)
Alverno C (WI)
Ball State U (IN)
Becker C (MA)
Bridgeport, U of (CT)
Burlington C (VT)
Chowan C (NC)
Cincinnati, U of (OH) (University College)
Colby-Sawyer C (NH)
Connecticut, U of
Defiance C (OH)
Elmira C (NY)
Emory U (GA) (Oxford College)
Endicott C (MA)
Evansville, U of (IN)
Fairleigh-Dickinson U (NJ) (Edward Williams College)
Franklin C (IN)
Indiana U, Bloomington (General Studies)
Johnson and Wales U (RI)
Keene State C (NH)
Kendall C (IL)
La Verne, U of (CA)
Lasell C (MA)
Lynn U (FL)
Maine, U of, Bangor (University College)
Maine, U of, Orono (University College)
Marquette U (WI)
Menlo C (CA)
Mesa State C (CO)
Montana, U of
Montreat C (NC)
Mt. Ida C (MA)
New Hampshire, U of (Thompson School)
New Haven, U of (CT)
New York Institute of Technology
Northeastern U (MA) (University College part-time division)
Ohio U, Athens
Ohio U, Chillicothe
Ohio U, Lancaster
Ohio U, Zanesville
Pennsylvania State U, University Park
Pine Manor C (MA)
Pittsburgh, U of (PA)
Quinnipiac C (CT)
Rider C (NJ)
Rio Grande, U of (OH)
Rochester Institute of Technology (NY)
Roger Williams C (RI)
St. Mary C (KS)
Southern Illinois U, Carbondale
Southern Vermont C
Stephens C (MO)
Tampa, U of (FL)
Thiel C (PA)

Four-Year Colleges Offering Two-Year Programs (continued)

Toledo, U of (OH)
Unity C (ME)
Villanova U (PA)
Washburn U (KS)
West Chester, U of (PA)
West Florida, U of
Widener U (PA)
Xavier U (OH)
York C (PA)

The Experts' Choice: Twenty Hot Colleges

These colleges were rated highest by counselors who were asked for schools particularly popular in recent years.

1. Duke U (NC)
2. Virginia, U of
3. Brown U (RI)
4. Emory U (GA)
*5. Georgetown U (DC)
6. Vermont, U of
7. Williams C (MA)
8. Richmond, U of (VA)
*9. Vanderbilt U (TN)
10. Pennsylvania, U of
*11. Tufts U (MA)
12. Bates C (ME)
*13. Washington U (MO)
14. Colgate U (NY)
*15. Colorado, U of
*16. Michigan, U of, Ann Arbor
*17. Northwestern U (IL)
*18. Wesleyan U (CT)
19. Boston C (MA)
*20. Colorado C

Numbers College Shoppers Should Know

The numbers below are estimates.

Number of high school graduates in 1995–96	2,800,000
Number of undergraduate students enrolled in college in 1995	12,250,000
Number of students who earned a bachelors degree in 1994–95	1,500,000
Percentage of students graduating from four-year institutions within five years of high school graduation	52.8%

Source: U.S. Department of Education and American College Testing, Inc.

*See Author's Note, p. xxv.

Colleges Using the Common Application

To simplify the application process and to eliminate the need for separate applications for every college to which a student is applying, several colleges and universities have developed a single form, called the Common Application. The following colleges accept the Common Application and consider it equal to their own.

Adelphi U (NY)
Agnes Scott C (GA)
Albertson C (ID)
Albion C (MI)
Albright C (PA)
Alfred U (NY)
Allegheny C (PA)
American U (DC)
Amherst C (MA)
Antioch C (OH)
Babson C (MA)
Bard C (NY)
Barnard C (NY)
Bates C (ME)
Beaver C (PA)
Beloit C (WI)
Bennington C (VT)
Bentley C (MA)
Boston U (MA)
Bowdoin C (ME)
Brandeis U (MA)
Bryn Mawr C (PA)
Bucknell U (PA)
Butler U (IN)
Carleton C (MN)
Case Western Reserve U (OH)
Centenary C (LA)
Centre C (KY)
Claremont McKenna C (CA)
Clark U (MA)
Coe C (IA)
Colby C (ME)
Colby-Sawyer C (NH)
Colgate U (NY)
Colorado C
Connecticut C
Cornell C (IA)
Dallas, U of (TX)
Dartmouth U (NH)
Davidson U (NC)
Denison U (OH)
Denver, U of (CO)
DePauw U (IN)
Dickinson C (PA)
Drew U (NJ)
Duke U (NC)
Earlham C (IN)
Eckerd C (FL)
Elizabethtown C (PA)
Elmira C (NY)
Emory U (GA)
Eugene Lang C (NY)
Fairfield U (CT)
Fisk U (TN)
Fordham U (NY)
Franklin and Marshall C (PA)
Furman U (SC)
George Washington U (DC)
Gettysburg C (PA)
Goucher C (MD)
Grinnell C (IA)
Guilford C (NC)
Gustavus Adolphus C (MN)
Hamilton C (NY)
Hampden-Sydney C (VA)
Hampshire C (MA)

Colleges Using the Common Application (continued)

Hanover C (IN)
Hartwick C (NY)
Harvard C (MA)
Harvey Mudd C (CA)
Haverford C (PA)
Hendrix C (AR)
Hiram C (OH)
Hobart C (NY)
Hofstra U (NY)
Hollins C (VA)
Holy Cross, C of the (MA)
Hood C (MD)
Ithaca C (NY)
Johns Hopkins U (MD)
Juniata C (PA)
Lake Forest C (IL)
Le Moyne C (NY)
Loyola C (MD)
Lynchburg C (VA)
Kalamazoo C (MI)
Kenyon C (OH)
Knox C (IL)
Lafayette C (PA)
Lawrence U (WI)
Lehigh U (PA)
Lewis and Clark C (OR)
Linfield C (OR)
Macalester C (MN)
Manhattan C (NY)
Manhattanville C (NY)
Marietta C (OH)
Marquette U (WI)
Miami, U of (FL)
Middlebury C (VT)
Mills C (CA)
Millsaps C (MS)
Moravian C (PA)
Morehouse C (GA)
Mt. Holyoke C (MA)
Muhlenberg C (PA)
New York U
Oberlin C (OH)
Occidental C (CA)
Ohio Wesleyan U
Pacific, U of the (CA)
Pitzer C (CA)
Pomona C (CA)
Portland, U of (OR)
Puget Sound, U of (WA)
Randolph-Macon C (VA)
Randolph-Macon Woman's C (VA)
Redlands, U of (CA)
Reed C (OR)
Regis C (MA)
Regis U (CO)
Rensselaer Polytechnic Institute (NY)
Rhodes C (TN)
Rice U (TX)
Richmond, U of (VA)
Ripon C (WI)
Rochester Institute of Technology (NY)
Rochester, U of (NY)
Rollins C (FL)
St. Benedict, C of/St. John's U (MN)
St. Joseph's (PA)
St. Lawrence U (NY)
St. Olaf C (MN)
Salem C (NC)
Santa Clara U (CA)
Sarah Lawrence C (NY)
Scripps C (CA)
Seattle U (WA)
Simmons C (MA)
Skidmore C (NY)

Smith C (MA)
South, U of the (TN)
Southern Methodist U (TX)
Southwestern U (TX)
Spelman C (GA)
Stetson U (FL)
Stonehill C (MA)
Suffolk U (MA)
Susquehanna U (PA)
Swarthmore C (PA)
Syracuse U (NY)
Texas Christian U
Trinity C (CT)
Trinity U (TX)
Tufts U (MA)
Tulane U (LA)
Tulsa, U of (OK)
Union C (NY)
Ursinus C (PA)
Valparaiso U (IN)
Vanderbilt U (TN)
Vassar C (NY)
Wabash C (IN)
Wagner C (NY)
Wake Forest U (NC)
Washington C (MD)
Washington U (MO)
Washington and Lee U (VA)
Wellesley C (MA)
Wells C (NY)
Wesleyan U (CT)
Western Maryland C
Wheaton C (MA)
Whitman C (WA)
Whittier C (CA)
Widener U (PA)
Willamette U (OR)
William Smith C (NY)
Williams C (MA)
Wittenberg U (OH)
Wooster, C of (OH)
Worcester Polytechnic Institute (MA)

Source: *The Common Application,* National Association of Secondary School Principals, Reston, VA.

ACADEMICS

LIBERAL ARTS

Strictly Liberal Arts Colleges

These private colleges offer no or very few professional programs (such as business or engineering); they are tailored for the student who wants a broadly based education.

Adrian C (MI)
Agnes Scott C (GA)
Albertus Magnus C (CT)
Albion C (MI)
Albright C (PA)
Allegheny C (PA)
Alma C (MI)
Amherst C (MA)
Atlantic, C of the (ME)
Augustana C (IL)
Austin C (TX)
Barat C (IL)
Bard C (NY)
Barnard C (NY)
Bates C (ME)
Beloit C (WI)
Benedictine C (KS)
Bennett C (NC)
Bennington C (VT)
Bethany C (WV)
Bethel C (KS)
Bethel C (TN)
Birmingham-Southern C (AL)
Blackburn C (IL)
Borromeo C (OH)
Bowdoin C (ME)
Bradford C (MA)
Bridgewater C (VA)
Bryan C (TN)
Burlington C (VT)
Caldwell C (NJ)
California Baptist C
Carleton C (MN)
Centenary C (LA)
Centre C (KY)
Chatham C (PA)
Chestnut Hill C (PA)
Christendom C (VA)
Claflin C (SC)
Claremont McKenna C (CA)
Coe C (IA)
Coker C (SC)
Colby C (ME)
Colgate U (NY)
Colorado C
Concordia C (MI)

Strictly Liberal Arts Colleges (continued)

Concordia C (NY)
Concordia U (CA)
Connecticut C
Cornell C (IA)
Dana C (NE)
Davidson C (NC)
Denison U (OH)
DePauw U (IN)
Dickinson C (PA)
Divine Word C (IA)
Earlham C (IN)
Emmanuel C (MA)
Emory and Henry C (VA)
Fisk U (TN)
Franklin C (IN)
Franklin and Marshall C (PA)
Furman U (SC)
Gettysburg C (PA)
Goddard C (VT)
Gordon C (MA)
Goshen C (IN)
Goucher C (MD)
Greensboro C (NC)
Greenville C (IL)
Grinnell C (IA)
Guilford C (NC)
Gustavus Adolphus C (MN)
Hamilton C (NY)
Hampden-Sydney C (VA)
Hampshire C (MA)
Hanover C (IN)
Hartwick C (NY)
Haverford C (PA)
Heidelberg C (OH)
Hendrix C (AR)
Hillsdale C (MI)
Hiram C (OH)
Hobart C/William Smith C (NY)
Hollins C (VA)
Holy Cross, C of the (MA)
Hope C (MI)
Houghton C (NY)
Howard Payne U (TX)
Huntingdon C (AL)
Illinois C
Immaculata C (PA)
Judson C (AL)
Judson C (IL)
Juniata C (PA)
Kalamazoo C (MI)
Kenyon C (OH)
King C (TN)
Knox C (IL)
Lafayette C (PA)
Lake Forest C (IL)
Lawrence U (WI)
Lebanon Valley C (PA)
Long Island U, Southampton (NY)
Luther C (IA)
Lycoming C (PA)
Macalester C (MN)
Manhattanville C (NY)
Marlboro C (VT)
Mary Baldwin C (VA)
Marymount Manhattan C (NY)
Maryville C (TN)
Middlebury C (VT)
Mills C (CA)
Millsaps C (MS)
Monmouth C (IL)
Morehouse C (GA)
Morris C (SC)
Mt. Holyoke C (MA)
Muhlenberg C (PA)
Mundelein C (IL)
Muskingum C (OH)
Nebraska Wesleyan U
Neumann C (PA)

Northland C (WI)
North Park C (IL)
Oberlin C (OH)
Occidental C (CA)
Oglethorpe U (GA)
Ohio Wesleyan U
Olivet C (MI)
Pine Manor C (MA)
Pitzer C (CA)
Pomona C (CA)
Presbyterian C (SC)
Principia C (IL)
Randolph-Macon C (VA)
Randolph-Macon Woman's C (VA)
Reed C (OR)
Regis C (MA)
Rhodes C (TN)
Ripon C (WI)
Roanoke C (VA)
Rockford C (IL)
Rosemont C (PA)
St. Andrews Presbyterian C (NC)
St. Anselm C (NH)
St. John's C (MD)
St. John's C (NM)
St. John's U (MN)
St. Lawrence U (NY)
St. Olaf C (MN)
Salem C (NC)
Sarah Lawrence C (NY)
Scripps C (CA)
Seton Hill C (PA)
Shorter C (GA)
Simon's Rock, of Bard (MA)
Skidmore C (NY)
Smith C (MA)
South, U of the (TN)
Southwestern U (TX)
Spelman C (GA)
Spring Hill C (AL)
Swarthmore C (PA)
Sweet Briar C (VA)
Talladega C (AL)
Thiel C (PA)
Thomas Aquinas C (CA)
Thomas More C (KY)
Tougaloo C (MS)
Transylvania U (KY)
Trinity C (CT)
Trinity C (DC)
Trinity C (IL)
Union C (NY)
Ursinus C (PA)
Vassar C (NY)
Virginia Wesleyan C
Voorhees C (SC)
Wabash C (IN)
Warner Pacific C (OR)
Warren Wilson C (NC)
Washington C (MD)
Washington and Jefferson C (PA)
Wellesley C (MA)
Wells C (NY)
Wesleyan C (GA)
Wesleyan U (CT)
Western Maryland C
Westminster C (MO)
Westmont C (CA)
Wheaton C (IL)
Wheaton C (MA)
Whitman C (WA)
Wilberforce U (OH)
Williams C (MA)
Wilson C (PA)
Wittenberg U (OH)
Wofford C (SC)
Wooster, C of (OH)

Source: Based on David W. Breneman, *Liberal Arts Colleges: Thriving, Surviving, or Endangered?* (Washington, DC: The Brookings Institution, 1994).

State Universities That Don't Shortchange the Liberal Arts

Many state universities have well-developed reputations for their programs in such professional areas as business and engineering. At the same time, these schools provide comparable attention to students interested in the liberal arts and sciences.

Alabama, U of, Tuscaloosa
Bloomsburg U (PA)
California State U, Humboldt
California State U, Sonoma
California, U of, Davis
California, U of, Riverside
Central Michigan U
Charleston, C of (SC)
Colorado State U
Evergreen State C (WA)
Idaho, U of
Illinois State U
James Madison U (VA)
Kansas, U of
Louisiana State U, Baton Rouge
Maine, U of, Farmington
Millersville U (PA)
Minnesota, U of, Morris
Montana, U of
Nevada, U of, Reno
New York, City U of, Lehman C
New York, City U of, Queens C
New York, State U of, Albany
New York, State U of, Empire State C
North Carolina, U of, Asheville
North Dakota, U of
Northeast Missouri State U
Northern Iowa, U of
Ohio State U, Columbus
Ohio U, Athens
Oklahoma, U of
Shippensburg U (PA)
South Carolina, U of, Columbia
South Dakota, U of
Western Washington U
Wisconsin, U of, Eau Claire

The Experts' Choice: The Top Twenty-five State Universities with Excellent Liberal Arts Programs

1. Virginia, U of
2. Michigan, U of, Ann Arbor
3. Wisconsin, U of, Madison
4. North Carolina, U of, Chapel Hill
5. Vermont, U of
*6. William and Mary, C of (VA)
7. Indiana U, Bloomington
8. New York, State U of, Binghamton
9. California, U of, Santa Cruz
10. California, U of, Berkeley
*11. Miami U (OH)
*12. New Hampshire, U of
13. Illinois, U of, Urbana
*14. Iowa, U of
15. Delaware, U of
*16. Mary Washington C (VA)
*17. New York, State U of, C at Geneseo
*18. Oregon, U of
*19. Texas, U of, Austin
20. California, U of, Irvine
*21. California, U of, Santa Barbara
*22. Kansas, U of
*23. Michigan State U
*24. Rutgers U (NJ)
*25. Washington, U of

*See Author's Note, p. xxv.

Colleges with Fine Social Science Programs

These colleges are noted for strength in such social science fields as history, political science, psychology, sociology, anthropology, economics, and geography. Particular strengths are indicated.

Beloit C (WI) (anthropology)
Bryn Mawr C (PA) (archeology)
Chicago, U of (IL)
Claremont McKenna C (CA)
Columbia U (NY)
Connecticut, U of
Drew U (NJ) (political science)
Earlham C (IN) (Japanese studies/peace studies)
Georgetown U (DC) (foreign service)
George Washington U (DC) (government)
Grinnell C (IA)
Hamline U (MN)
International Training, School for (VT)
Johns Hopkins U (MD) (government/global studies)
Lafayette C (PA) (global affairs)
Macalester C (MN)
Maine, U of, Orono (Canadian studies)
Nebraska, U of, Lincoln (Great Plains studies)
New Mexico, U of, Albuquerque (anthropology)
Occidental C (CA)
Pennsylvania, U of (anthropology)
Pitzer C (CA)
Princeton U (NJ) (global affairs)
St. Anselm C (NH)
Trinity C (DC)
Tufts U (MA) (global studies)
Willamette U (OR)

The Experts' Choice: Colleges with Fine Social Science Programs

Amherst C (MA)
Bates C (ME)
Bowdoin C (ME)
Bryn Mawr C (PA)
Carleton C (MN)
Chicago, U of (IL)
Claremont McKenna C (CA)
Columbia U (NY)
Davidson C (NC)
Duke U (NC)
Gettysburg C (PA)
Hamilton C (NY)
Kenyon C (OH)
Macalester C (MN)
Michigan, U of, Ann Arbor
Northwestern U (IL)
Oberlin C (OH)
Pitzer C (CA)
Pomona C (CA)
Rochester, U of (NY)
Smith C (MA)
South, U of the (TN)
Wake Forest U (NC)

Colleges with Fine Humanities Programs

These colleges are noted for strength in humanities fields such as English, philosophy, religion, languages, music, and art. Particular strengths are indicated.

Bard C (NY) (fine and performing arts)
Barnard C (NY)
Bennington C (VT) (art)
Birmingham-Southern C (AL) (fine and performing arts)
Bradford C (MA)
Brown U (RI) (graphic arts)
Bryn Mawr C (PA) (languages)
Bucknell U (PA) (Japanese studies)
Butler U (IN) (fine arts)
California State, U Hayward (philosophy)
Cardinal Stritch C (WI) (art)
Carnegie Mellon U (PA) (fine and performing arts)
Columbia U (NY)
Connecticut C
Dartmouth C (NH) (languages)
Earlham C (IN) (Japanese studies)
Grinnell C (IA)
Gustavus Adolphus C (MN) (art)
Hawaii, U of, Manoa (languages)
Hofstra U (NY) (drama)
Illinois Wesleyan U (fine arts)
Iowa, U of
Kenyon C (OH)
Knox C (IL)
Middlebury C (VT)
Millikin U (IL) (fine and performing arts)
Mills C (CA) (fine arts)
Mississippi, U of
Mt. St. Joseph, C of (OH) (fine arts)
New York, State U of, Purchase (visual and performing arts)
New York U (fine, visual, and performing arts)
North Carolina, U of, Greensboro (fine and performing arts)
Pittsburgh, U of (PA) (philosophy)
Redlands, U of (CA)
St. John's C (MD)
Santa Fe, C of (NM) (performing arts)
Scripps C (CA)
Skidmore C (NY) (fine and performing arts)
Smith C (MA)
Southern Methodist U (TX) (fine and performing arts)
Stephens C (MO) (performing arts)
Tufts U (MA) (performing arts)
Vassar C (NY)
Washington and Lee U (VA)
Yale U (CT) (fine and performing arts)

The Experts' Choice: Colleges with Fine Humanities Programs

Amherst C (MA)
Bowdoin C (ME)
Brown U (RI)
Bryn Mawr C (PA)
Carleton C (MN)
Chicago, U of (IL)
Colgate U (NY)
Columbia U (NY)
Connecticut C
Davidson C (NC)
Hamilton C (NY)
Haverford C (PA)
Kenyon C (OH)
Mt. Holyoke C (MA)
Pomona C (CA)
St. Johns C (MD)
Skidmore C (NY)
Swarthmore C (PA)
Trinity C (CT)
Vassar C (NY)
Wellesley C (MA)
Wesleyan U (CT)
Wheaton C (MA)
Williams C (MA)
Yale U (CT)

SPECIFIC LIBERAL ARTS FIELDS

ART

Best Colleges for Aspiring Artists

These four-year, two-year, or specialized schools are well known as training grounds for future artists.

Art Center C of Design (CA)
Art Institute of Boston (MA)
Art Institute of Chicago, School of the (IL)
California C of Arts and Crafts
Kansas City Art Institute (MO)
Maryland Institute C of Art
Moore C of Art and Design (PA)
New York U
North Carolina School of the Arts
Otis/Parsons School of Art and Design (CA)
Parsons School of Design (NY)
Penland School of Crafts (NC)
Pilchuck Glass School (Stanwood, WA) (glass art, summer only)
Pratt Institute (NY)
Rhode Island School of Design
Ringling School of Art and Design (FL)
Studio Art Centers International (Italy)

The Experts' Choice: The Top Fifteen Undergraduate Art Schools

Art Institute of Chicago, School of the (IL)
Boston U (MA)
Carnegie Mellon U (PA)
Cooper Union (NY)
Furman U (SC)
Maryland Institute C of Art
Michigan, U of, Ann Arbor
Museum of Fine Arts, School of the (MA)
New York U
Rhode Island School of Design
Skidmore C (NY)
Smith C (MA)
Syracuse U (NY)
Virginia Commonwealth U
Washington U (MO)

Association of Independent Colleges of Art and Design

These colleges offer excellent programs in art and design.

Art Academy of Cincinnati (OH)
Art Center C of Design (CA)
Art Institute of Boston (MA)
Art Institute of Chicago, School of the (IL)
Art Institute of Southern California
Arts, U of the (PA)
Atlanta C of Art (GA)
California C of Arts and Crafts
Center for Creative Studies, C of Art and Design (MI)
Cleveland Institute of Art (OH)
Columbus C of Art and Design (OH)
Cooper Union School of Art (NY)
Corcoran School of Art (DC)
Kendall C of Art and Design (MI)
Maryland Institute C of Art
Massachusetts C of Art
Memphis C of Art (TN)
Milwaukee Institute of Art and Design (WI)
Minneapolis C of Art and Design (MN)
Montserrat C of Art (MA)
Moore C of Art and Design (PA)
Museum of Fine Arts, School of the (MA)
Otis/Parsons School of Art and Design (CA)
Pacific Northwest C of Art (OR)
Parsons School of Design (NY)

Association of Independent Colleges of Art and Design (continued)

Pennsylvania Academy of the Fine Arts
Philadelphia C of Art and Design at the U of the Arts (PA)
Portland School of Art (ME)
Rhode Island School of Design
Ringling School of Art and Design (FL)
San Francisco Art Institute (CA)
Visual Arts, School of (NY)

COMMUNICATIONS/JOURNALISM

Top Journalism Programs

Alabama, U of, Tuscaloosa
American U (DC)
Arizona State U
Arizona, U of
Ball State U (IN)
Boston U (MA)
California State U, Northridge
California, U of, Berkeley
Carleton U (Canada)
Colorado State U
Colorado, U of
Columbia U (NY)
DePauw U (IN)
Drake U (IA)
Duke U (NC)
Duquesne U (PA)
Emerson C (MA)
Florida, U of
Georgia, U of
Idaho, U of
Illinois, U of, Urbana
Indiana U, Bloomington
Ithaca C (NY)
Kansas, U of
Kent State U (OH)
Louisiana State U, Baton Rouge
Loyola U (LA)
Maryland, U of, College Park
Michigan State U
Middle Tennessee State U
Midland Lutheran C (NE)
Minnesota, U of, Twin Cities
Mississippi, U of
Missouri, U of, Columbia
Montana, U of
Nebraska, U of, Lincoln
Nevada, U of, Reno
New York U
North Carolina, U of, Chapel Hill
Northwestern U (IL)
Ohio State U, Columbus
Ohio U, Athens
Oregon, U of
Pepperdine U (CA)
Santa Fe, C of (NM)
South Carolina, U of, Columbia
Southern California, U of
Southern Illinois U, Carbondale
Stanford U (CA)
Syracuse U (NY)
Tennessee, U of
Texas Christian U
Texas, U of, Austin
Washington and Lee U (VA)
Washington State U
Washington U of
Wisconsin, U of, Madison

DANCE

Excellent Dance Programs

Arizona State U
Arizona, U of
California State U, Long Beach
California, U of, Irvine
California, U of, Los Angeles
California, U of, Santa Barbara
Florida State U
Goucher C (MD)
Illinois, U of, Urbana
Juilliard School (NY)
New York U
Ohio U, Athens
Sarah Lawrence C (NY)
Southern Methodist U (TX)
Stephens C (MO)

ECONOMICS

Excellent Economics Departments

Agnes Scott C (GA)
Allegheny U (PA)
American U (DC)
Bates C (ME)
Bowdoin C (ME)
Brown U (RI)
Bryn Mawr C (PA)
California, U of, Berkeley
California, U of, Los Angeles
Carnegie Mellon U (PA)
Chicago, U of (IL)
Claremont McKenna C (CA)
Columbia U (NY)
Dartmouth C (NH)
Denison U (OH)
Hamilton C (NY)
Harvard U (MA)
Haverford C (PA)
Heidelberg C (OH)
Hendrix C (AR)
Illinois C
Johns Hopkins U (MD)
Lafayette C (PA)
Macalester C (MN)
Massachusetts Institute of Technology
Michigan, U of, Ann Arbor
Middlebury C (VT)
Mt. Holyoke C (MA)
Northwestern U (IL)
Pennsylvania, U of
Pomona C (CA)
Princeton U (NJ)
Rhodes C (TN)
Rochester, U of (NY)
Smith C (MA)
Stanford U (CA)
St. Lawrence U (NY)
St. Olaf C (MN)
Swarthmore C (PA)
Trinity C (CT)
Trinity U (TX)
Ursinus C (PA)
Vanderbilt U (TN)
Virginia, U of
Wake Forest U (NC)
Washington and Jefferson C (PA)
Washington and Lee U (VA)
Washington U (MO)
Wesleyan U (CT)
Whitman C (WA)
Willamette U (OR)
Williams C (MA)
Wisconsin, U of, Madison
Wofford C (SC)
Yale U (CT)

ENGLISH

Top Programs in English

Undergraduate and graduate programs in English are ranked highly at these colleges.

Amherst C (MA)
Beloit C (WI)
Bennington C (VT)
Brandeis U (MA)
Brown U (RI)
Bryn Mawr C (PA)
California, U of, Berkeley
Carleton C (MN)
Chicago, U of (IL)
Columbia U (NY)
Cornell U (NY)
Dartmouth C (NH)
Denver, U of (CO)
Dickinson C (PA)
Duke U (NC)
Harvard U (MA)
Haverford C (PA)
Iowa, U of
Johns Hopkins U (MD)
Kenyon C (OH)
Knox C (IL)
Michigan, U of, Ann Arbor
Middlebury C (VT)
Mt. Holyoke C (MA)
North Carolina, U of, Chapel Hill
North Carolina, U of, Wilmington
Oberlin C (OH)
Pennsylvania, U of
Pomona C (CA)
Princeton U (NJ)
Reed C (OR)
Smith C (MA)
Stanford U (CA)
Swarthmore C (PA)
Virginia, U of
Wesleyan U (CT)
Whitman C (WA)
Williams C (MA)
Wofford C (SC)
Yale U (CT)

Colleges with Excellent Writing Programs

Alabama, U of
Alaska, U of, Anchorage
Arizona, U of
Arkansas, U of, Fayetteville
Bard C (NY)
Bennington C (VT)
British Columbia, U of (Canada)
Brown U (RI)
Bryn Mawr C (PA)
Bucknell U (PA)
California, U of, Irvine
Carnegie Mellon U (PA)
Columbia C (IL)
Columbia U (NY)
Connecticut, U of
Cornell U (NY)
Denison U (OH)
Denver, U of (CO)
Emerson C (MA)
Florida International U
Florida State U
Florida, U of
George Mason U (VA)
Goddard C (VT)
Grinnell C (IA)
Hamilton C (NY)
Iowa, U of
Johns Hopkins U (MD)
Kenyon C (OH)
Loyola C (IL)
Maine, U of, Farmington
Miami U (OH)
Middlebury C (VT)
Mississippi, U of
Mt. Holyoke C (MA)
New York, State U of, Binghamton
New York U
North Carolina State U
Northwestern U (IL)
Oberlin C (OH)
Oregon, U of
Pittsburgh, U of (PA)
Pomona C (CA)
Redlands, U of (CA)
Roger Williams C (RI)
Santa Clara U (CA)
Sarah Lawrence C (NY)
Smith C (MA)
Trinity C (CT)
Tufts U (MA)
Warren Wilson C (NC)
Washington C (MD)
Washington U (MO)
Wittenberg C (OH)

FILM AND TV

Best Colleges for Film and TV

These colleges, ranging in both size and specialization, are well regarded for programs in film and television.

Art Center C of Design (CA)
Art Institute of Chicago, School of the (IL)
California Institute of the Arts
California State U, San Francisco
California, U of, Berkeley
California, U of, Los Angeles
Cincinnati, U of (OH)
Columbia C (IL) (film)
Columbia U (NY) (graduate)
Emerson C (MA)
Florida State U
Illinois, U of, Urbana
Indiana U, Bloomington
Iowa, U of
Ithaca C (NY)
Kansas, U of
Loras C (IA)
Loyola Marymount U (CA)
Maryland, U of, College Park
Memphis State U (TN)
Michigan, U of, Ann Arbor
New York U
North Carolina, U of, Chapel Hill
Northwestern U (IL)
Ohio U, Athens
Otis/Parsons School of Art and Design (CA)
Pennsylvania, U of
Santa Fe, C of (NM)
Southern California, U of
Syracuse U (NY)
Temple U (PA)
Texas, U of, Austin
Washington State U (television)
Washington, U of (television)
Wayne State U (MI)
Webster U (MO)
Wisconsin, U of, Madison

HISTORY

Colleges with Outstanding History Departments

Albion C (MI)
Allegheny C (PA)
Amherst C (MA)
Bates C (ME)
Birmingham Southern C (AL)
Boston C (MA)
Boston U (MA)
Brown U (RI)
Bryn Mawr C (PA)
California, U of, Berkeley
Calvin C (MI)
Carleton C (MN)
Chicago, U of (IL)
Claremont McKenna C (CA)
Colgate U (NY)
Colorado C
Columbia U (NY)
Connecticut C
Cornell U (NY)
Dallas, U of (TX)
Dartmouth C (NH)
Davidson C (NC)
Dickinson C (PA)
Drew U (NJ)
Duke U (NC)
Emory U (GA)
Georgetown U (DC)
George Washington U (DC)
Gettysburg C (PA)
Grinnell C (IA)
Hamilton C (NY)
Hampden-Sydney C (VA)
Harvard U (MA)
Haverford C (PA)
Hiram C (OH)
Indiana U, Bloomington
Johns Hopkins U (MD)
Kansas, U of
Lake Forest C (IL)
Lawrence U (WI)
Macalester C (MN)
Michigan, U of, Ann Arbor
Mt. Holyoke C (MA)
Muhlenberg C (PA)
North Carolina, U of, Chapel Hill
Pennsylvania, U of
Pittsburgh, U of (PA)
Pomona C (CA)
Princeton U (NJ)
Smith C (MA)
South, U of the (TN)
Southwestern U (TX)
Stanford U (CA)
Swarthmore C (PA)
Texas Christian U
Trinity U (TX)
Union C (NY)
Vanderbilt U (TN)
Vassar C (NY)
Vermont, U of
Virginia, U of
Wabash C (IN)
Washington and Lee U (VA)
Wellesley C (MA)
Whitman C (WA)
William and Mary, C of (VA)
Wittenberg U (OH)
Yale U (CT)

INTERNATIONAL RELATIONS/INTERNATIONAL BUSINESS

Colleges with Strong Programs in International Relations/International Business

Alma C (MI)
American U (DC)
Beloit C (WI)
California, U of, Berkeley
California, U of, Davis
Claremont McKenna C (CA)
Colorado C
Connecticut C
Drake U (IA)
Emory U (GA)
Georgetown U (DC)
George Washington U (DC)
Goucher C (MD)
Hamline U (MN)
Harvard U (MA)
Hiram C (OH)
Johns Hopkins U (MD)
Kalamazoo C (MI)
Kenyon C (OH)
Lewis and Clark C (OR)
Macalester C (MN)
Middlebury C (VT)
Moravian C (PA)
Northeastern U (MA)
Ohio Wesleyan U
Pennsylvania, U of
Princeton U (NJ)
Rochester, U of (NY)
St. Olaf C (MN)
Santa Clara U (CA)
South Carolina, U of, Columbia
Southern California, U of
Texas, U of, Austin
Tufts U (MA)
U.S. International U (CA)
Vassar C (NY)
Washington U (MO)
William and Mary, C of (VA)
Wisconsin, U of, Madison

MUSIC

Colleges with Outstanding Music Departments

Amherst C (MA)
Baldwin-Wallace C (OH)
Boston U (MA)
California, U of, Berkeley
Case Western Reserve U (OH)
Catholic U (DC)
Chicago, U of (IL)
Cincinnati, U of (OH)
Coe C (IA)
Cornell U (NY)
DePaul U (IL)
Gustavus Adolphus C (MN)
Hartford, U of (CT)
Heidelberg C (OH)
Hope C (MI)
Illinois, U of, Urbana
Indiana U, Bloomington
Iowa, U of
Ithaca C (NY)
Lawrence U (WI)
Loyola U (LA)
Miami, U of (FL)
Michigan, U of, Ann Arbor
Missouri, U of, Kansas City
Mt. St. Joseph, C of (OH)
New York, State U of, C at Fredonia
New York U
North Carolina, U of, Greensboro
North Texas, U of (including jazz studies)
Northern Colorado, U of
Northwestern U (IL)
Oberlin C (OH)
Pacific, U of the (CA)
Redlands, U of (CA)
Rice U (TX)
Rochester, U of (NY)
St. Olaf C (MN)
Shenandoah U (VA)
Skidmore C (NY)
Southern California, U of
Southern Methodist U (TX)
Susquehanna U (PA)
Temple U (PA)
Westminster Choir C (NJ)
Wyoming, U of
Yale U (CT)

Superior Music Conservatories

American Conservatory of Music (IL)
Arts, U of the (PA)
Berklee C of Music (MA)
Boston Conservatory (MA)
California Institute of the Arts
Cincinnati College Conservatory of Music (OH)
Cleveland Institute of Music (OH)
Cornish C of the Arts (WA)
Curtis Institute of Music (PA)
Eastman School of Music, Rochester, U of (NY)
Juilliard School (NY)
Manhattan School of Music (NY)
Mannes School of Music (NY)
New England C of Music (MA)
North Carolina School of the Arts
Oberlin C, Conservatory of Music (OH)
Peabody C of Music, Johns Hopkins U (MD)
San Francisco Conservatory of Music (CA)

PHYSICAL EDUCATION

Colleges with Outstanding Physical Education Programs

Bemidji State U (MN)
California, U of, Santa Barbara
Colorado, U of
Elon C (NC)
Linfield C (OR)
Michigan State U
New York, State U of, C at Cortland
North Carolina, U of, Chapel Hill
Norwich U (VT)
Occidental C (CA)
Pennsylvania State U, University Park
Springfield C (MA)
Texas, U of, Austin
Washington State U
Westmont C (CA)
Wisconsin, U of, La Crosse

PSYCHOLOGY

Excellent Colleges to Study Psychology

Allegheny C (PA)
Boston C (MA)
Carnegie Mellon U (PA)
Chicago, U of (IL)
Claremont McKenna C (CA)
Clark U (MA)
Connecticut College
Denison U (OH)
Denver, U of (CO)
Drew U (NJ)
Earlham C (IN)
Emory U (GA)
George Washington U (DC)
Hamline C (MN)
Hobart C (NY)
Mary Washington (VA)
New York, State U of, Binghamton
New York U
North Carolina, U of, Chapel Hill
Oregon, U of
Otterbein C (OH)
Pennsylvania, U of
Pitzer C (CA)
Randolph Macon C (VA)
Reed C (OR)
Roanoke C (VA)
Rochester, U of (NY)
St. Lawrence U (NY)
St. Olaf C (MN)
Santa Clara, U of (CA)
Stanford U (CA)
Trenton State C (NJ)
Tufts U (MA)
Tulsa, U of (OK)
Union C (NY)
Vanderbilt U (TN)
Vassar C (NY)
Virginia, U of
Wabash C (IN)
Wake Forest U (NC)
Wesleyan U (CT)
Westmont C (CA)
Wheaton C (MA)
Wisconsin, U of, Madison
Wittenberg C (OH)
Wofford C (SC)
Yale U (CT)

SOCIOLOGY

Top Undergraduate Sociology Programs

Amherst C (MA)
Beloit C (WI)
Brandeis U (MA)
Bryn Mawr C (PA)
California, U of, Berkeley
California, U of, Los Angeles
Chicago, U of (IL)
Columbia U (NY)
Cornell U (NY)
Dartmouth C (NH)
Duke U (NC)
Gettysburg C (PA)
Hartwick C (NY)
Harvard U (MA)
Illinois, U of, Urbana
Michigan, U of, Ann Arbor
North Carolina, U of, Chapel Hill
North Carolina U of, Wilmington
Northwestern U (IL)
Oberlin C (OH)
Pennsylvania, U of
Pittsburgh, U of (PA)
Princeton U (NJ)
San Francisco State U (CA)
Smith C (MA)
Stanford U (CA)
Swarthmore C (PA)
Tufts U (MA)
Washington, U of
Wheaton C (MA)
Wisconsin, U of, Madison
Wooster, C of (OH)
Yale U (CT)

THEATER

Colleges with Excellent Theater Programs

American Academy for Theater Arts (NY)
American Conservatory Theater, San Francisco (CA)
Baylor U (TX)
Boston Conservatory (MA)
Boston U (MA)
Brandeis U (MA)
California, U of, Los Angeles
California, U of, San Diego
Carnegie Mellon U (PA)
Case Western Reserve U (OH)
Cornell U (NY)
DePaul U (IL)
Evansville, U of (IN)
Florida State U
Illinois Wesleyan U
Indiana U, Bloomington
Iowa, U of
Juilliard School (NY)
Michigan State U
Missouri, U of, Kansas City
New York, State U of, Purchase
New York U
North Carolina School of the Arts
Northwestern U (IL)
Otterbein C (OH)
Southern California, U of
Southern Methodist U (TX)
Stephens C (MO)
Syracuse U (NY)
Temple U (PA)
Tufts U (MA)
Washington, U of
Whitman C (WA)
Wisconsin, U of, Milwaukee
Yale U (CT)

The Experts' Choice: The Fifteen Best Colleges for the Aspiring Actor

Boston U (MA)
Carnegie Mellon U (PA)
Catawba C (NC)
Catholic U (DC)
DePaul U (IL)
Emerson C (MA)
Kenyon C (OH)
Miami, U of (FL)
New York U
Northwestern U (IL)
Rollins C (FL)
Sarah Lawrence C (NY)
Southern California, U of
Southern Methodist U (TX)
Yale U (CT)

Consortium of Conservatory Theater Training Programs

These colleges have intensive, preprofessional theater programs.

Boston U (MA)
Carnegie Mellon U (PA)
New York, State U of, Purchase
North Carolina School of the Arts

SCIENCES

Top Undergraduate Science Programs

This is "the Oberlin group of fifty," a select group of undergraduate, liberal arts schools distinguished by their strong and productive undergraduate science curricula. Colleges were selected on the basis of the proportion of science graduates to graduates in other fields and undergraduate involvement in science research.

Albion C (MI)
Alma C (MI)
Amherst C (MA)
Antioch C (OH)
Barnard C (NY)
Bates C (ME)
Beloit C (WI)
Bowdoin C (ME)
Bryn Mawr C (PA)
Bucknell U (PA)
Carleton C (MN)
Colgate U (NY)
Colorado C
Davidson C (NC)
Denison U (OH)
DePauw U (IN)
Earlham C (IN)
Franklin and Marshall C (PA)
Grinnell C (IA)
Hamilton C (NY)
Hampton U (VA)
Harvey Mudd C (CA)
Haverford C (PA)
Holy Cross, C of the (MA)
Hope C (MI)
Kalamazoo C (MI)
Kenyon C (OH)
Lafayette C (PA)
Macalester C (MN)
Manhattan C (NY)
Middlebury C (VT)
Mt. Holyoke C (MA)
Oberlin C (OH)
Occidental C (CA)
Ohio Wesleyan U
Pomona C (CA)
Reed C (OR)
St. Olaf C (MN)
Smith C (MA)
Swarthmore C (PA)
Trinity C (CT)
Union C (NY)

Top Undergraduate Science Programs (continued)

Vassar C (NY)
Wabash C (IN)
Wellesley C (MA)
Wesleyan U (CT)
Wheaton C (IL)
Whitman C (WA)
Williams C (MA)
Wooster, C of (OH)

The Experts' Choice: Colleges with Fine Science Programs

In this list of colleges with well-respected science programs, counselors were asked to think beyond schools that are dominated by their science or engineering programs.

Bates C (ME)
Cornell U (NY)
Emory U (GA)
Franklin and Marshall C (PA)
Goucher C (MD)
Harvard U (MA)
Johns Hopkins U (MD)
Mt. Holyoke C (MA)
Oberlin C (OH)
Princeton U (NJ)
Reed C (OR)
Rhodes C (TN)
Rice U (TX)
Rochester, U of (NY)
Stanford U (CA)
Swarthmore C (PA)
Union C (NY)
Washington U (MO)
Wellesley C (MA)
Wooster, C of (OH)

Unexpectedly Strong Science Programs

Some colleges, like Massachusetts Institute of Technology, Rice U (TX), and California Institute of Technology, are well known for their science programs. The colleges listed below are recognized for the strength of their undergraduate programs in fields such as mathematics, chemistry, physics, biological sciences, geology, and computer science. Particular strengths are noted.

Alaska Pacific U, Anchorage (environmental science)
Alaska, U of, Fairbanks (fisheries and ocean studies)
Alfred U (NY) (glass study)
Allegheny C (PA)
Amherst C (MA)
Arizona, U of (astronomy)
Atlantic, C of the (ME) (environmental science, human ecology)
Austin C (TX)
California State U, Humboldt (natural resources/marine biology/forestry)
California State U, San Jose (nuclear science laboratory)
California, U of, Davis (botany)
California, U of, San Diego
California, U of Santa Barbara (marine biology)
California, U of, Santa Cruz (marine science)
Case Western Reserve U (OH) (environmental science)
Charleston, C of (SC) (marine biology)
Evergreen State C (WA) (environmental studies)
Fairleigh Dickinson U (NJ) (marine biology)
Florida Institute of Technology (marine biology, ocean engineering)
Franklin and Marshall C (PA) (geology)
Hamilton C (NY)
Hawaii, U of, Manoa (oceanography)
Hope C (MI)
Houston, U of (TX) (optometry)
Knox C (IL)
Lawrence U (WI)
Long Island U, Southampton (NY) (marine biology/ environmental science)
Miami, U of (FL) (marine biology)
Montana, U of (forestry)
Mt. Holyoke C (MA)
New Hampshire, U of (marine biology)
North Carolina, U of, Wilmington (marine biology)
Northland C (WI) (environmental studies)
Nova Southeastern U (FL) (ocean studies)
Oberlin C (OH)
Oklahoma, U of (meteorology)

Unexpectedly Strong Science Programs (continued)

Pennsylvania State U, University Park (meteorology)
Prescott C (AZ) (environmental science)
Rhode Island, U of (oceanography)
Rochester, U of (NY) (optics)
St. Mary's C (MD) (marine biology)
Smith C (MA)
South Carolina, U of, Coastal (marine science)
South Carolina, U of, Columbia (marine science)
Unity C (ME) (environmental studies)
Ursinus C (PA)
Utah, U of
Vermont, U of (environmental studies)
Warren Wilson C (NC) (environmental science)
Washington, U of (fisheries, oceanography)
Williams C (MA)
Wisconsin, U of, Stevens Point (natural resources)
Wyoming, U of (geology)

SPECIFIC SCIENCE FIELDS

BIOLOGY

The Top Undergraduate Programs in Biology

Amherst C (MA)
Austin C (TX)
Bates C (ME)
Bowdoin C (ME)
Brandeis U (MA)
Bryn Mawr C (PA)
Bucknell U (PA)
California Institute of Technology
California, U of, Berkeley
California, U of, San Diego
Carleton C (MN)
Chicago, U of (IL)
Colgate U (NY)
Colorado, U of
Colorado C
Cornell U (NY)
Creighton U (NE)
Davidson C (NC)
Dickinson C (PA)
Duke U (NC)
Emory U (GA)
Franklin and Marshall C (PA)
Gettysburg C (PA)
Grinnell C (IA)
Hamilton C (NY)
Harvey Mudd C (CA)
Harvard U (MA)
Haverford C (PA)
Indiana U, Bloomington
Iowa, U of
Johns Hopkins U (MD)
Kalamazoo C (MI)
Kenyon C (OH)
Lafayette C (PA)
Lawrence U (WI)
Macalester C (MN)
Massachusetts Institute of Technology
Michigan State U
Michigan, U of, Ann Arbor
Mt. Holyoke C (MA)
New York State U of, C at Geneseo
Oregon, U of
Pomona C (CA)
Presbyterian C (SC)
Princeton U (NJ)
Purdue U (IN)

The Top Undergraduate Programs in Biology (continued)

Reed C (OR)
Rhodes C (TN)
Rochester, U of (NY)
St. Olaf C (MN)
Southwestern U (TX)
Stanford U (CA)
Swarthmore C (PA)
Trinity C (CT)
Tufts U (MA)
Ursinus C (PA)
Union C (NY)
Wake Forest U (NC)
Washington U (MO)
Wellesley C (MA)
Whitman C (WA)
Williams C (MA)
Wisconsin, U of, Madison
Wooster, C of (OH)
Yale U (CT)

Sea Grant Colleges

These colleges have broad programs in marine sciences and related fields, such as biology, geology, economics, policy, law, and fisheries; programs emphasize practical approaches to sea/ocean/Great Lakes issues.

Alaska, U of, Fairbanks
California, U of, San Diego
Connecticut, U of, Groton
Delaware, U of, Newark
Florida, U of
Georgia, U of
Hawaii, U of, Manoa
Illinois, U of, Urbana
Louisiana State U, Baton Rouge
Maine, U of, Orono
Maryland, U of, College Park
Massachusetts Institute of Technology
Michigan, U of, Ann Arbor
Minnesota, U of, Twin Cities
New Hampshire, U of
New York, State U of, Stony Brook
North Carolina State U
Ohio State U, Columbus
Oregon State U
Puerto Rico, U of
Purdue U (IN)
Rhode Island, U of, Narragansett
Southern California, U of
Texas A&M U
Virginia, U of
Washington, U of
Wisconsin, U of, Madison

Source: National Oceanic and Atmospheric Administration, Silver Spring, MD.

BIOCHEMISTRY

Colleges with Excellent Biochemistry Programs

California, U of, Berkeley
California, U of, Los Angeles
California, U of, San Diego
Chicago, U of (IL)
Cornell U (NY)
Harvard U (MA)
Illinois, U of, Urbana
Iowa, U of
Kansas State U
Massachusetts Institute of Technology
Miami, U of (FL)
Mt. Holyoke C (MA)
New York, State U of, C at Geneseo
Pennsylvania State U, University Park
Princeton U (NJ)
Swarthmore C (PA)
Wisconsin, U of, Madison
Yale U (CT)

CHEMISTRY

Top Schools for Chemistry

Amherst C (MA)
Bowdoin C (ME)
California Institute of Technology
California, U of, Berkeley
California, U of, Los Angeles
California, U of, San Diego
Calvin C (MI)
Carleton C (MN)
Carnegie Mellon U (PA)
Carroll C (WI)
Case Western Reserve U (OH)
Chicago, U of (IL)
Colgate U (NY)
Columbia U (NY)
Cornell U (NY)
Dartmouth C (NH)
Davidson C (NC)
Franklin and Marshall C (PA)
Furman C (SC)
Grinnell C (IA)
Harvard U (MA)
Harvey Mudd C (CA)
Haverford C (PA)
Hope C (MI)
Illinois, U of, Urbana
Lafayette C (PA)
Lawrence U (WI)
Massachusetts Institute of Technology
Morningside C (IA)
Northwestern U (IL)
Oberlin C (OH)
Pittsburgh, U of (PA)
Pomona C (CA)
Princeton U (NJ)
Purdue U (IN)
Reed C (OR)
Rensselaer Polytechnic Institute (NY)
Rice U (TX)
Rochester, U of (NY)
Swarthmore C (PA)
Texas, U of, Austin
Tufts U (MA)
Union C (NY)
Utah, U of
Wellesley C (MA)
Whitman C (WA)
Williams C (MA)
Wisconsin, U of, Madison
Wooster, C of (OH)
Yale U (CT)

COMPUTER SCIENCE

Top Programs in Computer Science

These colleges have fine programs for students interested in careers in computer science.

Brandeis U (MA)
Brown U (RI)
California Institute of Technology
California Polytechnic State U, San Luis Obispo
California, U of, Berkeley
California, U of, Los Angeles
Carnegie Mellon U (PA)
Case Western Reserve U (OH)
Cornell U (NY)
Dartmouth C (NH)
Haverford C (PA)
Illinois, U of, Urbana
Mankato State U (MN)
Massachusetts Institute of Technology
Michigan, U of, Ann Arbor
New York, State U of, Stony Brook
Pennsylvania State U, University Park
Pittsburgh, U of (PA)
Princeton U (NJ)
Rensselaer Institute of Technology
Rice U (TX)
Rochester, U of (NY)
Southern California, U of
Stanford U (CA)
Texas, U of, Austin
Utah, U of
Washington, U of
Washington U (MO)
Williams C (MA)
Wisconsin, U of, Madison
Worcester Polytechnic Institute (MA)
Yale U (CT)

ENGINEERING

Outstanding Colleges with a Large Percentage of Engineering Students

Alfred U (NY)
California Institute of Technology
Carnegie Mellon U (PA)
Case Western Reserve U (OH)
Clarkson U (NY)
Colorado School of Mines
Columbia U, School of Engineering and Applied Science (NY)
Cooper Union (NY)
Drexel U (PA)
Embry-Riddle Aeronautical U (FL)
Georgia Institute of Technology
Harvey Mudd C (CA)
Illinois Institute of Technology
Kettering U (MI)
Lehigh U (PA)
Massachusetts Institute of Technology
Michigan Technological U
Missouri, U of, Rolla
Montana Tech
New Jersey Institute of Technology
New Mexico Institute of Mining and Technology
New York, State U of, Institute of Technology
Northrop U (CA)
Pennsylvania State U, Erie
Polytechnic U (NY)
Purdue U (IN)
Rensselaer Polytechnic Institute (NY)
Rutgers U, C of Engineering (NJ)
South Dakota School of Mines and Technology
Stevens Institute of Technology (NJ)
Texas A&M U, Kingsville
Virginia Polytechnic Institute and State U
Worcester Polytechnic Institute (MA)

Colleges with a Balance of Engineering and Liberal Arts

These are small or medium-sized colleges that offer engineering programs but also have a good mix of liberal arts and sciences courses.

Alfred U (NY)
Boston U (MA)
Bradley U (IL)
Brown U (RI)
Bucknell U (PA)
Calvin C (MI)
Catholic U (DC)
Cornell U (NY)
Dartmouth C (NH)
Dayton, U of (OH)
Detroit Mercy, U of (MI)
Duke U (NC)
Hartford, U of (CT)
Harvard U (MA)
Hofstra U (NY)
Johns Hopkins U (MD)
Lafayette C (PA)
Lehigh U (PA)
Loyola C (MD)
Loyola Marymount U (CA)
Marietta C (OH)
Marquette U (WI)
Miami, U of (FL)
Northwestern U (IL)
Notre Dame, U of (IN)
Pacific, U of the (CA)
Portland, U of (OR)
Princeton U (NJ)
Rice U (TX)
Santa Clara U (CA)
Seattle U (WA)
Stanford U (CA)
Swarthmore C (PA)
Trinity U (TX)
Tufts U (MA)
Tulane U (LA)
Tulsa, U of (OK)
Tuskegee U (AL)
Union C (NY)
Valparaiso U (IN)
Vanderbilt U (TN)
Villanova U (PA)
Washington U (MO)
Western New England C (MA)
Yale U (CT)

SPACE STUDIES

Top Programs in Aeronautics

These colleges offer bachelor of arts or bachelor of science degrees in aeronautical technology. They are designated space-related programs.

Arizona State U
Bowling Green State U (OH)
Central Missouri State U (MO)
Embry-Riddle Aeronautical U (FL)
Indiana State U (IN)
LeTourneau U (TX)
Lewis U (IL)
Moody Bible Institute (IL)
Northrop U (CA)
Parks C of St. Louis (IL)
Purdue U (IN)
Western Michigan U (MI)

Space Grant Colleges

Selected in 1989, these colleges have programs that are designed for students interested in learning more about space science and technology.

Alabama, U of, Huntsville
Arizona, U of
California, U of, Berkeley
California, U of, Los Angeles
California, U of, San Diego
Case Western Reserve U (OH)
Chicago, U of (IL)
Colorado, U of
Cornell U (NY)
Georgia Institute of Technology
Houston, U of (TX)
Houston, U of, Clear Lake (TX)
Illinois, U of, Urbana
Iowa, U of
Johns Hopkins U (MD)
Massachusetts Institute of Technology
Michigan, U of, Ann Arbor
New Mexico State U
Ohio State U, Columbus
Old Dominion U (VA)
Pennsylvania State University, University Park
Texas A&M U
Texas, U of, Austin
Virginia Polytechnic Institute and State U
Washington, U of

Source: National Aeronautics and Space Administration, Washington, DC.

Top Astrophysics Programs

Akron, U of (OH)
Bennington C (VT)
Boston U (MA)
Brown U (RI)
California State U, San Francisco
Chicago, U of (IL)
Colgate U (NY)
Columbia U (NY)
Harvard U (MA)
Indiana U, Bloomington
Marlboro C (VT)
Massachusetts Institute of Technology
Michigan State U
Minnesota, U of, Twin Cities
Montana State U
New Mexico Institute of Mining and Technology
New Mexico, U of, Albuquerque
New York, City U of, Brooklyn C
Northwestern U (IL)
Oklahoma, U of
Pennsylvania, U of
Princeton U (NJ)
Purdue U (IN)
U.S. Military Academy (NY)
Virginia, U of
Wesleyan U (CT)
Williams C (MA)
Wisconsin, U of, Madison
Wyoming, U of

Schools with the Most Graduates Who Became Astronauts

Massachusetts Institute of Technology	20
Purdue U (IN)	18
Stanford U (CA)	14
Colorado, U of	10
Southern California, U of	9
California Institute of Technology	8
Houston, U of	8

Source: National Aeronautics and Space Administration, Washington, DC.

BUSINESS

Colleges with Focused Business Administration Programs

These colleges are known for emphasizing undergraduate preparation in business administration.

Babson C (MA)
Bentley C (MA)
Bryant C (RI)
Daniel Webster C (NH)
Maharishi U (IA)
New Hampshire C
Nichols C (MA)
Northwood U (MI)
Robert Morris C (PA)
Tiffin U (OH)
Webber C (FL)

Fine Business Programs at Arts and Sciences Colleges

These liberal arts colleges offer business programs, as well as a good mix of liberal arts and sciences courses.

Adrian C (MI)
Albion C (MI)
Albright C (PA)
Averett C (VA)
Baker U (KS)
Birmingham-Southern C (AL)
Bucknell U (PA)
Buena Vista C (IA)
Carthage C (WI)
Chapman U (CA)
City U (WA)
DePauw U (IN) (management fellows program)
Eckerd C (FL)
Elizabethtown C (PA)
Elmhurst C (IL)
Florida Southern C
Fontbonne C (MO)
Franklin Pierce C (NH)
Furman U (SC)
Gettysburg C (PA)
Greensboro C (NC)
Hawaii Pacific U
Hillsdale C (MI)
Indiana Wesleyan U
La Verne, U of (CA)
Lewis and Clark C (OR)
Linfield C (OR)
Lynn U (FL)
Manhattanville C (NY)
Marietta C (OH)
Menlo C (CA)
Millsaps C (MS)
Moravian C (PA)
Morehouse C (GA)
Muhlenberg C (PA)
Muskingum C (OH)
Nichols C (MA)
Ohio Wesleyan U
Presbyterian C (SC)
Puget Sound, U of (WA)
Quinnipiac C (CT)
Randolph-Macon C (VA)
Redlands, U of (CA)
Regis U (CO)
Rhodes C (TN)
Roger Williams C (RI)
St. Bonaventure U (NY)
St. Joseph's U (PA)
Samford U (AL)
San Francisco, U of (CA)
Seattle U (WA)
Skidmore C (NY)
Southwestern U (TX)
Spring Hill C (AL)
Stetson U (FL)
Susquehanna U (PA)
Transylvania U (KY)
Trinity U (TX)
Tusculum C (TN)
U.S. International U (CA)
Washington and Jefferson C (PA)
Washington and Lee U (VA)
Western New England C (MA)

Excellent Business Programs at Comprehensive Colleges

Among the numerous academic programs offered at these medium-sized universities, the program in business administration is recognized for its quality and academic strength. (Also see page 46 for schools with strong programs in international relations/international business.)

Adelphi U (NY)
Alfred U (NY)
Baylor U (TX)
Bloomsburg U (PA)
Boston C (MA)
Bradley U (IL)
Denver, U of (CO)
DePaul U (IL)
Drexel U (PA)
Emory U (GA)
Fairfield U (CT)
Florida Institute of Technology
Florida International C
Fordham U (NY)
Georgetown U (DC)
Hartford, U of (CT)
Hofstra U (NY)
Jacksonville U (FL)
John Carroll U (OH)
La Salle U (PA)
Lehigh U (PA)
Loyola C (MD)
Loyola U (IL)
Loyola U (LA)
Marquette U (WI)
Miami U (OH)
Mississippi, U of
New Orleans, U of (LA)
New York U
Northwest Missouri State U
Notre Dame, U of (IN)
Pennsylvania, U of
Pepperdine U (CA)
Richmond, U of (VA)
Rochester, U of (NY) (management certificate)
Rutgers U, Newark (NJ)
San Diego, U of (CA)
Santa Clara U (CA)
Southern California, U of
Southern Methodist U (TX)
Texas Christian U
Truman State U (MO)
Tulane U (LA)
Tulsa, U of (OK)
Villanova U (PA)
Virginia, U of
Wake Forest U (NC)
Washington U (MO)
William and Mary, C of (VA)

The Toughest Graduate Business Schools to Get Into

California, U of, Berkeley
California, U of, Los Angeles
Chicago, U of (IL)
Columbia U (NY)
Cornell U (NY)
Dartmouth C (NH)
Duke U (NC)
Harvard U (MA)
Massachusetts Institute of Technology
Michigan, U of, Ann Arbor
New York U
Northwestern U (IL)
Pennsylvania, U of
Stanford U (CA)
Virginia, U of
Yale U (CT)

Colleges with Outstanding Programs in Specific Business Areas

American Graduate School of International Management (AZ) (international business)
Arizona, U of (accounting)
Babson C (MA) (entrepreneurship)
Carnegie Mellon U (PA) (accounting, management information systems)
Chicago, U of (IL) (accounting, finance)
Connecticut, U of (real estate, insurance)
Cornell U (NY) (accounting, management)
Duke U (NC) (management)
Florida State U (accounting)
Harvard U (MA) (international business, nonprofit management)
Houston, U of (TX) (management)
Kansas, U of (accounting)
Maryland, U of, College Park (management)
Massachusetts Institute of Technology (management information systems and production)
Michigan, U of, Ann Arbor (accounting, general business, marketing)
New York, State U of, Buffalo (management)
Northwestern U (IL) (management, marketing)
Pennsylvania U of (accounting, entrepreneurship, financial management)
Pittsburgh, U of (PA) (management)
Rochester, U of (NY) (accounting, general business)
Rutgers U (NJ) (real estate, insurance)
South Carolina, U of, Columbia (international business, marketing, real estate, insurance)
Southern California, U of (finance, real estate, insurance)
Southern Methodist U (TX) (real estate, insurance)
Texas A&M U (general business, management, marketing)
Virginia Polytechnic Institute and State U (management, marketing)
Yale U (CT) (finance, nonprofit management)

The Best Business Schools for Entrepreneurs

"Instead of stale case studies and dusty academic research," says *Success* magazine, "these schools are proving that entrepreneurship can be taught." These colleges offer "the freshest ideas, brilliant strategies, and innovative technologies" in teaching business students.

Arizona, U of
Babson C (MA)
Ball State U (IN)
Baylor, U (TX)
Brigham Young U (UT)
California State U, San Diego
California, U of, Los Angeles
Carnegie Mellon U (PA)
Colorado, U of
Cornell U (NY)
DePaul U (IL)
Georgia, U of
Harvard U (MA)
Illinois, U of, Chicago
Maryland, U of, College Park
Nebraska, U of, Lincoln
New York U
Northwestern U (IL)
Pennsylvania, U of
Rensselaer Polytechnic Institute (NY)
St. Louis U (MO)
St. Thomas, U of (MN)
South Carolina, U of, Columbia
Southern California, U of
Texas, U of, Austin

Source: First appeared in *Success* magazine September 1997. Reprinted with the permission of *Success* magazine. To subscribe, call 1-800-234-7324.

MORE ACADEMIC FIELDS

ARCHITECTURE

Comprehensive Undergraduate and Graduate Architecture Schools

These schools offer programs in architecture accredited by the National Architectural Accrediting Board, leading to both bachelor's and master's degrees in architecture.

California State Polytechnic U, Pomona
Carnegie Mellon U (PA)
Catholic U (DC)
Florida A&M U
Hawaii, U of, Manoa
Houston, U of (TX)
Illinois, U of, Chicago
Iowa State U
Kent State U (OH)
Minnesota, U of, Twin Cities
New Jersey Institute of Technology
North Carolina State U
Oklahoma State U
Oklahoma, U of
Oregon, U of
Rensselaer Polytechnic Institute (NY)
Rice U (TX)
Southern California Institute of Architecture
Syracuse U (NY)
Texas, U of, Austin
Virginia Polytechnic Institute and State U

Source: National Architectural Accrediting Board, Washington, DC.

Excellent Undergraduate Architecture Schools

These schools offer bachelor's of architecture degree programs accredited by the National Architectural Accrediting Board.

Andrews U (MI)
Arizona, U of
Arkansas, U of, Fayetteville
Auburn U (AL)
Ball State U (IN)
Boston Architectural Center (MA)
California Polytechnic State U, San Luis Obispo
Cincinnati, U of (OH)
Cooper Union (NY)
Cornell U (NY)
Detroit Mercy, U of (MI)
Drexel U (PA)
Hampton U (VA)
Howard U (DC)
Idaho, U of
Illinois Institute of Technology
Kansas State U
Kansas, U of
Kentucky, U of
Lawrence Technological U (MI)
Louisiana State U, Baton Rouge
Louisiana Tech U
Miami, U of (FL)
Mississippi State U
Montana State U
New York, City U of, City C
New York Institute of Technology
North Carolina, U of, Charlotte
North Dakota State U
Notre Dame, U of (IN)
Pennsylvania State U, University Park
Pratt Institute (NY)
Rhode Island School of Design
Roger Williams C (RI)
Southern California, U of
Southern U (LA)
Southwestern Louisiana, U of
Temple U (PA)
Tennessee, U of, Knoxville
Texas Tech U
Tulane U (LA)
Tuskegee U (AL)
Washington State U

Source: National Architectural Accrediting Board, Washington, DC.

EDUCATION

Top Education Programs at Liberal Arts Colleges

These liberal arts and sciences colleges offer a strong program in education and teacher training.

Akron, U of (OH)
Alice Lloyd C (KY)
Alma C (MI)
Ashland U (OH)
Audrey Cohen C (NY)
Augustana C (IL)
Averett C (VA)
Berea C (KY)
Bethany C (KS)
Birmingham-Southern C (AL)
Bloomsburg U (PA)
Bob Jones U (SC)
Boston C (MA)
Buena Vista C (IA)
Butler U (IN)
Calvin C (MI)
Cardinal Stritch U (WI)
Carroll C (WI)
Catawba C (NC)
Centenary C (LA)
Central C (IA)
Concordia U (CA)
Davidson C (NC)
Dayton, U of (OH)
Defiance C (OH)
DePauw (IN)
Dordt C (IA)
Drake U (IA)
East Stroudsburg U (PA)
Elon C (NC)
Fort Hays State U (KS)
Guilford C (NC)
Gustavus Adolphus C (MN)
Hamline U (MN)
Hanover C (IN)
Hastings C (NE)
High Point U (NC)
Hiram C (OH)
Ithaca C (NY)
Lenoir-Rhyne C (NC)
Lesley C (MA)
Linfield C (OR)
Loras C (IA)
Marietta C (OH)
Millikin C (IL)
Millsaps C (MS)
Muhlenberg C (PA)
Muskingum C (OH)
Nebraska Wesleyan U (NE)
New York, State U of,
C at Cortland
Ohio Wesleyan U (OH)
Oklahoma Baptist U
Otterbein C (OH)
Principia C (IL)
Redlands, U of (CA)
St. Michael's C (VT)
St. Olaf C (MN)
Samford U (AL)
Simmons C (MA)
Southeast Missouri State U
Springfield C (MA)
Stetson C (FL)
Wake Forest U (NC)
Wartburg C (IA)
Wheaton C (IL)

Wheelock C (MA)
Wilmington C (DE)
Wittenberg C (OH)
Vanderbilt U (TN)

GRAPHIC DESIGN

Excellent Graphic Design Schools

Art Center C of Design (CA)
Art Institute of Chicago, School of the (IL)
California Institute of the Arts
Cincinnati, U of (OH)
New York School of Visual Art
Otis/Parsons School of Art and Design (CA)
Parsons School of Design (NY)
Philadelphia C of Art (PA)
Rhode Island School of Design

HOTEL AND RESTAURANT MANAGEMENT

Fine Hotel and Restaurant Management Schools

California State Polytechnic U, Pomona, School of Hotel and Restaurant Management
Cornell U (NY), School of Hotel Administration
Denver, U of (CO), School of Hospitality Management and Tourism
Florida International U, School of Hospitality Management
Georgia State U, Cecil B. Day School of Hospitality Administration
Hawaii, U of, Manoa, School of Travel Industry Management
Houston, U of (TX), Conrad N. Hilton College of Hotel and Restaurant Management
Johnson and Wales U (RI), College of Hospitality
Nevada, U of, Las Vegas, William F. Harrah College of Hotel Administration
New Haven, U of (CT), School of Hotel, Restaurant, and Tourism Administration
Massachusetts, U of, Amherst, Department of Hotel, Restaurant, and Travel Management
Michigan State U, School of Hotel, Restaurant, and Institutional Management
Pennsylvania State U, University Park, School of Hotel, Restaurant, and Institutional Management
South Carolina, U of, Columbia, School of Hotel, Restaurant, and Tourism Administration
Swiss Hospitality Institute (Washington, CT)
Washington State U, Hotel and Restaurant Administration Program
Widener U (PA), School of Hotel and Restaurant Management

INTERIOR DESIGN

Recognized Interior Design Colleges

These schools are accredited by the Foundation for Interior Design Education Research (FIDER).

Academy of Art C (CA)
Akron, U of (OH)
Alabama, U of
Alexandria Technical C (MN)
American C (CA)
American Intercontinental U (GA)
Arizona State U
Arkansas, U of
Art Institute in Atlanta (GA)
Auburn U (AL)
Bauder C (GA)
Berkeley C (NJ)
Brenau U (GA)
Brooks C (CA)
California C of Arts and Crafts
California State U, Fresno
California State U, Scaramento
California, U of, Berkeley*
California, U of, Los Angeles*
Cincinnati, U of (OH)
Colorado State U
Cornell U (NY)
Dakota County Technical C (MN)
Dawson C (Canada)
Design Institute of San Diego (CA)
Drexel U (PA)
East Carolina U (NC)
Eastern Michigan U
El Centro C (TX)
Endicott C (MA)
Fashion Institute of Design and Merchandising (CA)
Fashion Institute of Technology (NY)
Florida State U
Florida, U of
Georgia, U of
Harrington Institute of Interior Design (IL)
Houston Community College System (TX)
Indiana U, Bloomington
Interior Designers Institute (CA)
International Academy of Merchandising and Design (Canada)
International Academy of Merchandising and Design (FL)
International Academy of Merchandising and Design (IL)
International Fine Arts College (FL)
Iowa State U of Science and Technology
James Madison U (VA)
Kansas State U
Kendall C of Art and Design (MI)
Kent State U (OH)
Kentucky, U of
La Roche C (PA)

Recognized Interior Design Colleges (continued)

Lakeland C (Canada)
Lawrence Technological U (MI)
Louisiana State U, Baton Rouge
Louisiana Tech U
Manitoba, U of (Canada)
Maryland Institute College of Art
Marymount U (VA)
Maryville U (MO)
Massachusetts, U of, Amherst
Meredith College (NC)
Michigan State U
Middle Tennessee State U
Minnesota, U of, Twin Cities
Mississippi State U
Missouri, U of, Columbia
Moore C of Art and Design (PA)
Mt. Ida C (MA)
Mt. Mary C (WI)
Mt. Royal C (Canada)
Nebraska, U of, Lincoln
New England School of Art and Design (MA)
New Jersey, C of
New York Institute of Technology
New York School of Interior Design
Newbury C (MA)
North Carolina, U of, Greensboro
North Dakota State U
North Texas, U of
Northern Alberta Institute of Technology (Canada)
Ohio State U, Columbus
Ohio U
Oklahoma State U
Oklahoma, U of
O'More C of Design (TN)
Oregon, U of
Philadelphia College of Textiles and Science (PA)
Pratt Institute (NY)
Purdue U (IN)
Ricks C (ID)
Ringling School of Art and Design (FL)
Rochester Institute of Technology (NY)
Ryerson Polytechnic U (Canada)
San Diego Mesa C (CA)
San Diego State U (CA)
Seminole Community C (FL)
Southern C (FL)
Southern Illinois U, Carbondale
Southern Mississippi, U of
Southwest Texas State U
Southwestern Louisiana, U of
Stephen F. Austin State U (TX)
Suffolk County Community C (NY)
Syracuse U (NY)
Tennessee, U of, Knoxville
Texas Christian U
Texas Tech U
Texas, U of, Arlington
Texas, U of, Austin
Utah State U
Villa Maria C (NY)
Virginia Commonwealth U
Virginia Polytechnic Institute and State U

Washington State U
Watkins Institute C of Art and Design (TN)
Wentworth Institute of Technology (MA)
West Valley C (CA)
West Virginia U
Western Carolina U (NC)
Western Michigan U (MI)
Winthrop U (SC)
Wisconsin, U of, Madison
Wisconsin, U of, Stevens Point
Woodbury U (CA)

*Note: Only the extension divisions of Berkeley and UCLA are recognized by FIDER.

OCCUPATIONAL THERAPY

Comprehensive Occupational Therapy Programs

These colleges offer both bachelor's and master's degrees and/or a combined program.

Boston U (MA), (Sargent C of Allied Health Professions)
California State U, San Jose
Colorado State U
D'Youville C (NY) (offers a five-year combined B.A./M.A. program)
New York U
Puget Sound, U of (WA)
Southern California, U of
Springfield C (MA) (offers a five-year combined B.A./M.A. program)
Texas Woman's U
Touro C (NY) (offers a three-year combined B.A./M.A. program)
Towson State U (MD)
Virginia Commonwealth U
Washington U (MO) (School of Medicine)
Western Michigan U

Source: American Occupational Therapy Association, Rockville, MD.

PHYSICAL THERAPY

Comprehensive Physical Therapy Programs

These colleges offer both undergraduate and graduate degrees in physical therapy.

Evansville, U of (IN)
Mt. St. Mary's C (CA)
North Dakota, U of
Old Dominion U (VA)
Pittsburgh, U of (PA)
Virginia Commonwealth U
Wichita State U (KS)

Source: American Physical Therapy Association, Alexandria, VA.

WOMEN'S STUDIES

Colleges with Fine Women's Studies Programs

Albion C (MI)
Amherst C (MA)
Antioch C (OH)
Appalachian State U (NC)
Arizona State U
Arizona, U of
Augsburg C (MN)
Augustana C (IL)
Barnard C (NY)
Bates C (ME)
Beloit C (WI)
Bennington C (VT)
Bowling Green State U (OH)
Burlington C (VT)
Cabrillo C (CA)
California State U, Long Beach
California State U, Northridge
California State U, Sacramento
California State U, San Diego
California State U, San Francisco
California State U, San Jose
California, U of, Berkeley
California, U of, Irvine
California, U of, Los Angeles
California, U of, Santa Barbara
California, U of, Santa Cruz
Carlow C (PA)
Cedar Crest C (PA)
Claremont Colleges Consortium (CA)
Clark Atlanta U (GA)
Colby C (ME)
Colby-Sawyer C (NH)
Colgate U (NY)
Colorado, U of, Boulder
Colorado, U of, Colorado Springs
Columbia U (NY)
Connecticut C
Connecticut, U of
Cornell C (IA)
Cornell U (NY)
Cosumnes River College (CA)
Curry College (MA)
Delaware, U of
Denison U (OH)
Denver, U of (CO)
Earlham C (IN)
Eckerd C (FL)
Emory U (GA)
Fordham U (NY)
Goucher C (MD)
Hamilton C (NY)
Harvard U (MA)
Hawaii, U of, Manoa
Illinois U of, Urbana
Iowa State U
Kansas State U
Kansas, U of
Lewis and Clark C (OR)
Lycoming C (PA)
Maine, U of
Mankato State U (MN)
Mary Washington C (VA)
Maryland, U of, Baltimore County
Maryland, U of, College Park
Massachusetts Institute of Technology
Massachusetts, U of, Amherst
Massachusetts, U of, Boston
Mercy C (NY)
Metropolitan State C (CO)
Michigan, U of, Ann Arbor
Middlebury C (VT)

Colleges with Fine Women's Studies Programs (continued)

Mills C (CA)
Minnesota, U of, Duluth
Minnesota, U of, Twin Cities
Missouri, U of, Columbia
Monterey Peninsula C (CA)
Mt. Holyoke C (MA)
Mt. St. Joseph, C of (OH)
Nebraska, U of, Lincoln
New York, City U, Brooklyn C
New York, City U, C of Staten Island
New York, City U, Hunter C
New York, City U, Queens C
New York, State U of, Albany
New York, State U of, C at Brockport
New York, State U of, C at Buffalo
New York U
North Carolina, U of, Greensboro
Northeastern Illinois U
Northern Colorado, U of
Oberlin C (OH)
Ohio State U, Columbus
Ohio Wesleyan U
Old Dominion U (VA)
Pennsylvania State U, University Park
Pennsylvania, U of
Pittsburgh, U of (PA)
Pitzer C (CA)
Pomona C (CA)
Princeton Theological Seminary (NJ)
Redlands, U of (CA)
Rhode Island C
Rhode Island, U of
Richmond, U of (VA)
Rochester, U of (NY)
Rutgers U, Douglass C (NJ)
Sacramento City C (CA)
St. Olaf C (MN)
Sangamon State U (IL)
Simmons C (MA)
Simon's Rock C of Bard (MA)
Smith C (MA)
South Carolina, U of, Columbia
South Florida, U of
Southeastern Massachusetts U
Southern Maine, U of
Southwestern U (TX)
Stanford U (CA)
Suffolk County Community C (NY)
Temple U (PA)
Tompkins Cortland Community C (NY)
Trinity C (CT)
Tulane U (LA)
Union C (NY)
Utah, U of
Vassar C (NY)
Washington U (MO)
Washington, U of
Wellesley C (MA)
Wesleyan U (CT)
Western Michigan U
Wichita State U (KS)
Wisconsin, U of, Madison
Wisconsin, U of, Platteville
Wisconsin, U of, Whitewater
Wooster, C of (OH)
Yale U (CT)

Source: Data compiled from information in *NWSA Directory of Women's Studies Programs, Women's Centers, and Women's Research Centers*, National Women's Studies Association, College Park, MD.

CLUSTERS OF COLLEGES

Often, colleges, particularly smaller ones, find they can offer expanded academic and social programs by forming clusters or consortia. Students at member schools may be able to cross-register, travel together, or make use of joint resources or facilities.

Associated Colleges of the Midwest

Beloit C (WI)
Carleton C (MN)
Chicago, U of (IL)
Coe C (IA)
Colorado C
Cornell C (IA)
Grinnell C (IA)
Knox C (IL)
Lake Forest C (IL)
Lawrence U (WI)
Macalester C (MN)
Monmouth C (IL)
Ripon C (WI)
St. Olaf C (MN)

Associated Colleges of the St. Lawrence Valley

Clarkson U (NY)
New York, State U of, C at Potsdam
New York, State U of, C of Technology, Canton
St. Lawrence U (NY)

Associated Colleges of the South

Birmingham-Southern C (AL)
Centenary C (LA)
Centre C (KY)
Furman U (SC)
Hendrix C (AR)
Millsaps C (MS)
Morehouse C (GA)
Rhodes C (TN)
Richmond, U of (VA)
Rollins C (FL)
South, U of the (TN)
Southwestern U (TX)
Trinity U (TX)
Washington and Lee U (VA)

Atlanta University Center

Clark Atlanta U (GA)
Interdenominational Theological Center (GA)
Morehouse C (GA)
Morehouse School of Medicine (GA)
Morris Brown C (GA)
Spelman C (GA)

The Claremont Colleges

Claremont McKenna C (CA)
Harvey Mudd C (CA)
Pitzer C (CA)
Pomona C (CA)
Scripps C (CA)

Five-College Consortium

Amherst C (MA)
Hampshire C (MA)
Massachusetts, U of, Amherst
Mt. Holyoke C (MA)
Smith C (MA)

Great Lakes Colleges Association

Albion C (MI)
Antioch C (OH)
Denison U (OH)
DePauw U (IN)
Earlham C (IN)
Hope C (MI)
Kalamazoo C (MI)
Kenyon C (OH)
Oberlin C (OH)
Ohio Wesleyan U
Wabash C (IN)
Wooster, C of (OH)

Lehigh Valley Association of Independent Colleges

Allentown C (PA)
Cedar Crest C (PA)
Lafayette C (PA)
Lehigh U (PA)
Moravian C (PA)
Muhlenberg C (PA)

Seven-College Exchange

Hampden-Sydney C (VA)
Hollins C (VA)
Mary Baldwin C (VA)
Randolph-Macon C (VA)
Randolph-Macon Woman's C (VA)
Sweet Briar C (VA)
Washington and Lee U (VA)

Southern Consortium

Agnes Scott C (GA)
Davidson C (NC)
Emory U (GA)
Furman U (SC)
Hollins C (VA)
Miami, U of (FL)
Rhodes C (TN)
Rice U (TX)
Richmond, U of (VA)
Rollins C (FL)
South, U of the (TN)
Southern Methodist U (TX)
Stetson U (FL)
Texas Christian U
Trinity U (TX)
Tulane U (LA)
Vanderbilt U (TN)
Wake Forest U (NC)
Washington and Lee U (VA)

Twelve-College Exchange

Amherst C (MA)
Bowdoin C (ME)
Connecticut C
Dartmouth C (NH)
Mt. Holyoke C (MA)
Smith C (MA)
Trinity C (CT)
Vassar C (NY)
Wellesley C (MA)
Wesleyan U (CT)
Wheaton C (MA)
Williams C (MA)

Washington Consortium

American U (DC)
Catholic U (DC)
District of Columbia, U of
Gallaudet U (DC)
George Mason U (VA)
George Washington U (DC)
Georgetown U (DC)
Howard U (DC)
Maryland, U of
Marymount U (VA)
Trinity C (DC)

Worcester Consortium

Anna Maria C (MA)
Assumption C (MA)
Becker C (MA)
Clark U (MA)
Holy Cross, C of the (MA)
Massachusetts, U of, Medical Center
Quinsigamond Community C (MA)
Tufts New England Veterinary Medical Center (MA)
Worcester Polytechnic Institute (MA)
Worcester State C (MA)

PROGRAMS FOR STUDENTS WITH LEARNING DISABILITIES

Top Schools for Students with Learning Disabilities

These colleges have strong, separate programs for students with learning disabilities or have significant forms of academic support services available.

Adelphi U (NY)—Program for College Students with Learning Disabilities
Alabama, U of, Birmingham—Horizons Program
American International C (MA)—Supportive Learning Services Program (SLSP)
American U (DC)—Learning Services Program
Arizona, U of—Strategic Alternative Learning Techniques (SALT)
Augsburg C (MN)—Center for Learning and Adaptive Student Services (CLASS)
Barat C (IL)—Learning Opportunities Program (LOP)
Beacon C (FL)—The college is devoted to students with learning disabilities.
Bradford C (MA)—College Learning Program (CLP)
Brenau U (GA)—Learning Center (LC)
California Polytechnic State U, San Luis Obispo—Disabled Student Services (DSS)
Curry C (MA)—Program for Advancement in Learning (PAL)
Davis and Elkins C (WV)—Learning Disability Special Services
Denver, U of (CO)—Learning Effectiveness Program (LEP)
DePaul U (IL)—Productive Learning Strategies (PLUS)
Fairleigh Dickinson U (NJ)—Regional Center for College Students with LD

Top Schools for Students with Learning Disabilities (continued)

Frostburg State U (MD)—Student Support Services
Hartford, U of (CT)—Learning Plus
Hofstra U (NY)—Program for Academic Learning Skills (PALS)
Indianapolis, U of (IN)—BUILD
Iona C (NY)—College Assistance Program (CAP)
Landmark C (VT)—The college is devoted to students with learning disabilities.
Lesley C (MA)—Threshold Program
Loras C (IA)—Learning Disabilities Program
Lynn U (FL)—The Advancement Program (TAP)
Marshall U (WV)—Higher Education for Learning Problems (HELP)
Mitchell C (CT)—Learning Resource Center (LRC)
Monmouth C (NJ)—Support Services for Students with LD
Mt. Ida C (MA)—Learning Opportunities Program (LOP)
Mt. St. Joseph, C of (OH)—Project Excel
Muskingum C (OH)—PLUS Program
National-Louis U (IL)—Center for Academic Development
New England C (NH)—College Skills Center
New England, U of (ME)—Individual Learning Program (ILP)
St. Ambrose U (IA)—Services for Students with Disabilities
St. Thomas Aquinas C (NY)—The STAC Exchange
Schreiner C (TX)—Learning Support Services
Southern Illinois U, Carbondale—Achieve Program
Southern Vermont C—Learning Disability Program
Truckee Meadows Community C (NV)—Learning Disability Program
Unity C (ME)—Learning Resource Center (LRC)
Vermont, U of—Office of Specialized Student Services
Vincennes U (IN)—Student Transition into Education Program (STEP)
West Virginia Wesleyan C—Special Support Services Program
Westminster C (MO)—Learning Disabilities Program
Wingate C (NC)—Specific Learning Disabilities
Wisconsin, U of, Madison—McBurney Disability Resource Center
Wisconsin, U of, Oshkosh—Project Success

The Experts' Choice: The Top Colleges for a Student with a Mild Learning Disability

1. West Virginia Wesleyan C
2. Curry C (MA)
3. American U (DC)
*4. Colorado, U of
*5. New England C (NH)
6. Muhlenberg C (PA)
*7. Ohio Wesleyan U
*8. Syracuse U (NY)
9. Adelphi U (NY)
*10. Elon C (NC)
*11. Muskingum C (OH)
*12. Vermont, U of

*See Author's Note, p. xxv.

Colleges with Excellent Support for Learning Disabled Students

Geraldine Fryer, educational consultant and expert on colleges with learning disabilities programs, selected the following schools as tops for LD students.

American International College (MA)
Arizona, U of
Denver, U of (CO)
Fairleigh Dickinson U (NJ)
Hofstra U (NY)
Lynn U (FL)
Manhattanville C (NY)
Marist C (NY)
Marshall U (WV)
Marymount C (CA)
Muhlenberg C (PA)
Northeastern U (MA)
Providence C (RI)
Seattle U (WA)
Syracuse U (NY)
Vermont, U of
Wittenberg U (OH)

Colleges with a Caring Attitude toward the Needs of Learning Disabled Students

Abilene Christian U (TX)
Alaska, U of, Anchorage
Alaska, U of, Fairbanks
California State Polytechnic U, San Luis Obispo
Calvin C (MI)
Champlain C (VT)
Colby-Sawyer C (NH)
Dean C (MA)
Drury C (MO)
East Stroudsburg U (PA)
Georgia Southern U
Green Mountain C (VT)
Hastings C (NE)
Huron C (SD)
Indiana Wesleyan U
Lenoir-Rhyne C (NC)
Liberty U (VA)
Louisiana State U, Baton Rouge
Maine, U of, Machias
Manhattanville C (NY)
Memphis, U of (TN)
Miami U (OH)
Misericordia C (PA)
Mitchell C (CT)
Montana State U, Billings
Mt. Ida C (MA)
National-Louis U (IL)
New Hampshire, U of
New York, State U of, C of Technology at Alfred
North Carolina, U of, Greensboro
Northern Arizona U
Northern Colorado, U of
Ozarks, U of the (AR)
Pacific, U of the (CA)
Redlands, U of (CA)
Rochester Institute of Technology (NY)
San Francisco, U of (CA)
Santa Fe, C of (NM)
Southwest Missouri State U
Springfield C (MA)
Tulsa, U of (OK)
Waldorf C (IA)
Washington State U
Western Maryland C
Whittier C (CA)
Widener U (PA)
Wisconsin, U of, La Crosse
Wyoming, U of

DIFFERENT CALENDARS

Colleges with Unique Calendars

Most colleges divide their academic year into two semesters of equal length. These colleges, on the other hand, have other types of academic calendars.

Alma C (MI): short spring term in May
Bard C (NY): Winter Field Experience is a six-week program starting at the end of December
Bates C (ME): after second semester, a five-week short term is offered
Carleton C (MN): three ten-week terms per year
Centre C (KY): a six-week winter term between the two semesters
Cincinnati, U of (OH): trimester
Colorado C: the Block Plan, in which students take one course every three and a half weeks
Cornell C (IA): one course at a time, each course lasting three and a half weeks
Dartmouth C (NH): flexible year-round calendar, four terms per year
Denison U (OH): optional May term
Earlham C (IN): trimester calendar, three classes per term
Elmira C (NY): Term 3 is six-week special study term starting at end of April
Florida Southern C: four-week term at the end of the school year
Furman U (SC): eight-week winter term
Hanover C (IN): one-month term at the end of the school year
Hendrix C (AR): trimester
Hobart C (NY): trimester

Colleges with Unique Calendars (continued)

Houghton C (NY): optional three-week term at the end of the school year
Indianapolis, U of (IN): short spring term at the end of the school year
Kalamazoo C (MI): parts of the four years available for career development, foreign study, internships, and research
Knox C (IL): three ten-week terms per year
Lawrence U (WI): trimester
Lewis and Clark C (OR): trimester
Maharishi U (IA): one course at a time
Northland C (WI): short spring term at the end of the school year
Occidental C (CA): three ten-week terms per year
Queens C (NC): one-month term at the end of the school year
Roanoke C (VA): early semester calendar
Transylvania U (KY): one-month May term
Tusculum C (TN): courses taught one at a time
Union C (NY): trimester
Vanderbilt U (TN): Maymester, which is a four-week May term
Wartburg C (IA): short spring term at the end of the school year
Washington and Lee U (VA): six-week spring term
William Smith C (NY): trimester
William Woods C (MO): a one-month short term at the end of the school year for intensive study in one class or travel
Wittenberg U (OH): three eleven-week terms
Worcester Polytechnic Institute (MA): four terms, each seven weeks, per year

Colleges with January Terms

These colleges provide opportunities in January (between the two semesters) for students to take special classwork, pursue internships, study abroad, or be involved in volunteer projects.

Albright C (PA)
Amherst C (MA)
Austin C (TX)
Baker U (KS)
Bard C (NY)
Bethany C (KS)
Birmingham-Southern C (AL)
Bucknell U (PA)
Buena Vista C (IA)
Calvin C (MI)
Colby C (ME)
Colgate U (NY)
Delaware, U of
DePauw U (IN)
Drew U (NJ)
Eckerd C (FL)
Gettysburg C (PA)
Gustavus Adolphus C (MN)
Hartwick C (NY)
Hofstra U (NY)
Hollins C (VA)
Illinois Wesleyan U
Johns Hopkins U (MD)
Lafayette C (PA)
Luther C (IA)
Macalester C (MN)
Massachusetts Institute of Technology
Massachusetts, U of, Amherst
Middlebury C (VT)
Mt. Holyoke C (MA)
New College (FL)
Oberlin C (OH)
Randolph-Macon C (VA)
Redlands, U of (CA)
Rhode Island School of Design
St. Benedict, C of/St. John's U (MN)
St. Lawrence U (NY)
St. Olaf C (MN)
San Francisco, U of (CA)
Stetson U (FL)
Sweet Briar C (VA)
Washington and Jefferson C (PA)
Wells C (NY)
Whittier C (CA)
Whitworth C (WA)
William Jewell C (MO)
Williams C (MA)
Wisconsin, U of, Green Bay
Wofford C (SC)

ACADEMIC POTPOURRI

Colleges with Special Course Offerings

These colleges have the unique, special, or unusual academic programs listed.

Adrian C (MI) (arts management)
Alfred U (NY) (ceramic engineering, art, glass study)
Arizona, U of (racetrack industry program)
Artisans College (VT) (shipbuilding)
California State U, San Jose (aviation)
Carthage C (WI) (entrepreneurial studies in the natural sciences)
Centre C (KY) (glassblowing)
Colorado School of Mines (geological engineering)
Concordia C (MN) (institute of German studies)
Connecticut, U of (puppetry)
Digipen Institute of Technology (WA) (four-year degree in computer game programming)
Embry-Riddle Aeronautical U (FL) (aviation studies)
Findlay, U of (OH) (equestrian studies)
Florida Institute of Technology (aviation/aeronautics)
Full Sail Center for the Recording Arts (FL) (recording engineering)
Hartwick C (NY) (equestrian studies)
Johns Hopkins U (MD) (sound recording [Peabody Conservatory])
Johnson County Community C (KS) (railroad training)
Kendall C (IL) (culinary program)
Liverpool Institute for Performing Arts (UK) (sound technology)
Lynn U (FL) (gerontology)

Miami, U of (FL) (sound recording)
Middle Tennessee State U (recording industry management)
New Hampshire C (sports management)
New Haven, U of (CT) (music and sound recording)
New York, City U of, John Jay C (criminal justice)
New York, State U of, Albany (criminal justice)
New York, State U of, C of Environmental Science and Forestry (ranger training)
New York, State U of, Morrisville (equine racing management)
North Carolina State U (textiles)
North Central C (IL) (leadership)
North Dakota, U of (aviation/aerospace)
Northeastern U (MA) (criminal justice)
Northwestern U (IL) (speech)
Ohio State U, Columbus (black studies)
Paradise Ranch Racing School for Jockeys (CA) (horse racing)
Penland School of Crafts (NC) (clay, metal, glass, fiber)
Renton Technical C (WA) (musical instrument repair)
Rivier C (NH) (exercise psychology and sports medicine)
Rochester Institute of Technology (NY) (photography, printing)
Roger Williams U (RI) (architecture)
Rutgers U (NJ) (ceramic engineering)
St. Mary's C (MN) (electronic publishing)
School for Mechanics (AZ) (Harley-Davidson repair)
Southern Illinois U, Carbondale (aviation)
Springfield C (MA) (allied health areas, physical education)
Stephens C (MO) (equestrian science)

Colleges with Innovative Academic Programs

These colleges have a nontraditional or alternative character. At some of the schools, the unique experience is campuswide; at others, it is limited to the particular unit or division indicated.

Alverno C (WI)—assessment areas instead of grades; most students have jobs; competency-based curriculum that encourages mastery of skills
Antioch C (OH)—individualistic; work quarters alternate with study quarters
Atlantic, C of the (ME)—focuses on the study of people's relationship to the environment, self-designed academic program
Bennington C (VT)—unstructured curriculum; progressive
Berea C (KY)—all students work
Blackburn C (IL)—students work fifteen hours a week
California, U of, San Diego—five colleges divided on the basis of educational philosophy, environments, and requirements for degrees
California, U of, Santa Barbara—the College of Creative Studies enrolls approximately 150 gifted students; classes are tutorial
California, U of, Santa Cruz—interdisciplinary programs; narrative evaluation system; residential college system
Clarkson School, Clark U (NY)—for high school–aged students ready for college work
Dallas, U of (TX)—Great Books program (Instead of traditional textbooks, students learn the liberal arts by studying the classics—Plato, Euclid, Shakespeare, the Bible, and so on.)
Deep Springs C (CA)—very small, intellectual, individualistic, community-oriented; campus is an active ranch
Elon C (NC)—more in-depth learning in fewer courses
Eugene Lang C (NY)—all classes taught as seminars; students design course of study
Evergreen State C (WA)—one interdisciplinary program at a time; learning contracts; no distribution requirements; written evaluations
Goddard C (VT)—program based on independent study and internships
Hampshire C (MA)—written assessments instead of grades; independent projects

Hofstra U (NY)—New College offers flexible requirements and individualized education
International Training, School for (VT)—offers bachelor's degrees in world issues/world studies
Kalamazoo C (MI)—students incorporate career internship, study abroad, and senior project into their college years
Long Island U, Southampton (NY)—Friends World program features a global perspective, volunteerism, field work, individual study plans
Manhattanville C (NY)—Portfolio Program lets students design plan of study
Marlboro C (VT)—no required courses; many tutorials and research projects; community government; independent study in final two years; no varsity sports
Metropolitan State U (MN)—individualized majors; few structured programs
Miami U (OH)—Western College provides individualized and interdisciplinary programs of study
New C (CA)—Humanities Program offers interdisciplinary study in discussion-oriented, tutorial classes; an autobiography and a senior project are required
New C (FL)—individualized learning contracts; independent study; tutorials
New C (part of Norwich U, VT)—off-campus experiences such as internships, volunteer work, and cross-country experiences
New York, State U of, Purchase—flexible; narrative evaluations
Pitzer C (CA)—few requirements; creative freedom
Prescott C (AZ)—experiential education; narrative evaluations; learning by doing
Redlands, U of (CA)—Johnston Center for Individualized Instruction, in which students create course of study on contract
Reed C (OR)—conference system; student-run workshops in January
St. John's C (MD) and (NM)—entire program based on reading and discussing major books of Western civilization; discussions instead of lectures
St. Olaf C (MN)—Paracollege, a college within a college, offers self-directed study including tutorials
Sarah Lawrence C (NY)—seminar/conference system; written evaluations; individualized

Colleges with Innovative Academic Programs (continued)

Shimer C (IL)—Great Books curriculum (see Dallas, U of, p. 96); Socratic method; small class discussion

Simon's Rock, C of Bard (MA)—for students of high school age ready to start college early

Sterling C (VT)—emphasizes ecology/forestry; hands-on work experiences; interaction with the environment

Thomas Aquinas C (CA)—Great Books curriculum (See Dallas, U of, p. 96); classes taught as seminars; no majors

Thomas More C (NH)—students read the classics; individualized education

United World C (NM)—for high school students who wish to pursue an international baccalaureate

Unity C (ME)—focus on environmental science and natural resources; cooperative education; outdoor experiences

Warren Wilson C (NC)—academic program plus student work experiences

Western Washington U—Fairhaven College allows for small classes, interdisciplinary course work, independent study, and student-designed majors

The Forty Largest College Libraries

The number of volumes in the library is given.

1. Harvard U (MA)	13,369,855
2. Yale U (CT)	9,758,341
3. Illinois, U of, Urbana	8,840,326
4. California, U of, Berkeley	8,462,123
5. Texas, U of, Austin	7,329,663
6. Toronto, U of (Canada)	6,905,360
7. Michigan, U of, Ann Arbor	6,874,648
8. Columbia U (NY)	6,792,274
9. California, U of, Los Angeles	6,772,851
10. Stanford U (CA)	6,746,550
11. Chicago, U of (IL)	5,982,101
12. Cornell U (NY)	5,952,217
13. Indiana U, Bloomington	5,790,384
14. Wisconsin, U of, Madison	5,737,834
15. Washington, U of	5,601,263
16. Princeton U (NJ)	5,405,087
17. Minnesota, U of, Twin Cities	5,376,090
18. Alberta, U of (Canada)	5,085,060
19. Ohio State U, Columbus	4,977,610
20. North Carolina, U of, Chapel Hill	4,674,502
21. Duke U (NC)	4,534,208
22. Pennsylvania, U of	4,437,523
23. Arizona, U of	4,343,130
24. Virginia, U of	4,276,435
25. Michigan State U	4,047,477
26. Northwestern U (IL)	3,840,439
27. Iowa, U of	3,751,596
28. British Columbia, U of (Canada)	3,745,735
29. Pittsburgh, U of (PA)	3,730,776
30. Pennsylvania State U (all campuses)	3,724,916
31. Rutgers U (NJ) (all campuses)	3,567,690
32. New York U	3,508,001
33. Kansas, U of	3,450,463
34. Georgia, U of	3,392,238
35. Southern California, U of	3,344,620
36. Florida, U of	3,258,300
37. Arizona State U	3,175,896

38. Johns Hopkins U (MD) 3,172,679
39. Washington U (MO) 3,164,136
40. New York, State U of, Buffalo 2,991,288

Source: *ARL Statistics*, Washington, DC: Association of Research Libraries, 1995–96.

Medium-Sized Colleges with Large Library Holdings

Alabama, U of, Tuscaloosa
Brown U (RI)
California, U of, Irvine
California, U of, San Diego
Case Western Reserve U (OH)
Cincinnati, U of (OH)
Connecticut, U of
Dartmouth C (NH)
Delaware, U of
Emory U (GA)
Georgetown U (DC)
Georgia Institute of Technology
Guelph, U of (Canada)
Hawaii, U of
Howard U (DC)
Massachusetts Institute of Technology
Miami, U of (FL)
New Mexico, U of
New York, State U of, Stony Brook
Notre Dame, U of (IN)
Oregon, U of
Queen's U (Canada)
Rice U (TX)
Rochester, U of (NY)
Syracuse U (NY)
Tulane U (LA)
Vanderbilt U (TN)

Source: *ARL Statistics*, Washington, DC: Association of Research Libraries, 1995–96.

Leaders in Integrating Computers into Academic Life

At these colleges, personal computers are required of every student, or the college emphasizes the advantage of technology in the classroom.

Clarkson U (NY)
Dartmouth C (NH)
Drew U (NJ)
Drexel U (PA)
Florida, U of
Hartwick C (NY)
Longwood C (VA)
Mayville State U (ND)
Minnesota, U of, Crookston
North Carolina, U of, Chapel Hill
Rose-Hulman Institute of Technology (IN)
Stevens Institute of Technology (NJ)
Virginia Polytechnic Institute and State U
Virginia, U of
Wake Forest (NC)
Waldorf C (IA)
Wesleyan C (GA)
West Virginia Wesleyan C

Campuses with Major Internet Access

Arizona, U of
Auburn U (AL)
Boston U (MA)
California Institute of Technology
California, U of, Berkeley
California, U of, Davis
California, U of, Santa Cruz
Carnegie Mellon U (PA)
Case Western Reserve U (OH)
Colby C (ME)
Connecticut, U of
Dartmouth C (NH)
Delaware, U of
Drexel U (PA)
Emerson C (MA)
Hamilton C (NY)
Holy Cross, C of the (MA)
Huntingdon C (AL)
Illinois, U of, Urbana
Indiana U
Iowa State U
Massachusetts Institute of Technology
Middlebury C (VT)
New Jersey Institute of Technology
New York U
Northwestern U (IL)
Oregon, U of
Pennsylvania, U of
Pomona C (CA)
Princeton U (NJ)
Reed C (OR)
Rensselaer Institute of Technology (NY)
Rhodes C (TN)
Rice U (TX)
Rochester, U of (NY)
St. Benedict, C of (MN)
Skidmore C (NY)
Stanford U (CA)
Stevens Institute of Technology (NJ)
Sweet Briar C (VA)
Texas, U of, Austin
Tulane U (LA)
Virginia Polytechnic Institute and State U
Wesleyan C (GA)
Worcester Polytechnic Institute (MA)

Pass/Fail Colleges

These schools offer pass/fail, credit/no credit, satisfactory/no credit options for first-year students.

Brown U (RI)
California Institute of Technology
Massachusetts Institute of Technology
Rochester, U of (NY)
Swarthmore C (PA)

Colleges with Special Senior Requirements

These colleges require either a senior thesis, a senior comprehensive project, or a senior comprehensive examination to complete an undergraduate degree.

Allegheny C (PA)—senior project
Bard C (NY)—senior project
Bethany C (WV)—senior examination and senior project
Bradford C (MA)—senior project
California, U of, Santa Cruz—senior thesis or examination
Carleton C (MN)—senior comprehensive project
Goddard C (VT)—senior project
Goucher C (MD)—every student completes an off-campus experience, such as a special project, internship, or foreign study
Hobart C (NY)—senior essay
Kalamazoo C (MI)—senior individualized project
Kenyon C (OH)—senior oral and written examinations
Marlboro C (VT)—senior project
New C (CA)—senior project
New C (FL)—senior thesis
Occidental C (CA)—senior comprehensive examination
Parsons School of Design (NY)—senior project
Princeton U (NJ)—senior thesis
Reed C (OR)—senior thesis
Scripps C (CA)—senior thesis
South, U of the (TN)—comprehensive examination
Stevens Institute of Technology (NJ)—senior project
Swarthmore C (PA)—senior oral and written examinations

Colleges with Special Senior Requirements (continued)

Sweet Briar C (VA)—senior comprehensive examination
Ursinus C (PA)—Capstone experience (senior research project)
Whitman C (WA)—senior examination
Wooster, C of (OH)—senior independent project

Colleges That Require a Swimming Test to Graduate

Berea C (KY)
Bryn Mawr C (PA)
Carleton C (MN)
Colgate U (NY)
Columbia U (NY)
Cornell U (NY)
Dartmouth C (NH)
Hamilton C (NY)

Colleges That Offer Opportunities to Study Autonomously

These schools offer students the opportunity to study on their own: to take courses outside the normal curriculum, to work on projects or extended papers, and so on.

Amherst C (MA)
Bard C (NY)
Barnard C (NY)
Coe C (IA)
Hampshire C (MA)
Marlboro C (VT)
Massachusetts Institute of Technology
Michigan, U of, Ann Arbor
Randolph-Macon C (VA)
Redlands, U of (CA)
Reed C (OR)
Sarah Lawrence C (NY)
Swarthmore C (PA)
Wooster, C of (OH)

Colleges Known for Offering a Bachelor's Degree in Three Years

Albertus Magnus C (CT)
Drury C (MO)
Longwood C (VA)
Middlebury C (VT)
New Hampshire C
Oberlin C (OH)
Upper Iowa U
Valparaiso U (IN)

State Schools with Honors Colleges for Top Students

Many public colleges and universities have honors programs (or separate honors colleges) for very good students. Honors programs typically incorporate smaller classes, top faculty, special course offerings, opportunities for individual research or independent study, and, occasionally, separate dorms. Some of these programs are open only to liberal arts students.

Alabama, U of, Birmingham
Alabama, U of, Tuscaloosa
Arizona State U
Arizona, U of
Arkansas, U of, Fayetteville
Boise State U (ID)
California, U of, Los Angeles
Central Michigan U
Clemson U (SC) (Calhoun College)
Colorado State U
Connecticut, U of
Delaware, U of
Florida, U of
Georgia, U of
Houston, U of (TX)
Illinois State U
Indiana U, Bloomington
Iowa State U
James Madison U (VA)
Kansas State U
Kansas, U of
Kent State U (OH)
Kentucky, U of
Louisiana State U, Baton Rouge
Maine, U of, Orono
Maryland, U of, College Park
Massachusetts, U of, Amherst
Miami U (OH) (Western College)
Michigan State U
Michigan, U of, Ann Arbor (Residential College)
Minnesota, U of, Twin Cities
Mississippi State U
Missouri, U of, Columbia
Montana, U of
Nebraska, U of, Lincoln
New Hampshire, U of
New Jersey Institute of Technology

State Schools with Honors Colleges for Top Students (continued)

New York, State U of, Buffalo
New York, State U of, Stony Brook
North Carolina, U of, Chapel Hill
Ohio State U, Columbus
Ohio U, Athens
Oregon, U of
Pennsylvania State U, University Park (University Scholars)
Pittsburgh, U of (PA)
Rutgers U (NJ) (Rutgers College)
St. Mary's C (MD) (a public honors college)
South Carolina, U of, Columbia
South Florida, U of (New C)
Tennessee, U of, Knoxville
Texas A&M U
Texas, U of, Austin (Plan 2)
Trenton State C (NJ)
Utah, U of
Virginia Polytechnic Institute and State U
Virginia, U of
Washington State U
Washington, U of
West Virginia U
Western Washington U (Fairhaven C)
Wyoming, U of

College Members of the National Student Exchange

Founded in 1968, the National Student Exchange is a "domestic alternative" to study abroad. Students may study for a full year at another member college. More than 2,000 students per year participate in the program.

Alabama A&M U
Alabama State U
Alabama, U of
Alaska, U of, Anchorage
Alaska, U of, Fairbanks
Alaska, U of, Southeast
Arizona, U of
Boise State U (ID)
Bowie State U (MD)
Bowling Green State U (OH)
California Polytechnic State U, San Luis Obispo
California State Polytechnic U, Pomona
California State U, Bakersfield
California State U, Chico
California State U, Dominguez Hills
California State U, Fresno
California State U, Hayward
California State U, Humboldt
California State U, Los Angeles
California State U, Northridge

California State U, San Bernardino
California State U, San Jose
California State U, Sonoma
California U (PA)
Central Washington U
Cleveland State U (OH)
Charleston, C of (SC)
Connecticut, U of
Delaware, U of
East Carolina U (NC)
East Central U (OK)
East Stroudsburg U (PA)
Eastern Connecticut State U
Eastern New Mexico U
Eastern Oregon U
Florida International U
Florida State U
Fort Hays State U (KS)
Fort Lewis C (CO)
Georgia, U of
Grambling State U (LA)
Guam, U of (Guam)
Hawaii, U of, Hilo
Hawaii, U of, Manoa
Howard U (DC)
Idaho State U
Idaho, U of
Illinois State U
Indiana U (PA)
Indiana U–Purdue U, Fort Wayne
Iowa State U
Johnson State C (VT)
Keene State C (NH)
Louisiana State U, Baton Rouge
Louisville, U of (KY)
Maine, U of
Maine, U of, Farmington
Maine, U of, Fort Kent
Mankato State U (MN)
Maryland, U of, College Park
Massachusetts, U of, Amherst
Massachusetts, U of, Boston
Memphis, U of (TN)
Mesa State C (CO)
Michigan Technological U
Minnesota, U of, Twin Cities
Missouri, U of, Columbia
Missouri, U of, St. Louis
Montana State U
Montana, U of
Moorhead State U (MN)
Morehead State U (KY)
Murray State U (KY)
Nebraska, U of, Kearney
Nevada, U of, Las Vegas
Nevada, U of, Reno
New Hampshire, U of
New Jersey, C of
New Mexico State U
New Mexico, U of
New Orleans, U of (LA)
New York, City U of, Hunter C
New York, State U of, Binghamton
New York, State U of, Buffalo
New York, State U of, Plattsburgh
New York, State U of, Potsdam
New York, State U of, Stony Brook
North Carolina Central U
North Carolina State U
North Carolina, U of, Wilmington
North Texas, U of
Northeastern Illinois U
Northern Arizona U
Nothern Colorado, U of
Northern Iowa, U of

College Members of the National Student Exchange (continued)

Northern State U (SD)
Oklahoma State U
Oregon State U
Oregon, U of
Portland State U (OR)
Puerto Rico, U of, Bayamon (Puerto Rico)
Puerto Rico, U of, Cayey (Puerto Rico)
Puerto Rico, U of, Humacao (Puerto Rico)
Puerto Rico, U of, Interamerican, San German (Puerto Rico)
Puerto Rico, U of, Mayaguez (Puerto Rico)
Puerto Rico, U of, Rio Piedras (Puerto Rico)
Rhode Island C
Rhode Island, U of
Rutgers U, Rutgers C (NJ)
Sagrado Corazón, Universidad del (Puerto Rico)
St. Mary's C (MD)
South Carolina State C
South Carolina, U of, Columbia
South Dakota State U
South Dakota, U of
Southern Colorado, U of
Southern Maine, U of
Southern Oregon U
Southern U (LA)
Southwest Missouri State U
Southwest Texas State U
Tennessee State U
Texas, U of, El Paso
Texas, U of, San Antonio
Towson State U (MD)
Utah State U
Utah, U of
Virginia Commonwealth U
Virginia Polytechnic Institute and State U
Virginia State U
Washington State U
Washington, U of
West Chester U (PA)
West Florida, U of
West Virginia U
Western State C (CO)
Western Washington U
Westfield State U (MA)
Wichita State U (KS)
William Paterson C (NJ)
Winthrop C (SC)
Wisconsin, U of, Eau Claire
Wisconsin, U of, Green Bay
Wisconsin, U of, Platteville
Wisconsin, U of, River Falls
Wisconsin, U of, Whitewater
Wyoming, U of

Source: National Student Exchange, Fort Wayne, IN.

Members of the Venture Consortium

Students who attend member colleges are aided in finding a job in nonprofit organizations after graduation or during a time off from college studies.

Bates C (ME)
Brown U (RI)
Franklin and Marshall C (PA)
Holy Cross, C of the (MA)
Sarah Lawrence C (NY)
Swarthmore C (PA)
Vassar C (NY)
Wesleyan U (CT)

Source: The College Venture Program, Providence, RI.

Colleges with Internet or Distance Learning Opportunities

These are colleges where you can earn a degree (associate or bachelor's) without leaving your hometown. Studies are conducted via video or satellite TV, faculty contact, and/or interaction via E-mail and course work at home in front of the computer. Some of these colleges specialize in distance learning; others provide only certain degrees, majors, or programs through these nontraditional methods.

Alabama, U of, Tuscaloosa
Alaska, U of, Fairbanks
Antioch U (OH)
Arkansas State U
Athabasca U (Canada)
Ball State U (IN)
Baker C (MI)
Bemidji State U (MN)
Berean U (MO)
Brigham Young U (UT)
Burlington C (VT)
Caldwell C (NJ)
California C for Health Sciences
California State U, Dominguez Hills
Central Michigan U
Champlain C (VT)
Charter Oak State C (CT)
Christopher Newport C (VA)
City U (WA)
Clarkson C (NE)
Colorado Electronic Community C
Columbia Union C (MD)
Dakota State U (SD)
Eastern Illinois U
Eckerd C (FL)
Electronic U (CA)
Embry-Riddle Aeronautical U (FL)

Colleges with Internet or Distance Learning Opportunities (continued)

Empire State C (NY)
Evansville, U of (IN)
Fielding Institute (CA)
Goddard C (VT)
Governors State U (IL)
Grantham C of Engineering (LA)
Griggs U (MD)
Indiana U, Bloomington
Indiana U, Southeast
Judson C (AL)
Kansas State U
London, U of (UK)
Mary Baldwin C (VA)
Monash U (Australia)
Murray State U (KY)
National Technological U (CO)
New Jersey Institute of Technology
New School for Social Research (NY)
Northern Iowa, U of
Northwood U (MI)
Norwich U (VT)
Nova Southeastern U (FL)
Ohio U
Oklahoma City U
Oklahoma, U of
Open U (Israel)
Open U (UK)
Phoenix U of (CA)
Pittsburgh, U of (PA)
Prescott C (AZ)
Preston U (KS)
Queen's U (Canada)
Regents C (NY)
Regent U (VA)
Regis U (CO)
Rochester Institute of Technology (NY)
St. Joseph's C (ME)
St. Mary-of-the-Woods C (IN)
Salve Regina U (RI)
Seattle Central Community C (WA)
Skidmore C (NY)
South Africa, U of (South Africa)
Southwestern Adventist U (TX)
Stephens C (MO)
Syracuse U (NY)
Thomas Edison State C (NJ)
Trinity C (CT)
Troy State U, Montgomery (AL)
Union Institute (OH)
Upper Iowa U
Washington State U
Waterloo, U of (Canada)
Western Governors U (UT)
Western Illinois U
Wisconsin, U of, Platteville
York U (Canada)

Colleges with Respected Art Museums

Strong museums or collections add a special dimension to the academic experience at these colleges.

Arizona State U (outer space materials)
Bowdoin C (ME) (arctic museum)
Brandeis U (MA) (American Judaica)
California, U of, Berkeley
California, U of, Los Angeles (outdoor sculpture and art museum)
Carnegie Mellon U (PA)
Colby C (ME)
Cornell U (NY)
Florida Southern C (Frank Lloyd Wright architecture)
Florida, U of (natural science museum)
Harvard U (MA)
Houston, U of (TX) (outdoor sculpture gallery)
Indiana U, Bloomington
Iowa, U of
Kansas, U of (natural history museum)
Michigan, U of, Ann Arbor
Nebraska, U of, Lincoln
North Carolina, U of, Chapel Hill (museum and planetarium)
Notre Dame, U of (IN)
Oberlin C (OH)
Pennsylvania, U of
Pepperdine U (CA)
Princeton U (NJ)
Smith C (MA)
Stanford U (CA)
Virginia, U of
Western Washington U (outdoor sculpture gallery)
William and Mary, C of (VA)
Williams C (MA)
Wisconsin, U of, Madison
Wyoming, U of (American West)
Yale U (CT)

QUALITY

IVYS AND OTHER CLIMBING VINES

Ivy League Colleges

These colleges belong to the Ivy League Athletic Conference.

Brown U (RI)
Columbia U (NY)
Cornell U (NY)
Dartmouth C (NH)
Harvard U (MA)
Pennsylvania, U of
Princeton U (NJ)
Yale U (CT)

The Experts' Choice: The Undergraduate Ivy League

When asked for top schools in overall quality and excellence specifically for an undergraduate (and, thus, excluding graduate or professional programs), these colleges were rated highest.

THE TOP COLLEGES

1. Williams C (MA)
2. Amherst C (MA)
3. Swarthmore C (PA)
4. Princeton U (NJ)
5. Pomona C (CA)
6. Bowdoin C (ME)
*7. Carleton C (MN)
8. Wellesley C (MA)
*9. Yale U (CT)
10. Haverford C (PA)
11. Stanford U (CA)
12. Bates C (ME)
*13. Duke U (NC)
*14. Middlebury C (VT)
*15. Smith C (MA)
16. Dartmouth C (NH)
*17. Oberlin C (OH)
*18. Wesleyan U (CT)

The Experts' Choice: The Undergraduate Ivy League (continued)

19. Bryn Mawr C (PA)
*20. Chicago, U of (IL)
*21. Davidson C (NC)

*See Author's Note, p. xxv.

RUNNERS-UP

Barnard C (NY)
Brown U (RI)
Colby C (ME)
Colgate U (NY)
Columbia U (NY)
Emory U (GA)
Grinnell C (IA)
Hamilton C (NY)
Harvard U (MA)
Kenyon C (OH)
Michigan, U of, Ann Arbor
Northwestern U (IL)
Pennsylvania, U of
Reed C (OR)
Rice U (TX)
Virginia, U of
Washington and Lee U (VA)
Washington U (MO)
William and Mary, C of (VA)

The Public Ivys

Colleges were selected on the basis of (1) admission selectivity, (2) quality of undergraduate academic program and the importance of the liberal arts, (3) money and resourcefulness in managing it, and (4) prestige and visibility. Top schools are called "the public ivys"; the next level is termed "the best of the rest."

THE PUBLIC IVYS

California, U of, Berkeley
California, U of, Davis
California, U of, Irvine
California, U of, Los Angeles
California, U of, Riverside
California, U of, San Diego
California, U of, Santa Barbara
California, U of, Santa Cruz
Miami U (OH)
Michigan, U of, Ann Arbor
North Carolina, U of, Chapel Hill
Texas, U of, Austin
Vermont, U of
Virginia, U of
William and Mary, C of (VA)

THE BEST OF THE REST

Colorado, U of
Georgia Institute of Technology
Illinois, U of, Urbana
New C (FL)
New York, State U of, Binghamton
Pennsylvania State U, University Park
Pittsburgh, U of (PA)
Washington, U of
Wisconsin, U of, Madison

Source: Richard Moll, *The Public Ivys* (New York: Viking, 1985), ix–x.

U.S. News's Best National Universities

The following *U.S. News and World Report* rankings are based on such factors as quality of the student body, strength of faculty, financial resources, retention, and reputation.

1. Princeton U (NJ)
2. Harvard U (MA)
3. Duke U (NC)
4. Yale U (CT)
5. Stanford U (CA)
6. Massachusetts Institute of Technology
7. Dartmouth C (NH)

U.S. News*'s Best National Universities (continued)*

*8. Pennsylvania, U of
9. Brown U (RI)
*10. California Institute of Technology
*11. Columbia U (NY)
*12. Emory U (GA)
*13. Northwestern U (IL)
14. Chicago, U of (IL)
*15. Cornell U (NY)
*16. Johns Hopkins U (MD)
17. Rice U (TX)
*18. Washington U (MO)
19. Notre Dame, U of (IN)
*20. Vanderbilt U (TN)
21. Georgetown U (DC)
*22. Virginia, U of
23. California, U of, Berkeley
*24. Carnegie Mellon U (PA)
*25. Michigan, U of, Ann Arbor
*26. Tufts (MA)

*See Author's Note, p. xxv.

Source: Copyright © 1997, *U.S. News and World Report.*

Superior Public Universities

The nation's public universities were rated on the basis of such factors as amount of federal grants and number of articles published by professors.

1. California, U of, Berkeley
2. California, U of, Santa Barbara
3. New York, State U of, Stony Brook
4. California, U of, Los Angeles
5. Michigan, U of
6. Wisconsin, U of, Madison
7. Illinois, U of, Urbana
8. Indiana U
9. California, U of, San Diego
10. Colorado, U of

Source: Hugh D. Graham and Nancy Diamond, *The Rise of American Research Universities* (Baltimore: Johns Hopkins University Press, 1997).

U.S. News's Best National Liberal Arts Colleges

The following *U.S. News and World Report* rankings are based on such factors as quality of the student body, strength of faculty, financial resources, retention, and reputation.

1. Swarthmore C (PA)
2. Amherst C (MA)
3. Wellesley C (MA)
*4. Williams C (MA)
5. Pomona C (CA)
6. Haverford C (PA)
7. Carleton C (MN)
8. Bowdoin C (ME)
*9. Bryn Mawr C (PA)
*10. Claremont McKenna C (CA)
*11. Davidson C (NC)
*12. Middlebury C (VT)
*13. Washington and Lee U (VA)
14. Grinnell C (IA)
*15. Smith C (MA)
*16. Wesleyan U (CT)
17. Vassar C (NY)
18. Colby C (ME)
*19. Mt. Holyoke C (MA)
20. Bates C (ME)
*21. Colgate U (NY)
22. Hamilton C (NY)
*23. Oberlin C (OH)
*24. Trinity C (CT)
25. Holy Cross, C of the (MA)
*26. Macalester C (MN)

*See Author's Note, p. xxv.

Source: Copyright © 1997, *U.S. News and World Report.*

National Review's Top Liberal Arts Colleges

Colleges were selected on the basis of (1) quality and availability of faculty, (2) the quality of the curriculum, with emphasis on schools with a liberal arts "core" requirement, and (3) the quality of the intellectual environment.

Adelphi U (NY)
Asbury C (KY)
Assumption C (MA)
Baylor U (TX)
Birmingham-Southern C (AL)
Boston U (MA)
Brigham Young U (UT)
Calvin C (MI)
Centre C (KY)
Chicago, U of (IL)
Claremont McKenna C (CA)
Columbia U (NY)
Dallas, U of (TX)
Davidson C (NC)

National Review's *Top Liberal Arts Colleges (continued)*

Eureka C (IL)
Franciscan U (OH)
Furman U (SC)
Gonzaga U (WA)
Grove City C (PA)
Gustavus Adolphus C (MN)
Hampden-Sydney C (VA)
Hanover C (IN)
Hastings C (NB)
Hillsdale C (MI)
Hope C (MI)
Houghton C (NY)
Lawrence U (WI)
Lynchburg C (VA)
Millsaps C (MS)
Mt. St. Mary's C (MD)
Notre Dame, U of (IN)
Oglethorpe U (GA)
Oklahoma City U
Pepperdine U (CA)
Providence C (RI)
Rhodes C (TN)
St. Anselm C (NH)
St. Benedict, C of/St. John's U (MN)
St. John's C (MD) and (NM)
St. Mary's C (CA)
St. Mary's C (MD)
St. Olaf C (MN)
St. Vincent C (PA)
South, U of the (TN)
Southwestern U (TX)
Stetson U (FL)
Thomas Aquinas C (CA)
Thomas More C (NH)
Transylvania U (KY)
Trinity U (TX)
Truman State U (MO)
Union C (NY)
Wabash C (IN)
Washington and Lee U (VA)
Wheaton C (IL)
Whitman C (WA)
William and Mary, C of (VA)
Wofford C (SC)

Source: Reprinted with the permission of Simon & Schuster from *The National Review College Guide*, edited by Charles Sykes and Brad Miner. Copyright © 1993 by National Review, Inc.

The Experts' Choice: Colleges That Students Rave About

These are the colleges that counselors said their students most frequently rave about.

1. Pennsylvania, U of
2. Duke U (NC)
3. Brown U (RI)
*4. Kenyon C (OH)
*5. Michigan, U of, Ann Arbor
*6. Northwestern U (IL)
*7. Tufts U (MA)

*8. Virginia, U of
9. Colgate U (NY)
*10. Hobart C/William Smith C (NY)
*11. Vanderbilt U (TN)
12. Bates C (ME)
*13. Cornell U (NY)
*14. Dartmouth C (NH)
*15. Princeton U (NJ)
*16. Syracuse U (NY)
*17. Vermont, U of
*18. Washington U (MO)
*19. Wesleyan U (CT)
*20. Williams C (MA)
21. Denison U (OH)
*22. Lehigh U (PA)
*23. New Hampshire, U of
*24. Rollins C (FL)
*25. Southern Methodist U (TX)
*26. Wheaton C (MA)

*See Author's Note, p. xxv.

Colleges Highly Rated by Students for Academic Excellence

These colleges receive consistently high marks among undergraduates for their academic quality.

California Institute of Technology
California, U of, Berkeley
California, U of, Los Angeles
California, U of, San Diego
Claremont McKenna C (CA)
Colorado C
Georgetown U (DC)
Johns Hopkins U (MD)
Lafayette C (PA)
Massachusetts Institute of Technology
Miami U (OH)
Mt. Holyoke C (MA)
Muhlenberg C (PA)
New York, State U of, Binghamton
North Carolina, U of, Chapel Hill
Notre Dame, U of (IN)
Rochester, U of (NY)
South, U of the (TN)
Trinity C (CT)
Tufts U (MA)
Vanderbilt U (TN)
Vermont, U of
Virginia, U of
Texas, U of, Austin
Washington, U of
Wisconsin, U of, Madison

Colleges That Change Lives

Loren Pope, educational consultant, identifies the following colleges as places where faculty and students work closely together, learning is collaborative rather than competitive, and there is discussion of values and a sense of family.

Allegheny C (PA)
Antioch C (OH)
Austin C (TX)
Bard C (NY)
Beloit C (WI)
Birmingham-Southern C (AL)
Clark U (MA)
Cornell C (IA)
Denison U (OH)
Earlham C (IN)
Eckerd C (FL)
Emory and Henry C (VA)
Evergreen State C (WA)
Franklin and Marshall C (PA)
Goucher C (MD)
Grinnell C (IA)
Guilford C (NC)
Hampshire C (MA)
Hendrix C (AR)
Hiram C (OH)
Hope C (MI)
Juniata C (PA)
Kalamazoo C (MI)
Knox C (IL)
Lawrence U (WI)
Lynchburg C (VA)
Marlboro C (VT)
Millsaps C (MS)
Ohio Wesleyan U
Reed C (OR)
Rhodes C (TN)
St. Andrews Presbyterian C (NC)
St. John's C (MD and NM)
St. Olaf C (MN)
Southwestern U (TX)
Western Maryland C
Wheaton C (IL)
Whitman C (WA)
Wooster, C of (OH)

Source: Loren Pope, *Colleges That Change Lives* (New York: Penguin Books, 1996).

The Experts' Choice: The Top Twenty-five Overrated Colleges

Counselors were asked to identify those colleges where the actual undergraduate experience doesn't measure up to the popular image of the school.

1. Harvard U (MA)
2. Stanford U (CA)
3. Boston C (MA)
4. Georgetown U (DC)
*5. Richmond, U of (VA)
*6. Yale U (CT)
7. California, U of, Berkeley
*8. Cornell U (NY)
*9. Tufts U (MA)
10. California, U of, Los Angeles
*11. Chicago, U of (IL)
*12. James Madison U (VA)
*13. Johns Hopkins U (MD)
*14. Michigan, U of, Ann Arbor
*15. Syracuse U (NY)
*16. Tulane U (LA)
*17. Virginia, U of
18. Brown U (RI)
*19. Colgate U (NY)
*20. Middlebury C (VT)
*21. North Carolina, U of, Chapel Hill
*22. Pennsylvania, U of
*23. Vermont, U of
24. Colorado, U of
25. Wisconsin, U of, Madison

*See Author's Note, p. xxv.

HONORS

Colleges with Phi Beta Kappa Chapters

Phi Beta Kappa is a national academic honor society. Election to Phi Beta Kappa represents commitment and scholarship in the liberal arts and sciences. As members, college chapters select undergraduate students who meet the academic criteria of the honorary. Less than 10 percent of colleges in the nation have been selected for membership. The date indicates the year the college was admitted to the society.

Agnes Scott C (GA) (1926)
Alabama, U of, Tuscaloosa (1851)
Albion C (MI) (1940)
Allegheny C (PA) (1902)
Alma C (MI) (1980)
American U (DC) (1994)
Amherst C (MA) (1853)
Arizona State U (1973)
Arizona, U of (1932)
Arkansas, U of, Fayetteville (1932)
Augustana C (IL) (1950)
Bates C (ME) (1917)
Baylor U (TX) (1977)
Beloit C (WI) (1911)
Birmingham-Southern C (AL) (1937)
Boston C (MA) (1971)
Boston U (MA) (1899)
Bowdoin C (ME) (1825)
Bowling Green State U (OH) (1983)
Brandeis U (MA) (1962)
Brown U (RI) (1830)
Bucknell U (PA) (1940)
California State U, Long Beach (1977)
California State U, San Diego (1974)
California State U, San Francisco (1977)
California, U of, Berkeley (1898)
California, U of, Davis (1968)
California, U of, Irvine (1974)

California, U of, Los Angeles (1930)
California, U of, Riverside (1965)
California, U of, San Diego (1977)
California, U of, Santa Barbara (1968)
California, U of, Santa Cruz (1986)
Carleton C (MN) (1914)
Carnegie Mellon U (PA) (1995)
Case Western Reserve U (OH) (1847)
Catholic U (DC) (1941)
Centre C (KY) (1971)
Chatham C (PA) (1962)
Chicago, U of (IL) (1899)
Cincinnati, U of (OH) (1899)
Claremont McKenna C (CA) (1983)
Clark U (MA) (1953)
Coe C (IA) (1949)
Colby C (ME) (1896)
Colgate U (NY) (1878)
Colorado C (1904)
Colorado State U (1973)
Colorado, U of (1904)
Columbia U, Barnard C (NY) (1901)
Columbia U, Columbia C (NY) (1869)
Connecticut C (1935)
Connecticut, U of (1956)
Cornell C (IA) (1923)
Cornell U (NY) (1882)
Dallas, U of (TX) (1989)
Dartmouth C (NH) (1787)
Davidson C (NC) (1923)
Delaware, U of (1956)
Denison U (OH) (1911)
Denver, U of (CO) (1940)
DePauw U (IN) (1889)
Dickinson C (PA) (1887)
Drake U (IA) (1923)
Drew U (NJ) (1980)
Duke U (NC) (1920)
Earlham C (IN) (1965)
Elmira C (NY) (1940)
Emory U (GA) (1929)
Fairfield U (CT) (1995)
Fisk U (TN) (1953)
Florida State U (1935)
Florida, U of (1938)
Fordham U (NY) (1962)
Franklin and Marshall C (PA) (1908)
Furman U (SC) (1973)
Georgetown U (DC) (1965)
George Washington U (DC) (1938)
Georgia, U of (1914)
Gettysburg C (PA) (1923)
Goucher C (MD) (1905)
Grinnell C (IA) (1908)
Gustavus Adolphus C (MN) (1983)
Hamilton C (NY) (1870)
Hamline U (MN) (1974)
Hampden-Sydney C (VA) (1949)
Harvard U (MA) (1781)
Haverford C (PA) (1899)
Hawaii, U of, Manoa (1952)
Hiram C (OH) (1971)
Hobart C/William Smith C (NY) (1871)
Hofstra U (NY) (1973)
Hollins C (VA) (1962)
Holy Cross, C of the (MA) (1974)
Hope C (MI) (1971)
Howard U (DC) (1953)

Colleges with Phi Beta Kappa Chapters (continued)

Idaho, U of (1926)
Illinois C (1932)
Illinois, U of, Chicago (1977)
Illinois, U of, Urbana (1907)
Indiana U, Bloomington (1911)
Iowa State U (1973)
Iowa, U of (1895)
Johns Hopkins U (MD) (1895)
Kalamazoo C (MI) (1958)
Kansas State U (1974)
Kansas, U of (1890)
Kent State U (OH) (1977)
Kentucky, U of (1926)
Kenyon C (OH) (1858)
Knox C (IL) (1917)
Lafayette C (PA) (1890)
Lake Forest C (IL) (1962)
Lawrence U (WI) (1914)
Lehigh U (PA) (1887)
Louisiana State U, Baton Rouge (1977)
Loyola C (MD) (1995)
Loyola U (IL) (1995)
Luther C (IA) (1983)
Macalester C (MN) (1968)
Maine, U of, Orono (1923)
Manhattan C (NY) (1971)
Marietta C (OH) (1860)
Marquette U (WI) (1971)
Mary Baldwin C (VA) (1971)
Maryland, U of, College Park (1964)
Mary Washington C (VA) (1971)
Massachusetts Institute of Technology (1971)
Massachusetts, U of, Amherst (1965)
Miami, U of (FL) (1983)
Miami U (OH) (1911)
Michigan State U (1968)
Michigan, U of, Ann Arbor (MI) (1907)
Middlebury C (VT) (1868)
Mills C (CA) (1929)
Millsaps C (MS) (1989)
Minnesota, U of, Twin Cities (1892)
Missouri, U of, Columbia (1901)
Morehouse C (GA) (1968)
Mt. Holyoke C (MA) (1905)
Muhlenberg C (PA) (1968)
Nebraska, U of, Lincoln (1895)
New Hampshire, U of (1952)
New Mexico, U of, Albuquerque (1965)
New York, City U of, Brooklyn C (1950)
New York, City U of, City C (1867)
New York, City U of, Hunter C (1920)
New York, City U of, Lehman C (1971)
New York, City of, Queens C (1950)
New York, State U of, Albany (1974)
New York, State U of, Binghamton (1971)
New York, State U of, Buffalo (1938)
New York, State U of, Stony Brook (1974)

New York U (1858)
North Carolina, U of, Chapel Hill (1904)
North Carolina, U of, Greensboro (1934)
North Dakota, U of (1914)
Northwestern U (IL) (1890)
Notre Dame, U of (IN) (1968)
Oberlin C (OH) (1907)
Occidental C (CA) (1926)
Ohio State U, Columbus (1904)
Ohio U, Athens (1929)
Ohio Wesleyan U (1907)
Oklahoma, U of (1920)
Oregon, U of (1923)
Pennsylvania State U, University Park (1937)
Pennsylvania, U of (1892)
Pittsburgh, U of (PA) (1953)
Pomona C (CA) (1914)
Princeton U (NJ) (1899)
Puget Sound, U of (WA) (1986)
Purdue U (IN) (1971)
Radcliffe C (MA) (1914)
Randolph-Macon C (VA) (1923)
Randolph-Macon Woman's C (VA) (1917)
Redlands, U of (CA) (1977)
Reed C (OR) (1938)
Rhode Island, U of (1977)
Rhodes C (TN) (1949)
Rice U (TX) (1929)
Richmond, U of (VA) (1929)
Ripon C (WI) (1952)
Rochester, U of (NY) (1887)
Rockford C (IL) (1953)
Rutgers U, Douglass C (NJ) (1921)
Rutgers U, Newark C (NJ) (1958)
Rutgers U, Rutgers C (NJ) (1869)
St. Catherine, C of (MN) (1938)
St. Lawrence U (NY) (1899)
St. Louis U (MO) (1968)
St. Olaf C (MN) (1949)
Santa Clara U (CA) (1977)
Scripps C (CA) (1962)
Skidmore C (NY) (1971)
Smith C (MA) (1904)
South Carolina, U of, Columbia (1926)
South Dakota, U of (1926)
South, U of the (TN) (1926)
Southern California, U of (1929)
Southern Methodist U (TX) (1949)
Southwestern U (TX) (1995)
Stanford U (CA) (1904)
Stetson U (FL) (1982)
Swarthmore C (PA) (1896)
Sweet Briar C (VA) (1950)
Syracuse U (NY) (1896)
Temple U (PA) (1974)
Tennessee, U of, Knoxville (1965)
Texas Christian U (1971)
Texas, U of, Austin (1905)
Trinity C (CT) (1845)
Trinity C (DC) (1971)
Trinity U (TX) (1974)
Tufts U (MA) (1892)
Tulane U (LA) (1909)
Tulsa, U of (OK) (1989)
Union C (NY) (1817)

Colleges with Phi Beta Kappa Chapters (continued)

Ursinus C (PA) (1992)
Utah, U of (1935)
Vanderbilt U (TN) (1901)
Vassar C (NY) (1899)
Vermont, U of (1848)
Villanova U (PA) (1986)
Virginia Polytechnic Institute and State U (1977)
Virginia, U of (1908)
Wabash C (IN) (1898)
Wake Forest U (NC) (1941)
Washington and Jefferson C (PA) (1937)
Washington and Lee U (VA) (1911)
Washington State U (1929)
Washington, U of (1914)
Washington U (MO) (1914)
Wayne State U (MI) (1953)
Wellesley C (MA) (1904)
Wells C (NY) (1932)
Wesleyan U (CT) (1845)
West Virginia U (1910)
Western Maryland C (1980)
Wheaton C (MA) (1932)
Whitman C (WA) (1920)
William and Mary, C of (VA) (1776)
Williams C (MA) (1864)
Wilson C (PA) (1950)
Wisconsin, U of, Madison (1899)
Wisconsin, U of, Milwaukee (1974)
Wittenberg U (OH) (1992)
Wofford C (SC) (1941)
Wooster, C of (OH) (1926)
Wyoming, U of (1940)
Yale U (CT) (1780)

Source: Phi Beta Kappa Society, Washington, DC.

Colleges Where National Merit Scholars Enroll

The following colleges enrolled the most Merit Scholars in 1997. Several of these colleges sponsor Merit Scholarships for finalists in the National Merit Scholarship Program who will attend their institution.

Alabama, U of, Tuscaloosa
Baylor U (TX)
Boston U (MA)
Brigham Young U (UT)
Brown U (RI)
California, U of, Berkeley
Carleton C (MN)
Case Western Reserve U (OH)
Chicago, U of (IL)
Dartmouth C (NH)
Duke U (NC)
Florida, U of
Georgia Institute of Technology
Harvard U/Radcliffe C (MA)
Iowa State U
Kansas, U of
Massachusetts Institute of Technology
Michigan State U
New York U
Northwestern U (IL)
Oberlin C (OH)
Ohio State U, Columbus
Oklahoma, U of
Princeton U (NJ)
Purdue U (IN)
Rice U (TX)
Southern California, U of
Stanford U (CA)
Texas A&M U
Texas, U of, Austin
Trinity U (TX)
Vanderbilt U (TN)
Washington U (MO)
Yale U (CT)

Source: *The Chronicle of Higher Education,* February 6, 1998.

Forty Colleges Where National Science Foundation Fellows Attend

These colleges enrolled at least five students who received National Science Foundation Fellowships. These highly competitive fellowships are awarded to students based on their academic performance, recommendations, and test scores. The foundation awards three-year grants for graduate study and research in the sciences, mathematics, and engineering.

Brigham Young U (UT)
Brown U (RI)
California Institute of Technology
California, U of, Berkeley
California, U of, Davis
California, U of, Los Angeles
California, U of, San Diego
Chicago, U of (IL)
Cornell U (NY)
Dartmouth C (NH)
Delaware, U of
Duke U (NC)
Florida, U of
Georgia Institute of Technology
Harvard U (MA)
Illinois, U of, Urbana
Indiana U, Bloomington
Iowa State U
Massachusetts Institute of Technology
Michigan State U
Michigan, U of, Ann Arbor
New York, State U of, Buffalo
North Carolina State U
Northwestern U (IL)
Pennsylvania State U, University Park
Pennsylvania, U of
Princeton U (NJ)
Purdue U (IN)
Rice U (TX)
Rutgers U (NJ)
Stanford U (CA)
Swarthmore C (PA)
Texas A&M U
Texas, U of, Austin
Trinity U (TX)
Virginia Polytechnic Institute and State U
Virginia, U of
Washington, U of
Wisconsin, U of, Madison
Yale U (CT)

Source: Data compiled from information provided by the National Science Foundation, Washington, DC.

Colleges Where Rhodes Scholars Enroll

The highly prized Rhodes Scholarship entitles the recipient to study at Oxford University in England for two years. Winners are selected in nationwide competition on the basis of intellectual and academic excellence and personal qualities, including leadership. Rhodes Scholars for 1997 represented the following colleges.

Arkansas, U of, Little Rock
California, U of, Los Angeles
Colorado C
Columbia U (NY)
Cornell U (NY)
Duke U (NC)
Georgetown U (DC)
Harvard U (MA)
Massachusetts Institute of Technology
Michigan State U
Nebraska, U of, Lincoln
Notre Dame, U of (IN)
Pennsylvania State U, University Park
Princeton U (NJ)
Rice U (TX)
St. Olaf C (MN)
Stanford U (CA)
U.S. Military Academy (NY)
Wake Forest U (NC)
Washington U (MO)
William and Mary, C of (VA)
Wisconsin, U of, Madison

Source: Rhodes Scholarship Trust, Claremont, CA.

Distinguished Junior Colleges

These are junior colleges with distinguished chapters of Phi Theta Kappa, the national two-year college honor society. Applications are judged on annual reports, leadership, service, fellowship, and scholarship.

Andrew C (GA)
Anoka-Ramsey Community C (MN)
Brazosport C (TX)
Broward Community C (FL)
Cambridge Community C Center (MN)
Connors State C (OK)
Copiah-Lincoln Community C (MS)
Florida Community C
Gulf Coast Community C (FL)
Harold Washington C (IL)
Jefferson State Community C (AL)
Kirtland Community C (MI)
Miami-Dade Community C (FL)
Mott Community C (MI)
Normandale Community C (MN)
Oakland Community C (MI)
Palm Beach Community C (FL)
St. Petersburg Junior C (FL)
Sinclair Community C (OH)
Southern Union State Community C (FL)
South Mountain Community C (AZ)
Southside Virginia Community C
Trident Technical C (SC)
Western Oklahoma State C
Wharton Community Junior C (TX)

Source: Phi Theta Kappa, Jackson, MS.

PROFESSORS

Colleges with a Low Ratio of Students to Faculty Members

Student/faculty ratio at these colleges is approximately ten to one.

Academy of Art C (CA)
Academy of the New Church (PA)
Alaska, U of, Southeast
Andrews U (MI)
Arkansas Baptist C
Bennington C (VT)
Brandeis U (MA)
Brenau Women's C (GA)
Bridgeport Engineering Institute (CT)
California Institute of Technology
California Institute of the Arts
Carnegie Mellon U (PA)
Case Western Reserve U (OH)
Catholic U (DC)
Cedar Crest C (PA)
Centenary C (LA)
Chicago, U of (IL)
Christian Brothers U (TN)
Cleveland Institute of Art (OH)
Cleveland Institute of Music (OH)
Cogswell Polytechnical C (CA)
Columbia U (NY)
Converse C (SC)
Corcoran School of Art (DC)
Cornell U (NY)
Creighton U (NE)
Denver, U of (CO)
Detroit Mercy, U of (MI)
Fairleigh Dickinson U (NJ)
Felician C (NJ)
Gallaudet U (DC)
Gwynedd-Mercy C (PA)
Harvard U (MA)
Hawaii, U of, Manoa
Holy Names C (CA)
Howard U (DC)
Illinois Institute of Technology
Illinois, U of, Chicago
Judaism, U of (CA)
Maharishi International U (IA)
Marlboro C (VT)

Colleges with a Low Ratio of Students to Faculty Members (continued)

Massachusetts Institute of Technology
Michigan, U of, Ann Arbor
Moore C of Art and Design (PA)
New Mexico Institute of Mining and Technology
New Rochelle, C of (NY)
North Carolina School of the Arts
Notre Dame, C of (CA)
Notre Dame, C of (MD)
Oakland City C (IN)
Pennsylvania, U of
Prescott C (AZ)
Princeton U (NJ)
Rice U (TX)
Rosemont C (PA)
Russell Sage C (NY)
St. John's C (MD)
St. Joseph C (CT)
St. Louis U (MO)
St. Martin's C (WA)
St. Mary-of-the-Woods C (IN)
St. Xavier U (IL)
San Francisco Conservatory of Music (CA)
Sarah Lawrence C (NY)
Sheldon Jackson C (AK)
Shimer C (IL)
Silver Lake C (WI)
Spalding U (KY)
Sweet Briar C (VA)
U.S. Air Force Academy (CO)
U.S. Coast Guard Academy (CT)
U.S. International U (CA)
U.S. Merchant Marine Academy (NY)
U.S. Military Academy (NY)
U.S. Naval Academy (MD)
Ursuline C (OH)
Vanderbilt U (TN)
Vandercook C of Music (IL)
Virgin Islands, U of
Washington U (MO)
Washington, U of
Wayne State U (MI)
Webb Institute of Naval Architecture (NY)
Wells C (NY)
Westbrook C (ME)
Westminster Choir C (NJ)
Williams C (MA)
Wilson C (PA)
Yale U (CT)

The Experts' Choice: Colleges with Particularly Accessible Teachers

Allegheny C (PA)
Amherst C (MA)
Bard C (NY)
Bates C (ME)
Bowdoin C (ME)
Clark U (MA)
Colby C (ME)
Colgate U (NY)
Connecticut C
Davidson C (NC)
DePauw U (IN)
Dickinson C (PA)
Earlham C (IN)
Franklin and Marshall C (PA)
Grinnell C (IA)
Guilford C (NC)
Hampshire C (MA)
Hartwick C (NY)
Haverford C (PA)
Hood C (MD)
Kenyon C (OH)
Lawrence U (WI)
Lynchburg C (VA)
Macalester C (MN)
Marlboro C (VT)
Middlebury C (VT)
Mt. Holyoke C (MA)
Muhlenberg C (PA)
New College (FL)
New England C (NH)
Oberlin C (OH)
Occidental C (CA)
Pine Manor C (MA)
Pitzer C (CA)
Pomona C (CA)
Randolph-Macon C (VA)
Rice U (TX)
Sarah Lawrence C (NY)
Skidmore C (NY)
Smith C (MA)
South, U of the (TN)
Wesleyan U (CT)
Wheaton C (MA)
Williams C (MA)
Wooster, C of (OH)

Colleges Where Teachers Work Closely with Students

Students report an unusually close working relationship with their professors at these colleges.

Albion C (MI)
Alma C (MI)
Asbury C (KY)
Baker U (KS)
Bard C (NY)
Barnard C (NY)
Beloit C (WI)
Bennington C (VT)
Bryn Mawr C (PA)
Bucknell U (PA)
California Institute of Technology
Calvin C (MI)
Carleton C (MN)
Centre C (KY)
Chicago, U of (IL)
Claremont McKenna C (CA)
Clark U (MA)
Clarkson U (NY)
Coe C (IA)
Colorado C
Duke U (NC)
Furman U (SC)
Goucher C (MD)
Grinnell C (IA)
Guilford C (NC)
Gustavus Adolphus C (MN)
Hamilton C (NY)
Hampden-Sydney C (VA)
Hampshire C (MA)
Harvey Mudd C (CA)
Haverford C (PA)
Hendrix C (AR)
Hiram C (OH)
Hope C (MI)
Knox C (IL)
Lafayette C (PA)
Lawrence U (WI)
Liberty U (VA)
Marlboro C (VT)
Middlebury C (VT)
Millsaps C (MS)
Monmouth C (IL)
Mt. Holyoke C (MA)
Muhlenberg C (PA)
Oglethorpe U (GA)
Ohio Wesleyan U
Oral Roberts U (OK)
Otterbein C (OH)
Phillips U (OK)
Pitzer C (CA)
Pomona C (CA)
Providence C (RI)
Randolph-Macon Woman's C (VA)
Reed C (OR)
Regis U (CO)
Rhodes C (TN)
Rochester, U of (NY)
Rollins C (FL)
St. Anselm C (NH)
St. Benedict, C of/St. John's U (MN)
St. John's C (MD)
St. John's C (NM)
St. Mary's C (MD)
Santa Clara U (CA)
Sarah Lawrence C (NY)
Scripps C (CA)
Simmons C (MA)

Smith C (MA)
South, U of the (TN)
Spelman C (GA)
Swarthmore C (PA)
Sweet Briar C (VA)
Tomlinson C (TN)
Trinity C (CT)
Trinity U (TX)
Ursinus C (PA)
Vassar C (NY)
Wabash C (IN)
Washington and Jefferson C (PA)
Washington U (MO)
Wellesley C (MA)
Wells C (NY)
Wesleyan U (CT)
Wheaton C (IL)
Wheaton C (MA)
Whitman C (WA)
Whittier C (CA)
Willamette U (OR)
William and Mary, C of (VA)
Williams C (MA)
Wittenberg U (OH)
Wofford C (SC)
Worcester Polytechnic Institute (MA)

Ten Schools with Satisfied Professors

These are colleges where faculty morale and satisfaction are high. Colleges were selected, in part, on the basis of their diversity.

Eastern Mennonite C (VA)
Gordon C (MA)
Greenville C (IL)
Lenoir-Rhyne C (NC)
Nebraska Wesleyan U
Notre Dame, C of (MD)
St. Scholastica, C of (MN)
Simpson C (IA)
Smith C (MA)
William Jewell C (MO)

Source: Ann E. Austin, R. Eugene Rice, Allen P. Splete, et al., *A Good Place to Work: Sourcebook for the Academic Workplace* (Washington, DC: Council of Independent Colleges, 1991).

Twenty Colleges with Highest Salaries for Professors

In a survey of faculty salaries at 2,200 institutions, these are the highest average salaries for full professors for the school year 1996–97. Exclusively graduate or professional schools are not included. Salaries are given in thousands of dollars.

1. Harvard U (MA)	$112.2
2. California Institute of Technology	106.9
3. Stanford U (CA)	106.4
4. Princeton U (NJ)	106.0
5. Yale U (CT)	104.7
6. New York U	102.5
7. Chicago, U of (IL)	101.6
8. Columbia U (NY)	101.2
9. Massachusetts Institute of Technology	100.1
10. Pennsylvania, U of	100.0
11. Rutgers U, Newark (NJ)	96.9
12. Northwestern U (IL)	96.1
13. Duke U (NC)	95.8
14. Georgetown U (DC)	94.4
15. Rutgers U, Camden (NJ)	91.3
16. Carnegie Mellon U (PA)	91.1
17. Notre Dame, U of (IN)	90.3
18. Vanderbilt U (TN)	89.3
19. Southern California, U of	88.8
20. California, U of, Berkeley	87.0

Source: Data gathered from information in *Academe*, the bulletin of the American Association of University Professors, March/April 1997.

Liberal Arts Colleges with the Highest Salaries for Professors

In a survey of faculty salaries at 2,200 institutions, these are the highest average salaries for full professors at primarily undergraduate colleges for the school year 1996–97. These schools essentially exist to teach undergraduate students. **Note:** Schools that have a business, science, or engineering focus typically have higher faculty salaries. Salaries are given in thousands of dollars.

1. Babson C (MA)	$95.5
2. Wellesley C (MA)	86.3
3. Harvey Mudd C (CA)	86.0
4. Williams C (MA)	84.9
5. Barnard C (NY)	83.9
6. Colby C (ME)	83.8
7. Swarthmore C (PA)	83.1
8. Pomona C (CA)	81.8
9. Claremont McKenna C (CA)	81.3
10. Bowdoin C (ME)	80.0
11. Amherst C (MA)	79.2
12. Colgate U (NY)	78.9
13. Cooper Union (NY)	77.8
14. Trinity C (CT)	77.4
15. Washington and Lee U (VA)	76.9
16. Grinnell C (IA)	75.9
17. Mt. Holyoke C (MA)	75.5
18. Bates C (ME)	75.1
19. Holy Cross, C of (MA)	74.8
20. Middlebury C (VT)	74.0
21. Richard Stockton C (NJ)	73.9
22. Lafayette C (PA)	73.5
*23. Vassar C (NY)	73.5
24. Cheyney U (PA)	73.1
25. Jersey City State C (NJ)	72.8
26. Pitzer C (CA)	72.6
27. Lock Haven U (PA)	72.5
28. Ramapo C (NJ)	72.3
29. Bryant C (RI)	72.1
30. Whittier C (CA)	71.7
31. Carleton C (MN)	71.6

Liberal Arts Colleges with the Highest Salaries for Professors (continued)

*32. Haverford C (PA)	71.6
33. Dowling C (NY)	71.2
*34. Franklin and Marshall C (PA)	71.2
35. Macalester C (MN)	71.0
*36. Mansfield U (PA)	71.0
37. Hamilton C (NY)	70.4
38. Connecticut C	70.3
*39. Occidental C (CA)	70.3
40. Lewis and Clark C (OR)	70.1
41. Colorado C	69.6
42. Bard C (NY)	69.5
43. Puget Sound, U of (WA)	69.3
44. Skidmore C (NY)	68.9
45. Scripps C (CA)	68.8
46. Wabash C (IN)	68.6
47. Davidson C (NC)	68.1
*48. Gettysburg C (PA)	68.1
49. Park C, St. Louis U (MO)	67.5
50. Oberlin C (OH)	67.1

*See Author's Note, p. xxv.

Source: Data gathered from information in *Academe*, the bulletin of the American Association of University Professors, March/April 1997.

Colleges with High Faculty Salaries

These colleges are known for high pay for teachers.

California Institute of Technology
California, U of, Berkeley
California, U of, Los Angeles
Chicago, U of (IL)
Colgate U (NY)
Columbia U (NY)
Duke U (NC)
Georgetown U (DC)
Harvard U (MA)
Harvey Mudd C (CA)
Johns Hopkins U (MD)
Massachusetts Institute of Technology
New Jersey Institute of Technology
New York, State U of, Binghamton
New York U
Northwestern U (IL)
Notre Dame, U of (IN)
Oberlin C (OH)
Pennsylvania, U of
Princeton U (NJ)
Rensselaer Polytechnic U (NY)
Rice U (TX)
Rutgers U, Camden (NJ)
Rutgers U, Newark (NJ)
Southern California, U of
Stanford U (CA)
Vanderbilt U (TN)
Washington U (MO)
Yale U (CT)

ENDOWMENTS

Colleges with large endowments are typically those whose financial futures are secure. Schools may have large endowments because individuals, corporations, and foundations have given gifts (of money, stocks, or property) or because the college has invested its money wisely. Schools with large endowments are typically not entirely dependent on tuition for their income and may be able to provide scholarship help to deserving students.

Top Thirty College and University Endowments

Listed are 1997 values of the endowments.

1. Harvard U (MA)	$10,919,670
2. Texas, U of (all campuses)	6,709,945
3. Yale U (CT)	5,742,000
4. Princeton U (NJ)	4,940,900
5. Stanford U (CA)	4,473,825
6. Emory U (GA)	4,273,543
7. California, U of	3,133,252
8. Massachusetts Institute of Technology	3,045,756
9. Columbia U (NY)	3,038,907
10. Texas A&M U	2,951,463
11. Washington U (MO)	2,798,221
12. Pennsylvania, U of	2,535,312
13. Rice U (TX)	2,321,757

14. Cornell U (NY)	2,125,070
15. Chicago, U of (IL)	2,031,131
16. Michigan, U of, Ann Arbor	1,988,835
17. Northwestern U (IL)	1,798,900
18. Notre Dame, U of (IN)	1,467,808
19. Vanderbilt U (TN)	1,339,788
20. Dartmouth C (NH)	1,277,753
21. Southern California, U of	1,204,672
22. Case Western Reserve U (OH)	1,157,600
23. Johns Hopkins U (MD)	1,156,598
24. Duke U (NC)	1,134,290
25. Virginia, U of	1,098,539
26. Minnesota, U of	992,726
27. California Institute of Technology	978,192
28. Brown University (RI)	949,574
29. Rochester, U of (NY)	947,648
30. Purdue U (IN)	856,693

Source: *The Chronicle of Higher Education Almanac*, February 20, 1998.

The Largest Endowments per Student

On this list, the size of the endowment has been adjusted for the size of the student body. Based on 1997 data, the numbers below represent the amount of money in the endowment per student enrolled.

PRIVATE INSTITUTIONS

1. Princeton U (NJ)	$775,773
2. Academy of the New Church (PA)	712,527
3. Webb Institute of Naval Architecture (NY)	638,690
4. Agnes Scott C (GA)	611,496
5. Harvard U (MA)	610,140
6. Curtis Institute of Music (PA)	610,025
7. Rice U (TX)	578,127
8. Grinnell C (IA)	564,819
9. Yale U (CT)	525,920
10. Swarthmore C (PA)	520,664

Private Institutions (continued)

11.	California Institute of Technology	514,297
12.	Juilliard School (NY)	449,912
13.	Colgate Rochester Divinity School (NY)	448,659
14.	Emory U (GA)	420,542
15.	Pomona C (CA)	411,150
16.	Berea C (KY)	351,646
17.	Stanford U (CA)	346,593
18.	Washington and Lee U (VA)	319,487
19.	Massachusetts Institute of Technology	309,969
20.	Wellesley C (MA)	306,877

PUBLIC INSTITUTIONS

1.	Virginia Military Institute Foundation	$156,981
2.	Oregon Health Sciences Foundation	120,755
3.	Georgia Institute of Technology and Foundation	62,887
4.	Texas, U of, System	62,131
5.	Virginia, U of	59,736
6.	Michigan, U of, Ann Arbor	44,833
7.	Delaware, U of	44,454
8.	Texas A&M U, System and Foundations	43,558
9.	William and Mary, C of, Endowment Association (VA)	41,404
10.	North Carolina, U of, Chapel Hill	36,369
11.	South Alabama, U of	32,259
12.	Kansas, U of, Endowment Association	28,193
13.	New Jersey, U of, Medicine and Dentistry	28,099
14.	Cincinnati, U of (OH)	25,626
15.	Colorado School of Mines Foundation	23,931
16.	Oklahoma, U of, Foundation	21,400
17.	California, U of, System	19,615
18.	New York, State U of, Brooklyn C, C of Medicine	19,401
19.	Washburn U (KS)	18,465
20.	Mississippi, U of, Foundation	18,173

Source: 1997 NACUBO Endowment Study, published by the National Association of College and University Business Officers, Washington, DC.

DONATIONS AND FUNDING

Another indication of the financial stability, reputation, and excellence of a college is its ability to secure money from individuals or groups. The donations and funding received by a school can affect the level of teaching and research, as well as the resources and facilities available to students.

Top Gifts to Colleges

These are the largest gifts through January 1998. The amount of the gift is noted in millions of dollars along with the donor.

1. Emory U (GA), $295, 1996, Lettie Pate Evans, Joseph B. Whitehead, Robert W. Woodruff
2. California, U of, San Francisco, $240, 1998, Larry L. Hillblom
3. New York U, $125, 1994, Sir Harold Acton
4. Franklin W. Olin College of Engineering (MA), $200, 1997, F. W. Olin
5. Louisiana State U, Baton Rouge, $125, 1981, Claude B. Pennington
6. Pennsylvania, U of, $120, 1993, Walter H. Annenberg

*7. Southern California, U of, $120, 1993, Walter H. Annenberg

8. Emory U (GA), $105, 1979, Robert Woodruff
9. California, U of, Los Angeles, $100, 1998, Alfred E. Mann

*10. Pennsylvania, U of, $100, 1997, Abramson Family Foundation

Top Gifts to Colleges (continued)

*11. Princeton U (NJ), $100, 1995, Gordon Y. S. Wu
*12. Regent U (VA), $100, 1992, Christian Broadcasting Network
*13. Rowan U (NJ), $100, 1992, Henry and Betty Rowan
*14. Scripps Research Institute, $100, 1996, L. Samuel and Aline W. Skaggs
*15. Southern California, U of, $100, 1998, Alfred E. Mann
*16. Washington U (MO), $100, 1986, Danforth Foundation
*17. Washington U (MO), $100, 1997, Danforth Foundation
*18. Utah, U of, $100, 1995, Jon M. Huntsman
19. Stanford U (CA), $77, 1994, W. R. Hewlett and David Packard
20. Harvard U (MA), $75.5, 1982, Edward Mallinckrodt
*21. Florida International U, $75.5, 1995, Mitchell Wolfson
22. Harvard U (MA), $70.5, 1995, John L. and Frances Lehman Loeb
23. Stanford U (CA), $70, 1986, David and Lucile Packard
24. Columbia U, $60, 1993, John W. Kluge
*25. Georgetown U Medical Center (DC), $60, 1997, Harry A. Toulmin, Jr.
*26. Harvard U Medical School (MA), $60, 1994, Isabelle and Leonard Goldenson
*27. Illinois Institute of Technology, $60, 1996, Robert W. Galvin
*28. Illinois Institute of Technology, $60, 1996, Robert A. Pritzker
*29. Mississippi, U of, $60, 1997, Joseph C. Bancroft Charitable and Educational Fund

*See Author's Note, p. xxv.

Source: Copyright © 1998, *The Chronicle of Higher Education Almanac.* Reprinted with permission.

Top Twenty-five Recipients of Grants in Higher Education

More than 66,000 grants of $10,000 or more were awarded in 1995–96 by more than 1,000 foundations to all U.S. and foreign nonprofit organizations, including colleges and universities. The list does not represent the total foundation dollars received by each school.

1.	Emory U (GA) (Health Sciences Center)	$223,853,070
2.	Harvard U (MA)	52,537,983
3.	Duke U (NC)	43,008,890
4.	Columbia U (NY)	38,570,084
5.	Michigan, U of, Ann Arbor	37,317,006
6.	California, U of, Berkeley	35,842,611
7.	Stanford U (CA)	35,797,805
8.	Yale U (CT)	28,670,806
9.	Cornell U (NY)	26,792,884
10.	Central European U (Hungary)	25,600,921
11.	Pennsylvania, U of	25,400,875
12.	New York U	25,173,276
13.	Texas, U of, Austin	24,370,039
14.	Johns Hopkins U (MD)	24,234,012
15.	Case Western Reserve U (OH)	21,561,329
16.	Northwestern U (IL)	19,635,528
17.	California, U of, Los Angeles	18,941,871
18.	Massachusetts Institute of Technology	18,280,992
19.	Washington U (MO)	17,831,092
20.	Brown U (RI)	16,434,040
21.	Pittsburgh, U of (PA)	15,148,131
22.	Southern California, U of	14,349,800
23.	Rice U (TX)	14,040,837
24.	Chicago, U of (IL)	13,883,988
25.	Minnesota, U of, Minneapolis	13,480,545

Source: The Foundation Center, *Who Gets Grants, Foundation Grants to Nonprofit Organizations, 5th Edition,* page xi. Foundation Center, 79 Fifth Avenue, New York, NY.

Top Twenty Institutions in Alumni Support

These are colleges with the most overall alumni support in 1995–96.

1. Stanford U (CA)	$170,718,875
2. Harvard U (MA)	132,104,519
3. Cornell U (NY)	94,738,327
4. Yale U (CT)	94,093,962
5. Princeton U (NJ)	68,640,191
6. Pennsylvania, U of	57,048,301
7. Richmond, U of (VA)	51,590,715
8. Dartmouth C (NH)	50,876,986
9. Columbia U (NY)	50,066,480
10. Michigan, U of	47,607,596
11. Massachusetts Institute of Technology	47,520,748
12. Virginia, U of	44,540,495
13. California, U of, Berkeley	40,048,689
14. Illinois, U of, Urbana	36,818,602
15. Wisconsin, U of, Madison	36,429,217
16. Chicago, U of (IL)	35,341,282
17. Ohio State U, Columbus	34,058,874
18. Duke U (NC)	33,239,549
19. North Carolina, U of, Chapel Hill	31,214,562
20. Notre Dame, U of (IN)	29,963,386

Source: Reprinted with the permission of the Council for Aid to Education from the 1995–96 Voluntary Support of Education Survey.

Top Twenty Institutions in Alumni Support per Student

These colleges have the most alumni support per student in 1995–96.

1. Wells C (NY)	$12,004
2. Richmond, U of (VA)	11,942
3. Washington and Lee U (VA)	11,733
4. Stanford U (CA)	11,201
5. Princeton U (NJ)	10,632
6. California Institute of Technology	9,890
7. Dartmouth C (NH)	9,803

8. Amherst C (MA)	9,713
9. Swarthmore C (PA)	9,516
10. Williams C (MA)	9,483
11. Yale U (CT)	8,565
12. Pine Manor C (MA)	8,411
13. Mt. Holyoke C (MA)	7,873
14. Randolph-Macon Woman's C (MA)	7,777
15. Wellesley C (MA)	7,728
16. Bowdoin C (MA)	7,298
17. Harvard U (MA)	7,215
18. Vassar C (NY)	7,091
19. Grinnell C (IA)	6,653
20. Smith C (MA)	6,610

Source: *The Chronicle of Higher Education Almanac,* August 29, 1997.

Colleges Compared to Other Charities in Fund-Raising

These are the leading recipients of charitable contributions in the United States. Figures listed are for private support in 1991.

1. United Jewish Appeal, National	$668,061,000
2. Salvation Army	648,963,493
3. Second Harvest	404,453,743
4. American Red Cross	386,065,000
5. Catholic Charities U.S.A.	368,278,040
6. American Cancer Society	346,346,000
7. American Heart Association	235,673,000
8. United Jewish Appeal, New York City	235,516,978
9. YMCA of the U.S.A.	214,527,189
10. Boy Scouts of America	209,598,000
11. Harvard U (MA)	195,582,616
12. Shriners Hospitals for Crippled Children	186,783,000
13. Stanford U (CA)	180,922,245
14. Public Broadcasting Service	179,979,314
15. Cornell U (NY)	177,054,933
16. Boys and Girls Clubs of America	164,758,902
17. Brigham Young U (UT)	160,426,163
18. Pennsylvania, U of	156,646,159
19. World Vision	154,688,531
20. Catholic Relief Services	150,396,000
21. Nature Conservancy	146,396,719
22. Campus Crusade for Christ	134,983,000
23. Yale U (CT)	132,417,000
24. Duke U (NC)	127,151,510
25. Minnesota, U of, Twin Cities	126,893,000

Source: Philip W. Semas (ed.), "The Philanthropy 400," *The Chronicle of Philanthropy* 5 (2) (November 1992): 27.

Universities Receiving Federal Research and Development Expenditures

These colleges received the most money from the U.S. government in fiscal year 1996.

1. Johns Hopkins U (MD)	$710,119,000
2. Washington, U of	312,645,000
3. California, U of, San Diego	291,917,000
4. Stanford U (CA)	281,641,000
5. Michigan, U of	281,062,000
6. Massachusetts Institute of Technology	271,544,000
7. California, U of, Los Angeles	236,635,000
8. Wisconsin, U of, Madison	233,174,000
9. California, U of, San Francisco	221,864,000
10. Pennsylvania, U of	216,167,000
11. Cornell U (NY)	203,082,000
12. Harvard U (MA)	203,047,000
13. Minnesota, U of	198,927,000
14. Columbia U (NY)	195,652,000
15. Pennsylvania State U, University Park	190,688,000
16. Southern California, U of	179,281,000
17. Colorado, U of	177,517,000
18. Yale U (CT)	176,994,000
19. California, U of, Berkeley	168,171,000
20. North Carolina, U of, Chapel Hill	157,034,000
21. Washington U (MO)	155,197,000
22. Arizona, U of	154,004,000
23. Pittsburgh, U of (PA)	149,960,000
24. Duke U (NC)	149,631,000
25. Texas A&M U	148,675,000

Source: National Science Foundation.

FOCUS ON UNDERGRADUATES

Many factors influence the nature of the undergraduate experience at a particular college. A large percentage of undergraduates, in comparison to graduate students, may suggest that the college or university focuses its resources and personnel on undergraduate teaching and the undergraduate experience.

Ivy League Colleges Ranked by Percentage of Undergraduates to Total Enrollment

Figures reflect approximate numbers of full-time students.

1. Dartmouth C (NH)	80%	5,334 total	4,285 undergraduates
2. Brown U (RI)	78%	7,626 total	5,963 undergraduates
3. Cornell U (NY)	72%	18,849 total	13,512 undergraduates
*4. Princeton U (NJ)	72%	6,340 total	4,593 undergraduates
5. Pennsylvania, U of	52%	21,171 total	11,024 undergraduates
6. Yale U (CT)	49%	10,986 total	5,326 undergraduates
7. Harvard U (MA)	37%	17,579 total	6,634 undergraduates
8. Columbia U (NY)	36%	19,664 total	8,072 undergraduates

*See Author's Note, p. xxv.

Source: Enrollment data compiled from information in *Barron's Profiles of American Colleges, 22nd Edition.*

Big 10 Colleges Ranked by Percentage of Undergraduate Students to Total Enrollment

Figures reflect approximate numbers of full-time students.

College	Percentage	Total	Undergraduates
1. Pennsylvania State U, University Park	83%	39,782 total	33,163 undergraduates
2. Purdue U (IN)	81%	35,156 total	28,567 undergraduates
3. Michigan State U	78%	41,545 total	32,318 undergraduates
4. Indiana U, Bloomington	77%	32,981 total	25,451 undergraduates
5. Illinois, U of, Urbana	76%	35,218 total	26,738 undergraduates
6. Ohio State U, Columbus	73%	48,352 total	35,486 undergraduates
7. Iowa, U of	67%	27,921 total	18,586 undergraduates
*8. Wisconsin, U of, Madison	67%	39,883 total	26,950 undergraduates
9. Minnesota, U of, Twin Cities	66%	35,481 total	23,689 undergraduates
10. Michigan, U of, Ann Arbor	65%	36,525 total	23,587 undergraduates
11. Northwestern U (IL)	63%	12,213 total	7,645 undergraduates

*See Author's Note, p. xxv.

Source: Enrollment data compiled from information in *Barron's Profiles of American Colleges, 22nd Edition.*

Atlantic Coast Conference Colleges Ranked by Percentage of Undergraduate Students to Total Enrollment

Figures reflect approximate numbers of full-time students.

College	Percentage	Total	Undergraduates
1. North Carolina State U	78%	27,169 total	21,154 undergraduates
2. Clemson U (SC)	77%	16,537 total	12,717 undergraduates
3. Florida State U	76%	30,264 total	23,051 undergraduates
4. Maryland, U of, College Park	75%	31,471 total	23,758 undergraduates

Atlantic Coast Conference Colleges Ranked by Percentage of Undergraduate Students to Total Enrollment (continued)

5. Georgia Institute of Technology	73%	13,242 total	9,671 undergraduates
6. North Carolina, U of, Chapel Hill	69%	21,937 total	15,063 undergraduates
7. Virginia, U of	67%	17,959 total	12,040 undergraduates
8. Wake Forest U (NC)	64%	5,910 total	3,771 undergraduates
9. Duke U (NC)	55%	11,589 total	6,326 undergraduates

Source: Enrollment data compiled from information in *Barron's Profiles of American Colleges, 22nd Edition.*

Big 12 Colleges Ranked by Percentage of Undergraduate Students to Total Enrollment

Figures reflect approximate numbers of full-time students.

1. Baylor U (TX)	85%	12,391 total	10,500 undergraduates
2. Kansas State U	83%	20,325 total	16,935 undergraduates
*3. Texas Tech U	83%	24,717 total	20,420 undergraduates
4. Iowa State U	82%	24,899 total	20,503 undergraduates
*5. Texas A&M U	82%	41,892 total	34,342 undergraduates
6. Colorado, U of	81%	24,622 total	18,845 undergraduates
7. Nebraska, U of, Lincoln	79%	23,877 total	18,954 undergraduates
8. Oklahoma State U	77%	18,917 total	14,640 undergraduates
*9. Oklahoma, U of	77%	19,026 total	14,732 undergraduates
*10. Texas, U of, Austin	77%	46,495 total	35,789 undergraduates
11. Missouri, U of, Columbia	76%	22,483 total	17,165 undergraduates
12. Kansas, U of	68%	27,407 total	18,652 undergraduates

*See Author's Note, p. xxv.

Source: Enrollment data compiled from information in *Barron's Profiles of American Colleges, 22nd Edition.*

Selective Colleges Listed in Order of Percentage of Undergraduate Students to Total Enrollment

This list includes schools with the highest admission standards and the very selective colleges (see page 4). Figures reflect approximate numbers of full-time students.

	College	%	Total	Undergraduates
1.	Amherst C (MA)	100%	1,607 total	all undergraduates
*2.	Bates C (ME)	100%	1,672 total	all undergraduates
*3.	Bowdoin C (ME)	100%	1,581 total	all undergraduates
*4.	Carleton C (MN)	100%	1,714 total	all undergraduates
*5.	Colby C (ME)	100%	1,812 total	all undergraduates
*6.	Claremont McKenna C (CA)	100%	952 total	all undergraduates
*7.	Colgate U (NY)	100%	2,859 total	all undergraduates
*8.	Hamilton C (NY)	100%	1,727 total	all undergraduates
*9.	Haverford C (PA)	100%	1,137 total	all undergraduates
*10.	Lafayette C (PA)	100%	2,184 total	all undergraduates
*11.	Middlebury C (VT)	100%	2,148 total	all undergraduates
*12.	Pomona C (CA)	100%	1,421 total	all undergraduates
*13.	Swarthmore C (PA)	100%	1,437 total	all undergraduates
*14.	Vassar C (NY)	100%	2,330 total	all undergraduates
*15.	Wellesley C (MA)	100%	2,319 total	all undergraduates
16.	Oberlin C (OH)	99%	2,793 total	2,776 undergraduates
17.	Connecticut C	97%	1,730 total	1,682 undergraduates
*18.	Williams C (MA)	97%	2,048 total	1,992 undergraduates
19.	Bucknell U (PA)	95%	3,585 total	3,390 undergraduates
20.	Cooper Union (NY)	94%	927 total	872 undergraduates
21.	Wesleyan U (CT)	84%	3,255 total	2,725 undergraduates
22.	Richmond, U of (VA)	82%	4,366 total	3,586 undergraduates
23.	California, U of, San Diego	81%	18,119 total	14,623 undergraduates
24.	Dartmouth C (NH)	80%	5,334 total	4,285 undergraduates
25.	Brown U (RI)	78%	7,626 total	5,963 undergraduates
26.	Notre Dame, U of (IN)	73%	10,500 total	7,700 undergraduates

Selective Colleges Listed in Order of Percentage of Undergraduate Students to Total Enrollment (continued)

College	%	Total	Undergraduates
*27. William and Mary, C of (VA)	73%	7,908 total	5,805 undergraduates
28. California, U of, Berkeley	72%	29,797 total	21,358 undergraduates
*29. Cornell U (NY)	72%	18,849 total	13,512 undergraduates
*30. Princeton U (NJ)	72%	6,340 total	4,593 undergraduates
31. North Carolina, U of, Chapel Hill	69%	21,937 total	15,063 undergraduates
32. Bryn Mawr C (PA)	68%	1,776 total	1,205 undergraduates
33. Virginia, U of	67%	17,959 total	12,040 undergraduates
34. Boston C (MA)	66%	13,618 total	8,958 undergraduates
35. California, U of, Los Angeles	65%	34,935 total	23,914 undergraduates
*36. Michigan, U of, Ann Arbor	65%	36,525 total	23,587 undergraduates
37. Rice U (TX)	64%	4,071 total	2,665 undergraduates
*38. Wake Forest U (NC)	64%	5,910 total	3,771 undergraduates
39. Carnegie Mellon U (PA)	63%	7,546 total	4,737 undergraduates
*40. Northwestern U (IL)	63%	12,213 total	7,645 undergraduates
41. Johns Hopkins U (MD)	61%	5,866 total	3,606 undergraduates
42. Juilliard School (NY)	58%	832 total	484 undergraduates
43. Vanderbilt U (TN)	57%	10,253 total	5,877 undergraduates
44. Tufts U (MA)	56%	8,183 total	4,539 undergraduates
45. Duke U (NC)	55%	11,589 total	6,326 undergraduates
46. Pennsylvania, U of	52%	21,171 total	11,024 undergraduates
47. Georgetown U (DC)	50%	12,629 total	6,338 undergraduates
48. Yale U (CT)	49%	10,986 total	5,326 undergraduates
49. Stanford U (CA)	47%	13,811 total	6,550 undergraduates
50. California Institute of Technology	46%	1,902 total	882 undergraduates
51. Massachusetts Institute of Technology	45%	9,947 total	4,429 undergraduates

52. Harvard U (MA)	38%	17,579 total	6,634 undergraduates
53. Columbia U (NY)	36%	19,664 total	8,072 undergraduates
54. Chicago, U of (IL)	29%	12,117 total	3,561 undergraduates

*See Author's Note, p. xxv.

Source: Enrollment data compiled with information in *Barron's Profiles of American Colleges, 22nd Edition.*

GRADUATION RECORD

National Universities with the Highest Graduation Rates

		PERCENT
1.	Harvard U (MA)	97
2.	Princeton U (NJ)	94
*3.	Stanford U (CA)	94
4.	Dartmouth C (NH)	93
*5.	Duke U (NC)	93
*6.	Emory U (GA)	93
*7.	Notre Dame, U of (IN)	93
*8.	Yale U (CT)	93
9.	Brown U (RI)	91
*10.	Northwestern U (IL)	91
*11.	Virginia, U of	91
*12.	William and Mary, C of (VA)	91
13.	Georgetown U	90
*14.	Rice U (TX)	90
15.	Cornell U (NY)	89
*16.	Massachusetts Institute of Technology	89
17.	Johns Hopkins U (MD)	88
*18.	Pennsylvania, U of	88
*19.	Tufts U (MA)	88
20.	Columbia U (NY)	87
21.	Boston C (MA)	86
*22.	Washington U (MO)	86
23.	Lehigh U (PA)	85

*24.	Wake Forest U (NC)	85
25.	Michigan, U of	84

*See Author's Note, p. xxv.

Source: Copyright © 1997, *U.S. News and World Report.*

Liberal Arts Colleges with the Highest Graduation Rates

		PERCENT
1.	Amherst C (MA)	98
2.	William C (MA)	95
3.	Bucknell U (PA)	92
4.	Hamilton C (NY)	91
*5.	Haverford C (PA)	91
*6.	Pomona C (CA)	91
*7.	Swarthmore C (PA)	91
8.	Holy Cross, C of the (MA)	90
9.	Bryn Mawr C (PA)	89
*10.	Davidson C (NC)	89
*11.	Trinity C (CT)	89
12.	Bowdoin C (ME)	88
*13.	Carleton C (MN)	88
*14.	Colby C (ME)	88
*15.	Colgate U (NY)	88
*16.	Middlebury C (VT)	88
*17.	South, U of the (TN)	88
18.	Barnard C (NY)	87
*19.	Lafayette C (PA)	87
*20.	Washington and Lee U (VA)	87
21.	Bates C (ME)	86
*22.	Claremont McKenna C (CA)	86
*23.	Kenyon C (OH)	86
*24.	Wellesley C (MA)	86
*25.	Wesleyan U (CT)	86

*See Author's Note, p. xxv.

Source: Copyright © 1997, *U.S. News and World Report.*

National Universities with the Lowest Graduation Rates

		PERCENT
1.	Texas Southern U	12
2.	Alaska, U of, Fairbanks	26
*3.	Louisville, U of (KY)	26
*4.	New Orleans, U of (LA)	26
5.	Southwestern Louisiana, U of	27
*6.	Texas, U of, Arlington	27
*7.	Wichita State U (KS)	27
8.	Cleveland State U (OH)	28
9.	Portland State U (OR)	29
10.	Alabama, U of, Birmingham	31
11.	Tennessee State U	32
*12.	Texas Woman's U	32
*13.	Texas, U of, Dallas	32
*14.	Wright State U (OH)	32
15.	Georgia State U	33
*16.	New Mexico, U of	33
17.	Akron, U of (OH)	34
*18.	California, State U of, San Diego	34
*19.	Illinois, U of, Chicago	34
*20.	Memphis, U of (TN)	34
21.	Houston, U of (TX)	35
*22.	North Texas, U of	35

*See Author's Note, p. xxv.

Liberal Arts Colleges with the Lowest Graduation Rates

		PERCENT
1.	Simon's Rock C of Bard (MA)	28
2.	Virginia Wesleyan C	37
3.	Marlboro C (VT)	39
4.	North Carolina, U of, Asheville	40
5.	Shepherd C (WV)	41
6.	Huntingdon C (AL)	43
7.	Monmouth C (IL)	45
*8.	Wesleyan C (GA)	45
9.	Georgetown C (KY)	47
10.	Antioch C (OH)	49
11.	Oglethorpe U (GA)	50
12.	Chatham C (PA)	51
*13.	Hastings C (NE)	51
*14.	Morehouse C (GA)	51
*15.	St. Andrews Presbyterian C (NC)	51
16.	Franklin C (IN)	52
*17.	Illinois C	52
*18.	Judson C (AL)	52
19.	Bethany C (WV)	54
*20.	St. John's C (NM)	54
21.	Wartburg C (IA)	55
22.	Bennington C (VT)	56
*23.	Salem C (NC)	56
*24.	William Jewell C (MO)	56

*See Author's Note, p. xxv.

Source: Copyright © 1997, *U.S. News and World Report.*

QUALITY POTPOURRI

The Experts' Choice: Hidden Treasures

Counselors were asked for colleges that provide an excellent education and student experience but are not well known by the general public.

THE TOP TWENTY-FIVE

1. Davidson C (NC)
2. Kenyon C (OH)
*3. Macalester C (MN)
4. Grinnell C (IA)
*5. Wooster, C of (OH)
6. Centre C (KY)
*7. Lawrence U (WI)
8. Drew U (NJ)
*9. Kalamazoo C (MI)
*10. South, U of the (TN)
11. Carleton C (MN)
*12. Earlham C (IN)
*13. Rhodes C (TN)
*14. Wheaton C (MA)
15. Guilford C (NC)
*16. Haverford C (PA)
*17. Muhlenberg C (PA)
*18. Occidental C (CA)
*19. Rochester, U of (NY)
*20. Washington C (MD)
*21. Washington U (MO)
*22. Willamette U (OR)
23. Allegheny C (PA)
*24. DePauw U (IN)
*25. Hartwick C (NY)

*See Author's Note, p. xxv.

ADDITIONAL HIGHLY RANKED COLLEGES

Bates C (ME)
Beloit C (WI)
Bethany C (WV)
Clark U (MA)
Colgate U (NY)
Colorado C

Connecticut C
Dickinson C (PA)
Eckerd C (FL)
Elizabethtown C (PA)
Emory U (GA)
Franklin and Marshall C (PA)
Goucher C (MD)
Hamilton C (NY)
Hendrix C (AR)
Hiram C (OH)
Hobart C/William Smith C (NY)
James Madison U (VA)
Lafayette C (PA)
Lewis and Clark C (OR)
Marietta C (OH)
Mary Washington C (VA)
Mt. Holyoke C (MA)
Pitzer C (CA)
Redlands, U of (CA)
Reed C (OR)
Rice U (TX)
St. Anselm C (NH)
St. Lawrence U (NY)
St. Olaf C (MN)
Trinity U (TX)
Union C (NY)
Ursinus C (PA)
Wittenberg U (OH)

Most Interesting Colleges for the New Millennium

Due to the program, emphasis, or atmosphere described, these are colleges that are moving up through the ranks of colleges at the start of the 2000s.

Bates C (ME)—individualism, egalitarianism, and acceptance have always been prized. Bates educates bright people even if some march to a different drummer.

California, U of, Los Angeles—who says Berkeley is the "best" of the California system? The decades have been good to UCLA. Balanced athletics, major as well as minor, have gone hand in hand with an increased emphasis on undergraduate teaching.

Chicago, U of (IL)—still on top in liberal arts education, and with the new millennium there is an increased emphasis on student life here as well.

Champlain C (VT)—increasingly, students want solid career preparation in college. Champlain has been a leader in career-focused education for more than one hundred years.

Cincinnati, U of (OH)—as students want a good education along with career preparation, Cincinnati's huge cooperative

Most Interesting Colleges for the New Millennium (continued)

education program combines a broad education with internships in industry.

Clark U (MA)—instead of building a cage around the campus, Clark has forged a partnership with Worcester, which has made the Clark experience a real-life one.

Denver, U of (CO)—a respectable place for years, but the school has revved its motors with a core curriculum, new facilities, Division I athletics, and more student immersion in the city and the state.

Emory U (GA)—keeps getting better; it has gone from a good Southern school to an excellent national university over the last decades. The quality of the faculty and the students continues to rise.

Florida, U of—being the first major state university to have a computer for every student is one example of Florida's innovation. Hey, Mom, it's not just a party school anymore.

Indiana U, Bloomington—what? A huge state school with good advising? Yes, and that is just part of a broad emphasis on helping and caring here.

Marlboro C (VT)—there is still a place in 2000 for the 1960s: Here's a progressive alternative school that is finally earning academic respect.

Michigan, U of, Ann Arbor—as students look increasingly to expand their horizons during college, Michigan students are bombarded with curricular and extracurricular options and resources that rival many Ivy League schools.

New York U—so, New York City is unsafe and overwhelming and students should look elsewhere for college? Hogwash. NYU uses the resources of its city, yet stands on its own with a fine teaching faculty and loads of interesting diversions.

Pepperdine U (CA)—for those students who don't see themselves in the wild party scene of many colleges, and who have some spiritual identity, look no farther than Malibu! A highly moral atmosphere makes teaching and learning here unique.

Pittsburgh, U of (PA)—perhaps the least recognized "Public Ivy," Pittsburgh has great sciences, increasingly strong majors in the arts and humanities, and a safe, city campus.

Portland, U of (OR)—the Northwest is popular, and so is this small Catholic school that understates its accessible faculty and accepting atmosphere.

Syracuse U (NY)—known for sports and its communication school, Syracuse has come of age. A more academically focused student body and a lot of student involvement makes for sunny days in oft-cloudy Syracuse.

Washington, U of—there's more than coffee in Seattle. The university has a superior faculty, an increasingly strong student body, good links to industry, and a tolerant spirit.

Wellesley C (MA)—who said women's colleges don't compete with coeducational schools? Compare the success of Wellesley grads with any top school—coeducational or women's.

Western Washington U—here's one to watch: a traditional public school with some funky elements like Fairhaven; a successful alternative college.

Yale U (CT)—while some Ivy schools have stood on their reputations, Yale has bettered its undergraduate faculty, its resources, and its city. There are reasons why Yalies have such high praise for their school.

Thirty College Gems

Arizona, U of—the sun and academic rigor coexist successfully at the U of A, where talented teachers bring the ivory tower into the real world.

Birmingham-Southern C (AL)—bridging the traditions of Northeastern and Southern colleges, Birmingham-Southern is committed to developing both character and mind.

Bradley U (IL)—a college in the heartland offers a well-regarded, comprehensive academic program and plenty of athletic and extracurriculars to cheer about.

Chicago, U of (IL)—sometimes overshadowed by Ivy League colleges, the undergraduate experience here is rigorous and intense, but ultimately rewarding.

Cornell C (IA)—Cornell students take only one course at a time, work hard, and enjoy the supportiveness and involvement of the entire college community.

DePauw U (IN)—DePauw is characterized by high-energy students, a wide range of academic programs, and a sensitive faculty.

Duke U (NC)—few schools offer the balance available at Duke: world-class academics, diverse and engaging activities, and a comprehensive athletic program.

Franklin and Marshall C (PA)—close relationships with teachers, even extending to coauthoring a journal article, contribute to students' academic confidence here.

Furman U (SC)—the tranquillity of the Furman campus adds to the pleasure of studying and learning in a community that promotes student growth.

Grinnell C (IA)—founded by reformers, Grinnell conveys acceptance, supports individuality, and teaches students how to problem-solve.

Gustavus Adolphus C (MN)—here is a college with a Lutheran heritage and Swedish tradition that expects a lot of its students, yet gives them time to explore and analyze themselves and their world.

Hamilton C (NY)—Clinton, New York, may not be a vacation destination, but four years at Hamilton can teach students to think, to create, and to smile.

Kalamazoo C (MI)—Kalamazoo's unique calendar combines teaching, internships, research, and foreign study in a neat package and produces students ready for the real world.

Kenyon C (OH)—Gambier, Ohio, is small and isolated, but Kenyon is a gentle giant, offering intriguing academic, social, and athletic possibilities for students.

Linfield C (OR)—despite Linfield's small size and small-town location, its students, sometimes underachievers, tally big gains in academic self-assurance.

Macalester C (MN)—individualists and participants are plentiful at Mac where the international flavor, in composition of students, foreign study opportunities, and classes themselves, not only enrich the four years, but also increase employment possibilities.

Mills C (CA)—the push to remain a college of women underscores the passion and the concern students possess about their small and vibrant college.

New England C (NH)—learning is easy and college is fun in rural New Hampshire, thanks to New England's friendliness and resources for improved study skills.

New York U—Greenwich Village, New York City, diverse students, acclaimed teachers, and a wide range of programs blend to make NYU right for the discoverer.

Ohio U, Athens—sometimes overshadowed by other Midwestern universities, OU has a sense of community rare in a public university.

Ohio Wesleyan U—a contented and active student body is found at OWU; students grow academically, but they also learn how to relate to other people.

Pacific Lutheran U (WA)—a family, community atmosphere exists at PLU; its advising is excellent, and students gain from the excitement of the Northwest.

Rochester, U of (NY)—Rochester provides a stellar faculty and motivated students who want top academics without the pressure of an Ivy League college.

St. Michael's C (VT)—with an emphasis on values, community service, and caring, St. Mike's is a place where young people feel engaged and trusted.

Smith C (MA)—far from the stereotype of a traditional women's school, Smith students find a place to be challenged, supported, and active.

Southwestern U (TX)—conservative and value-centered, South-

Thirty College Gems (continued)

western students are supportive of one another and, over four years, become confident about their academic potential.

Transylvania U (KY)—Transy, the first college west of the Allegheny Mountains, has a high participation rate in student organizations and activities and puts priority on knowledge instead of grades.

Tulsa, U of (OK)—with a wide range of programs and a medium size, Tulsa is a school on the move; it provides a big-university experience within a caring climate.

Washington C (MD)—doers and participants do well at this college rich in heritage (George Washington helped to endow it) and academic spice.

Whitman C (WA)—while Walla Walla is small and isolated, the beautiful countryside encourages highly motivated students to enjoy the beauty of learning.

Top Colleges in Graduate and Professional Education

These are the member colleges of the Association of American Universities (AAU). The AAU consists of a select group of fifty-six American and two Canadian universities with strong programs of graduate and professional education and research. Approximately half are public institutions and half private.

Arizona, U of
Brandeis U (MA)
Brown U (RI)
California Institute of Technology
California, U of, Berkeley
California, U of, Los Angeles
California, U of, San Diego
Carnegie Mellon U (PA)
Case Western Reserve U (OH)
Catholic U (DC)
Chicago, U of (IL)
Clark U (MA)
Colorado, U of
Columbia U (NY)
Cornell U (NY)
Duke U (NC)
Florida, U of
Harvard U (MA)
Illinois, U of, Urbana
Indiana U, Bloomington
Iowa State U
Iowa, U of
Johns Hopkins U (MD)
Kansas, U of
Maryland, U of, College Park
Massachusetts Institute of Technology
McGill U (Canada)
Michigan State U
Michigan, U of, Ann Arbor
Minnesota, U of, Twin Cities
Missouri, U of, Columbia
Nebraska, U of, Lincoln
New York, State U of, Buffalo
New York U
North Carolina, U of, Chapel Hill
Northwestern U (IL)
Ohio State U, Columbus
Oregon, U of
Pennsylvania State U, University Park
Pennsylvania, U of
Pittsburgh, U of (PA)
Princeton U (NJ)
Purdue U (IN)
Rice U (TX)
Rochester, U of (NY)
Rutgers U (NJ)
Southern California, U of
Stanford U (CA)
Syracuse U (NY)
Texas, U of, Austin
Toronto, U of (Canada)
Tulane U (LA)
Vanderbilt U (TN)
Virginia, U of
Washington, U of
Washington U (MO)
Wisconsin, U of, Madison
Yale U (CT)

Source: Association of American Universities, Washington, DC.

SOCIAL

THE SOCIAL FIT

Colleges for the Lover of Ideas

These schools provide many opportunities through colloquia and interdisciplinary study to explore and connect ideas; professors are attuned to the academic needs of the very brightest students. Students tend to be alert, quick thinking, and enjoy talking about ideas.

Amherst C (MA)
Antioch C (OH)
Bard C (NY)
Barnard C (NY)
Bates C (ME)
Bennington C (VT)
Bryn Mawr C (PA)
Carleton C (MN)
Chicago, U of (IL)
Columbia U (NY)
Deep Springs C (CA)
Grinnell C (IA)
Harvard U (MA)
Haverford C (PA)
New C (FL)
Oberlin C (OH)
Pomona C (CA)
Princeton U (NJ)
St. John's C (MD)
St. John's C (NM)
Sarah Lawrence C (NY)
Swarthmore C (PA)
Thomas Aquinas C (CA)
Thomas More C (NH)
Vassar C (NY)
Wellesley C (MA)
Wesleyan U (CT)
Yale U (CT)

Colleges for the Independent/Mature Student

These schools provide many academic and social options, have high expectations, and are appropriate for those who can make reasoned and adult decisions.

Antioch C (OH)
Bard C (NY)
Barnard C (NY)
Bennington C (VT)
Berklee C of Music (MA)
Brown U (RI)
California State U, Humboldt
California, U of, Berkeley
California, U of, Santa Cruz
Chicago, U of (IL)
Clark U (MA)
Columbia U (NY)
Cooper Union (NY)
Eugene Lang C (NY)
Evergreen State C (WA)
Goddard C (VT)
Hampshire C (MA)
Harvard U (MA)
Haverford C (PA)
International Training, School for (VT)
Juilliard School (NY)
Marlboro C (VT)
McGill U (Canada)
New C (FL)
New York U
Oberlin C (OH)
Prescott C (AZ)
Princeton U (NJ)
Ramapo C (NJ)
Reed C (OR)
Rhode Island School of Design
Sarah Lawrence C (NY)
Swarthmore C (PA)
Warren Wilson C (NC)
Wellesley C (MA)
Wesleyan U (CT)
Western Washington U, Fairhaven C

Colleges for the Shy Person

Because of their unusually friendly atmosphere, these schools make it easier for a shy student to fit in quickly and easily.

Allegheny C (PA)
Alma C (MI)
Augustana C (IL)
Austin C (TX)
Azusa Pacific U (CA)
Bates C (ME)
Biola U (CA)
Birmingham-Southern C (AL)
Bryn Mawr C (PA)
Buena Vista C (IA)
Central C (IA)
Cornell C (IA)
Dallas, U of (TX)
Dean C (MA)
Eckerd C (FL)
Elizabethtown C (PA)
Elms C (MA)
Gustavus Adolphus C (MN)
Hampden-Sydney C (VA)
Hanover C (IN)
Harvey Mudd C (CA)
Haverford C (PA)
Hendrix C (AR)
Hillsdale C (MI)
Hiram C (OH)
Hollins C (VA)
Hood C (MD)
Illinois Wesleyan U
Knox C (IL)
Lewis and Clark C (OR)
Loras C (IA)
Luther C (IA)
Lyndon State C (VT)
Marietta C (OH)
Marymount C (CA)
Minnesota, U of, Morris
Mt. St. Mary's C (CA)
Mt. St. Vincent, C of (NY)
Otterbein C (OH)
St. Andrews Presbyterian C (NC)
St. Anselm C (NH)
St. Benedict, C of/St. John's U (MN)
St. Mary's C (MN)
Scripps C (CA)
Simmons C (MA)
Spring Hill C (AL)
Stetson U (FL)
Wartburg C (IA)
Western State C (CO)
Westmont C (CA)
Wheaton C (IL)
Wittenberg U (OH)

Colleges for the Student Interested in Building Leadership Skills

By encouraging a wide representation in student clubs and activities, these schools provide many opportunities for leadership roles. Often, these are smaller colleges with easy entry to participation in campus life.

Agnes Scott C (GA)
Albion C (MI)
Appalachian State U (NC)
Babson C (MA)
Bentley C (MA)
Bowdoin C (ME)
Brandeis U (MA)
Brown U (RI)
Bryn Mawr C (PA)
Cedar Crest C (PA)
Claremont McKenna C (CA)
Coe C (IA)
Colgate U (NY)
Cornell C (IA)
Dartmouth C (NH)
Defiance C (OH)
Denison U (OH)
DePauw U (IN)
Dickinson C (PA)
Drew U (NJ)
Duke U (NC)
Duquesne U (PA)
Eckerd C (FL)
Evansville, U of (IN)
Fairfield U (CT)
Franklin and Marshall C (PA)
Furman U (SC)
George Washington U (DC)
Georgetown U (DC)
Guilford C (NC)
Gustavus Adolphus C (MN)
Hartwick C (NY)
Haverford C (PA)
Hiram C (OH)
Hobart C/William Smith C (NY)
Hollins C (VA)
Ithaca C (NY)
Kalamazoo C (MI)
Lawrence U (WI)
Lesley C (MA)
Linfield C (OR)
Marist C (NY)
Millikin U (IL)
Mt. Holyoke C (MA)
Mt. St. Mary's C (CA)
Muhlenberg C (PA)
North Carolina, U of, Chapel Hill
North Carolina, U of, Charlotte
North Central C (IL)
Northwestern U (IL)
Notre Dame, U of (IN)
Oxford C/Emory U (GA)
Pacific, U of the (CA)
Pepperdine U (CA)
Presbyterian C (SC)
Puget Sound, U of (WA)
Richmond, U of (VA)
St. Michael's C (VT)
Santa Clara U (CA)
Scripps C (CA)
Simmons C (MA)
Skidmore C (NY)
Smith C (MA)

South, U of the (TN)
Stephens C (MO)
Texas Christian U
Trinity C (DC)
Truman State U (MO)
Union C (NY)
Wabash C (IN)
Warren Wilson C (NC)
Washington and Lee U (VA)
Washington C (MD)
Washington U (MO)
Wellesley C (MA)
Westminster C (MO)
Whittier C (CA)
Williams C (MA)
Wofford C (SC)
Wooster, C of (OH)

Colleges for the Student Interested in Building Confidence

These schools are unusually supportive and caring and encourage students to try many activities.

Agnes Scott C (GA)
Albion C (MI)
Albright C (PA)
Alfred U (NY)
Allentown C (PA)
Alverno C (WI)
Amherst C (MA)
Arkansas C
Babson C (MA)
Baldwin-Wallace C (OH)
Bates C (ME)
Bradley U (IL)
Brevard C (NC)
Carleton C (MN)
Catawba C (NC)
Cedar Crest C (PA)
Coe C (IA)
Colby-Sawyer C (NH)
Colorado C
Connecticut C
Cottey C (MO)
Curry C (MA)
Deep Springs C (CA)
Defiance C (OH)
Drake U (IA)
Earlham C (IN)
Elmira C (NY)
Elon C (NC)
Franklin and Marshall C (PA)
George Fox C (OR)
Goucher C (MD)
Green Mountain C (VT)
Hamilton C (NY)
Hartford, U of (CT)
Hastings C (NE)
High Point U (NC)
Holy Cross, C of the (MA)
Holy Names C (CA)
Hope C (MI)
Kalamazoo C (MI)
Kenyon C (OH)
Knox C (IL)
Lake Forest C (IL)
Lasell C (MA)
Lawrence U (WI)

Colleges for the Student Interested in Building Confidence (continued)

Linfield C (OR)
Lycoming C (PA)
Lynchburg C (VA)
Marietta C (OH)
Mary Baldwin C (VA)
Mary Washington C (VA)
Marymount C (CA)
Mills C (CA)
Millsaps C (MS)
Moravian C (PA)
Mt. Ida C (MA)
Muhlenberg C (PA)
Muskingum C (OH)
New England C (NH)
Newbury C (MA)
North Carolina, U of, Ashville
Northwestern C (IA)
Oxford C/Emory U (GA)
Portland, U of (OR)
Presbyterian C (SC)
Providence C (RI)
Randolph-Macon C (VA)
Randolph-Macon Woman's C (VA)
Rhodes C (TN)
Roger Williams C (RI)
Rollins C (FL)
St. Andrews Presbyterian C (NC)
St. Benedict, C of/ St. John's U (MN)
St. Olaf C (MN)
Salve Regina U (RI)
Santa Clara U (CA)
Seattle Pacific U (WA)
Simmons C (MA)
Southwestern U (TX)
Spring Hill C (AL)
Stephens C (MO)
Sweet Briar C (VA)
Transylvania C (KY)
Utica C (NY)
Valparaiso U (IN)
Wabash C (IN)
Wake Forest U (NC)
Washington C (MD)
Washington U (MO)
Wheaton C (MA)
Whitman C (WA)
Whitworth C (WA)
William Jewell C (MO)
Wooster, C of (OH)

Colleges for the Friendly Student

These schools encourage student-to-student interaction; their people are unusually caring, outgoing, and supportive.

Albertson C (ID)
Albright C (PA)
Alma C (MI)
Augustana C (IL)
Baker U (KS)
Bradley U (IL)
Bryant C (RI)
Campbell U (NC)
Carroll C (MT)
Catawba C (NC)
Concordia U (CA)
Cornell C (IA)
Creighton U (NE)
Duke U (NC)
Evansville, U of (IN)
Fort Hays State U (KS)
Georgia Southern U
Gonzaga U (WA)
Grove City C (PA)
Guilford C (NC)
Gustavus Adolphus C (MN)
Hamline U (MN)
Hampden-Sydney C (VA)
Hanover C (IN)
Hawaii Pacific U
Heidelberg C (OH)
John Carroll U (OH)
Kansas State U
Knox C (IL)
Luther C (IA)
Missouri, U of, Columbia
Monmouth C (IL)
Morningside C (IA)
Mt. Ida C (MA)
Muhlenberg C (PA)
Muskingum C (OH)
Nebraska, U of, Lincoln
New York, State U of, C at Old Westbury
North Carolina, U of, Ashville
Northwestern U (IL)
Otterbein C (OH)
Pacific Lutheran U (WA)
Portland, U of (OR)
Quinnipiac C (CT)
Ripon C (WI)
Roanoke C (VA)
Rocky Mountain C (MT)
St. Bonaventure U (NY)
St. Mary of the Plains (KS)
St. Mary's C (CA)
Schreiner C (TX)
South Carolina, U of, Columbia
Southern Illinois U, Carbondale
Southwestern U (TX)
Susquehanna U (PA)
Tulsa, U of (OK)
Ursinus C (PA)
Utah, U of
Washington C (MD)
West Virginia Wesleyan C
Western Maryland C
Westmont C (CA)
Whitman C (WA)
Whitworth C (WA)
Wisconsin, U of, Eau Claire
Wisconsin, U of, Oshkosh
Wittenberg U (OH)

Colleges for the Student Interested in the Outdoors

Primarily, but not entirely, due to their locations, these schools are attractive to those who enjoy athletics, nature, and the environment.

Alaska, U of, Fairbanks
Appalachian State U (NC)
Atlantic, C of the (ME)
Bates C (ME)
Bowdoin C (ME)
Brevard C (NC)
British Columbia, U of (Canada)
California State U, Humboldt
California, U of, Davis
California, U of, Los Angeles
California, U of, Santa Barbara
California, U of, Santa Cruz
Charleston, C of (SC)
Chowan C (NC)
Clarkson U (NY)
Colby C (ME)
Colgate U (NY)
Colorado C
Colorado State U
Colorado, U of
Dartmouth C (NH)
Denver, U of (CO)
Evergreen State C (WA)
Fort Lewis C (CO)
Green Mountain C (VT)
Hampden-Sydney C (VA)
Idaho State U
Lehigh U (PA)
Lewis and Clark C (OR)
Maine, U of, Orono
Mankato State U (MN)
Miami, U of (FL)
Middlebury C (VT)
Montana State U
Montana, U of
Mt. Holyoke C (MA)
New Hampshire, U of
New Mexico State U
New Mexico, U of, Albuquerque
North Carolina, U of, Chapel Hill
North Florida, U of
Northern Arizona U
Northland C (WI)
Oregon, U of
Paul Smith's C (NY)
Pennsylvania State U, University Park
Prescott C (AZ)
Puget Sound, U of (WA)
Rocky Mountain C (MT)
St. Lawrence U (NY)
St. Michaels C (VT)
Skidmore C (NY)
Southern Illinois U, Carbondale
Southern Vermont C
Stephen F. Austin State U (TX)
Tennessee, U of, Knoxville
Unity C (ME)
Utah State U
Utah, U of
Vermont, U of
Washington State U
Washington, U of

Weber State U (UT)
Western State C (CO)
Western Washington U
Whitman C (WA)
Williams C (MA)
Wisconsin, U of, Madison
Wisconsin, U of, Stevens Point
Wyoming, U of

Colleges for the Free Spirit

These schools are for those who consider themselves unconventional, even somewhat eccentric or funky. Their students give the impression that they are impervious to peer influence.

Antioch C (OH)
Art Center C of Design (CA)
Atlantic, C of the (ME)
Bard C (NY)
Barnard C (NY)
Beloit C (WI)
Bennington C (VT)
Berklee C of Music (MA)
Bradford C (MA)
Brown U (RI)
California Institute of the Arts
California State U, Humboldt
California State U, San Francisco
California, U of, Santa Cruz
Carleton C (MN)
Chicago, U of (IL)
Clark U (MA)
Columbia U (NY)
Cooper Union (NY)
Earlham C (IN)
Eckerd C (FL)
Eugene Lang C (NY)
Evergreen State C (WA)
Goddard C (VT)
Grinnell C (IA)
Hampshire C (MA)
Iowa, U of
Lewis and Clark C (OR)
Macalester C (MN)
Marlboro C (VT)
Montana, U of
New C (CA)
New C (FL)
New York, State U of, Purchase
New York U
Oberlin C (OH)
Oregon, U of
Parsons School of Design (NY)
Pitzer C (CA)
Redlands, U of (CA) (Johnston Center)
Reed C (OR)
Rhode Island School of Design
St. John's C (MD)
St. John's C (NM)
Sarah Lawrence C (NY)
Simon's Rock of Bard C (MA)
Sterling C (VT)
Vassar C (NY)
Wesleyan U (CT)

Colleges Particularly Broad-Minded and Accepting of Students Who Are Different

These schools foster an unusual degree of acceptance. Students are affirmed for the way they look, dress, or behave.

Alverno C (WI)
Amherst C (MA)
Bard C (NY)
Bates C (ME)
Beloit C (WI)
Bennington C (VT)
Berklee C of Music (MA)
Bradford C (MA)
Brown U (RI)
Bryn Mawr C (PA)
California Institute of Technology
California State U, San Jose
California, U of, Berkeley
California, U of, Riverside
California, U of, Santa Cruz
Carleton C (MN)
Carnegie Mellon U (PA)
Chicago, U of (IL)
Cincinnati, U of (OH)
Clark U (MA)
Columbia U (NY)
Drew U (NJ)
Drexel U (PA)
Earlham C (IN)
Eckerd C (FL)
Emerson C (MA)
Eugene Lang C (NY)
Evergreen State C (WA)
Fairleigh Dickinson U (NJ)
Goddard C (VT)
Goucher C (MD)
Grinnell C (IA)
Guilford C (NC)
Hampshire C (MA)
Harvard U (MA)
Harvey Mudd C (CA)
Haverford C (PA)
Juilliard School (NY)
Lewis and Clark C (OR)
Macalester C (MN)
Marlboro C (VT)
Massachusetts Institute of Technology
McGill U (Canada)
New Mexico, U of, Albuquerque
New York U
Oberlin C (OH)
Oregon, U of
Parsons School of Design (NY)
Pittsburgh, U of (PA)
Pitzer C (CA)
Pratt Institute (NY)
Princeton U (NJ)
Ramapo C (NJ)
Reed C (OR)
Rhode Island School of Design
Rochester Institute of Technology (NY)
Rutgers U (NJ)
Sarah Lawrence C (NY)
Smith C (MA)
St. John's C (MD)
St. John's C (NM)
Sterling C (VT)

Stevens Institute of Technology (NJ)
Swarthmore C (PA)
Warren Wilson C (NC)
Wesleyan U (CT)
Yale U (CT)

Colleges with a Diverse Student Body

Large colleges and universities, as well as schools that are either very selective or focused on art and design, are often diverse. In addition, students at these schools represent a variety of economic, racial, ethnic, and attitudinal backgrounds and dispositions.

American U (DC)
Antioch C (OH)
Bard C (NY)
Barnard C (NY)
Bates C (ME)
Bennington C (VT)
Boston U (MA)
Brown U (RI)
Bryn Mawr C (PA)
California State U, Humboldt
California, U of, Berkeley
California, U of, Santa Cruz
Carleton C (MN)
Chicago, U of (IL)
Cincinnati, U of (OH)
Clark U (MA)
Colorado C
Columbia U (NY)
Cornell U (NY)
Earlham C (IN)
Eckerd C (FL)
Emerson C (MA)
Eugene Lang C (NY)
George Washington U (DC)
Goucher C (MD)
Grinnell C (IA)
Hampshire C (MA)
Harvard U (MA)
Lewis and Clark C (OR)
Macalester C (MN)
Massachusetts, U of, Amherst
New C (FL)
New York, City U of, Hunter C
New York U
Oberlin C (OH)
Oregon, U of
Prescott C (AZ)
Princeton U (NJ)
Reed C (OR)
St. John's C (MD)
St. John's C (NM)
St. John's U (NY)
Sarah Lawrence C (NY)
Smith C (MA)
Stanford U (CA)
Swarthmore C (PA)
Vassar C (NY)
Wellesley C (MA)
Wesleyan U (CT)
Yale U (CT)

Colleges with Active Gay or Lesbian Student Communities

These colleges have either an active gay or lesbian organization on campus or students who report support and acceptance of alternative lifestyles from the student body.

Antioch C (OH)
Atlantic, C of the (ME)
Bard C (NY)
Barnard C (NY)
Beloit C (WI)
Bennington C (VT)
Boston U (MA)
Brandeis U (MA)
Brown U (RI)
Bryn Mawr C (PA)
California State U, Los Angeles
California State U, San Francisco
California, U of, Berkeley
California, U of, Los Angeles
Carleton C (MN)
Chicago, U of (IL)
Colorado C
Cornell U (NY)
Earlham C (IN)
East Texas State U
Emerson C (MA)
Evergreen State C (WA)
Florida State U
Florida, U of
Goddard C (VT)
Grinnell C (IA)
Hampshire C (MA)
Harvard U (MA)
Haverford C (PA)
Hofstra U (NY)
Illinois, U of, Urbana
Indiana U, Bloomington
Iowa, U of
Macalester C (MN)
Maryland, U of, College Park
Massachusetts, U of, Amherst
Minnesota, U of, Twin Cities
Nevada, U of, Las Vegas
New C (FL)
New York, State U of, Purchase
New York U
Oberlin C (OH)
Ohio State U, Columbus
Ohio U, Athens
Oregon, U of
Parsons School of Design (NY)
Pennsylvania, U of
Pittsburgh, U of (PA)
Pratt Institute (NY)
Reed C (OR)
Rensselaer Polytechnic Institute (NY)
Rhode Island School of Design
Rollins C (FL)
Rutgers U (NJ)
Sarah Lawrence C (NY)
Smith C (MA)
Southern California, U of
Stanford U (CA)
Swarthmore C (PA)

Texas, U of, Austin
Vassar C (NY)
Washington, U of
Wesleyan U (CT)
Williams C (MA)
Wisconsin, U of, Madison
Yale U (CT)

Colleges with a Work-Hard/ Play-Hard Philosophy

The student experience at these schools is characterized by the blending of academics and social activities.

Alabama, U of, Tuscaloosa
Boston C (MA)
Bucknell U (PA)
California, U of, Davis
California, U of, Santa Barbara
Campbell U (NC)
Colby C (ME)
Colgate U (NY)
Colorado, U of
Connecticut, U of
Dartmouth C (NH)
Dayton, U of (OH)
Denison U (OH)
Denver, U of (CO)
DePauw U (IN)
Drake U (IA)
Duke U (NC)
East Carolina U (NC)
Emory U (GA)
Florida State U
Franklin and Marshall C (PA)
George Washington U (DC)
Georgetown U (DC)
Gettysburg C (PA)
Guenther C (LA)
Gustavus Adolphus C (MN)
Hartwick C (NY)
Hobart C/William Smith C (NY)
Iowa State U
Ithaca C (NY)
Keene State C (NH)
Kentucky, U of
Lafayette C (PA)
Lehigh U (PA)
Louisiana State U, Baton Rouge
Miami U (OH)
Miami, U of (FL)
New Hampshire, U of
North Carolina, U of, Chapel Hill
Northwestern U (IL)
Ohio Wesleyan U
Pacific, U of the (CA)
Pennsylvania State U, University Park
Pennsylvania, U of
Puget Sound, U of (WA)
Rensselaer Polytechnic Institute (NY)
Rhode Island, U of
Richmond, U of (VA)
Rochester, U of (NY)
Rollins C (FL)
Rutgers U (NJ)
St. Lawrence U (NY)
San Diego, U of (CA)
Scripps C (CA)
Skidmore C (NY)
South, U of the (TN)
Southern Illinois U, Carbondale
Southern Methodist U (TX)
Stephen F. Austin State U (TX)
Syracuse U (NY)
Texas Christian U
Trinity C (CT)

Trinity U (TX)
Tufts U (MA)
Tulane U (LA)
Union C (NY)
Ursinus C (PA)
Valparaiso U (IN)
Vanderbilt U (TN)
Vermont, U of
Villanova C (PA)
Virginia, U of
Washington U (MO)
Williams C (MA)
Wooster, C of (OH)
Xavier U (OH)

Colleges with a Balance of Academics and Social Life

Baylor U (TX)
Bentley C (MA)
Boston C (MA)
Bradley U (IL)
Brandeis U (MA)
Bucknell U (PA)
California State U, Long Beach
California, U of, Davis
Charleston, C of (SC)
Clarkson U (NY)
Clemson U (SC)
Colby C (ME)
Colgate U (NY)
Colorado State U
Colorado, U of
Creighton U (NE)
Dartmouth C (NH)
Dayton, U of (OH)
Denison U (OH)
Denver, U of (CO)
DePauw U (IN)
Drake U (IA)
Elon C (NC)
Emory U (GA)
Florida State U
Fordham U (NY)
Gettysburg C (PA)
George Washington U (DC)
Hartwick C (NY)
Hobart C (NY)
Holy Cross, C of the (MA)
Indiana U
Ithaca C (NY)
Kansas, U of
Lafayette C (PA)
Lawrence U (WI)
Lehigh U (PA)
Loyola Marymount (CA)
Miami U (OH)
Miami, U of (FL)
Michigan, U of
Monmouth U (NJ)
Muhlenberg C (PA)
New Hampshire, U of
North Carolina, U of, Chapel Hill
Northern Arizona U
Ohio State U, Columbus
Ohio Wesleyan U
Pacific, U of the (CA)
Pennsylvania State U, University Park
Pepperdine U (CA)
Portland, U of (OR)

Colleges with a Balance of Academics and Social Life (continued)

Puget Sound, U of (WA)
Richmond, U of (VA)
Roanoke C (VA)
Rollins C (FL)
St. Lawrence U (NY)
St. Mary's C (CA)
St. Michael's C (VT)
St. Olaf C (MN)
San Diego, U of (CA)
Simmons C (MA)
Skidmore C (NY)
South, U of the (TN)
Southern Methodist U (TX)
Syracuse U (NY)
Texas Christian U
Texas Tech U
Texas, U of, Austin
Trinity C (CT)
Tulane U (LA)
Union C (NY)
Valparaiso U (IN)
Vermont, U of
Villanova U (PA)
Virginia, U of
Whittier C (CA)
Xavier U (OH)

Colleges with Lots of Campus Spirit

Colleges with campus spirit exhibit the camaraderie and sense of community that come from groups of active, enthusiastic students.

Alabama, U of, Tuscaloosa
Alfred U (NY)
Boston C (MA)
Brigham Young U (UT)
Clemson U (SC)
Colby C (ME)
Colgate U (NY)
Colorado, U of
Cornell U (NY)
Dartmouth C (NH)
Denison U (OH)
Duke U (NC)
East Carolina U (NC)
Elon C (NC)
Florida, U of
Georgia Institute of Technology
Georgia, U of
Ithaca C (NY)
Kansas, U of
Lincoln C (IL)
Michigan State U
Michigan, U of, Ann Arbor
Mt. Holyoke C (MA)
New Hampshire, U of
New Mexico State U
New York, State U of, C at Oneonta
North Texas, U of
Northern Illinois U
Notre Dame, U of (IN)
Ohio State U, Columbus
Pennsylvania State U, University Park
Pennsylvania, U of
St. Lawrence U (NY)
St. Olaf C (MN)
South Carolina, U of, Columbia
South, U of the (TN)
Syracuse U (NY)
Tennessee, U of, Knoxville
Texas A&M U
Texas Tech U
Texas, U of, Austin
Valparaiso U (IN)
Villanova U (PA)
Virginia, U of
Washington, U of
Williams C (MA)
Wisconsin, U of, Green Bay
Wisconsin, U of, Madison

The Experts' Choice: The Top Fifteen Party Schools

1. Denison U (OH)
2. Tulane U (LA)
3. Hobart C/William Smith C (NY)
4. Colorado, U of
5. Arizona State U
*6. Dartmouth C (NH)
*7. Lehigh U (PA)

The Experts' Choice: The Top Fifteen Party Schools (continued)

*8. Virginia, U of
9. California, U of, Santa Barbara
*10. Lafayette C (PA)
11. Miami, U of (FL)
12. Rollins C (FL)
*13. St. Lawrence U (NY)
*14. Southern Methodist U (TX)
*15. Vermont, U of

*See Author's Note, p. xxv.

Colleges for the Fashion-Conscious Student

At these schools students tend to be concerned about their choice of clothing and dress in a "socially correct" way.

Agnes Scott C (GA)
Babson C (MA)
Baylor U (TX)
Boston C (MA)
Brandeis U (MA)
Brigham Young U (UT)
Bryant C (RI)
Bucknell U (PA)
Catholic U (DC)
Claremont McKenna C (CA)
Colgate U (NY)
Connecticut C
Cottey C (MO)
Dallas, U of (TX)
Dartmouth C (NH)
Denison U (OH)
Denver, U of (CO)
DePauw U (IN)
Duke U (NC)
Emory U (GA)
Franklin and Marshall C (PA)
Furman U (SC)
Georgetown U (DC)
Hampden-Sydney C (VA)
Hartford, U of (CT)
Hillsdale C (MI)
Hobart C/William Smith C (NY)
Hollins C (VA)
Illinois Wesleyan U
Ithaca C (NY)
Lake Forest C (IL)
Manhattanville C (NY)
Miami U (OH)
Northwestern U (IL)
Notre Dame, U of (IN)
Pepperdine U (CA)
Pine Manor C (MA)
Randolph-Macon Woman's C (VA)
Richmond, U of (VA)
Roanoke C (VA)
Rochester, U of (NY)
Rollins C (FL)
St. Lawrence U (NY)
St. Mary's C (CA)
St. Olaf C (MN)
San Diego, U of (CA)
Savannah C of Art and Design (GA)

Skidmore C (NY)
Southern Methodist U (TX)
South, U of the (TN)
Stephens C (MO)
Susquehanna U (PA)
Sweet Briar C (VA)
Syracuse U (NY)
Texas Christian U
Trinity C (CT)
Trinity U (TX)
Tulane U (LA)
Union C (NY)
Utah, U of
Vanderbilt U (TN)
Virginia, U of
Wabash C (IN)
Wake Forest U (NC)
Washington and Jefferson C (PA)
Washington and Lee U (VA)
Wheaton C (IL)
Williams C (MA)
Wittenberg U (OH)

Colleges with Large Fraternity/Sorority Systems

The social life at these schools is influenced by Greek-letter societies either because there are many students involved in them or because the societies' activities dominate the overall campus social life.

Alabama, U of, Tuscaloosa
Albion C (MI)
Allegheny C (PA)
Arizona, U of
Babson C (MA)
Birmingham-Southern C (AL)
Bowdoin C (ME)
Bucknell U (PA)
California State U, Fresno
California, U of, Los Angeles
Carnegie Mellon U (PA)
Centre C (KY)
Colgate U (NY)
Cornell U (NY)
Dartmouth C (NH)
Davidson C (NC)
Denison U (OH)
DePauw U (IN)
Dickinson C (PA)
Duke U (NC)
Emory U (GA)
Florida State U
Georgia Institute of Technology
Georgia, U of
Gettysburg C (PA)
Hamilton C (NY)
Hampden-Sydney C (VA)
Idaho, U of
Illinois, U of, Urbana
Indiana U, Bloomington
Iowa State U
James Madison U (VA)
Kansas State U
Kansas, U of
Kenyon C (OH)
Kettering U (MI)

Colleges with Large Fraternity/Sorority Systems (continued)

Lafayette C (PA)
Lehigh U (PA)
Loyola U (LA)
Massachusetts Institute of Technology
Miami U (OH)
Michigan, U of, Ann Arbor
Millsaps C (MS)
Mississippi, U of
Missouri, U of, Columbia
Muhlenberg C (PA)
New York, State U of, Buffalo
North Carolina State U
North Carolina, U of, Chapel Hill
North Dakota, U of
Northwestern U (IL)
Ohio Wesleyan U
Pennsylvania, U of
Puget Sound, U of (WA)
Purdue U (IN)
Rensselaer Polytechnic Institute (NY)
Rhode Island, U of
Rhodes C (TN)
Richmond, U of (VA)
Rochester, U of (NY)
St. Lawrence U (NY)
South, U of the (TN)
Southern California, U of
Southern Methodist U (TX)
Stetson U (FL)
Susquehanna U (PA)
Texas Christian U
Transylvania U (KY)
Trinity C (CT)
Tulane U (LA)
Tulsa, U of (OK)
Union C (NY)
Valparaiso U (IN)
Vanderbilt U (TN)
Villanova U (PA)
Virginia, U of
Wabash C (IN)
Wake Forest U (NC)
Washington and Jefferson C (PA)
Washington and Lee U (VA)
Whitman C (WA)
William and Mary, C of (VA)
Wittenberg U (OH)
Wofford C (SC)
Worcester Polytechnic Institute (MA)
Wyoming, U of

Colleges with No Fraternities or Sororities

These schools do not have Greek-letter organizations but offer other opportunities for involvement.

Amherst C (MA)
Antioch C (OH)
Bates C (ME)
Bennington C (VT)
Boston C (MA)
Brandeis U (MA)
Bryn Mawr C (PA)
California Institute of Technology
Carleton C (MN)
Claremont McKenna C (CA)
Clark U (MA)
Connecticut C
Dallas, U of (TX)
Drew U (NJ)
Earlham C (IN)
Eckerd C (FL)
Evergreen State C (WA)
Fairfield U (CT)
Fordham U (NY)
Furman U (SC)
Georgetown U (DC)
Goucher C (MD)
Grinnell C (IA)
Guilford C (NC)
Gustavus Adolphus C (MN)
Hampshire C (MA)
Harvard U (MA)
Harvey Mudd C (CA)
Haverford C (PA)
Hendrix C (AR)
Hiram C (OH)
Holy Cross, C of the (MA)
Houghton C (NY)
Kalamazoo C (MI)
Loyola C (MD)
Macalester C (MN)
Manhattanville C (NY)
Mt. Holyoke C (MA)
New C (FL)
North Central C (IL)
Notre Dame, U of (IN)
Oberlin C (OH)
Pitzer C (CA)
Princeton U (NJ)
Providence C (RI)
Reed C (OR)
Rhode Island School of Design
Rice U (TX)
Roger Williams C (RI)
St. Michael's C (VT)
St. Norbert C (WI)
St. Olaf C (MN)
Sarah Lawrence C (NY)
Scripps C (CA)
Skidmore C (NY)
Smith C (MA)
Sweet Briar C (VA)
Vassar C (NY)
Wellesley C (MA)
Wheaton C (IL)
Williams C (MA)
Yeshiva U (NY)

Colleges That Build Moral Character

These are members of the John Templeton Foundation Honor Roll for Character-Building Colleges. As a result of a survey of presidents of four-year colleges and a review by a six-member panel, the foundation identified colleges that emphasize character building as an integral part of the undergraduate experience.

Abilene Christian U (TX)
Albright C (PA)
Alma C (MI)
Alvernia C (PA)
Anderson U (IN)
Atlantic Union C (MA)
Austin C (TX)
Azusa Pacific U (CA)
Baylor U (TX)
Bethel C (IN)
Bethune-Cookman C (FL)
Birmingham-Southern C (AL)
Bluffton C (OH)
Boston U (MA)
Brigham Young U (UT)
Brown U (RI)
Cabrini C (PA)
California Lutheran U
California U (PA)
Calvin C (MI)
Canisius C (NY)
Catawba C (NC)
Catholic U (DC)
Central Methodist C (MO)
Central U (IA)
Claflin C (SC)
Clarkson C (NE)
Colorado State U
Connecticut C
Dakota Wesleyan U (SD)
Dallas Baptist U (TX)
Davidson C (NC)
Defiance C (OH)
DePauw U (IN)
Dillard U (LA)
Dominican U (IL)
Dordt C (IA)
Duquesne U (PA)
Earlham C (IN)
Eastern Mennonite U (VA)
Eckerd C (FL)
Fairfield U (CT)
Florida State U
Franciscan U (OH)
Franklin Pierce C (NH)
Gardner Webb C (NC)
Geneva C (PA)
Gonzaga U (WA)
Goshen C (IN)
Hampton U (VA)
Hillsdale C (MI)
Holy Cross, C of the (MA)
Hope C (MI)
Huntington C (IN)
Iowa Wesleyan C
John Brown U (AR)
John Carroll C (OH)
Johnson C. Smith U (NC)
King's C (PA)
La Sierra U (CA)
Lee U (TN)
Louisiana C
Loyola C (MD)
Loyola Marymount U (CA)
Lubbock Christian U (TX)
Lycoming C (PA)

Lynchburg C (VA)
Manchester C (IN)
Mary, U of (ND)
Marymount Manhattan C (NY)
Marymount U (VA)
Maryville C (TN)
McPherson C (KS)
Messiah C (PA)
Midway C (KY)
Millikin U (IL)
Mississippi C
Montreat C (NC)
Mt. St. Mary's C (CA)
Nebraska Wesleyan U
New York, City U of, John Jay C
New York, State U of, C at Oneonta
Niagara U (NY)
Northwestern C (IA)
Notre Dame, U of (IN)
Ohio Wesleyan U
Oklahoma, U of
Olivet C (MI)
Park C (MO)
Pennsylvania State U, University Park
Pepperdine U (CA)
Pittsburgh, U of, Bradford (PA)
Portland, U of (OR)
Ramapo C (NJ)
Rhodes C (TN)
Rosemont C (PA)
Rust C (MS)
St. Benedict, C of (MN)
St. Edwards U (TX)
St. Francis C (IN)
St. John Fisher C (NY)
St. John's U (MN)
St. John's U (NY)
St. Louis U (MO)
St. Michael's C (VT)
St. Norbert C (WI)
St. Olaf C (MN)
St. Thomas, U of (MN)
Salem C (NC)
San Diego, U of (CA)
Seattle Pacific U (WA)
Simpson C (IA)
Southern Methodist U (TX)
Southwest Missouri State U
Spalding U (KY)
Spelman C (GA)
Spring Arbor C (MI)
Trinity International U (IL)
U.S. Air Force Academy (CO)
U.S. Naval Academy (MD)
Ursuline C (OH)
Voorhees C (SC)
Wake Forest U (NC)
Wartburg C (IA)
Waynesburg C (PA)
Westmont C (CA)
Wheaton C (IL)
Whitworth C (WA)
William Jewell C (MO)
William Penn C (IA)
Wilmington C (OH)
Winston-Salem State U (NC)
Wittenberg C (OH)
Xavier U (OH)
Yale U (CT)

Source: The John Templeton Foundation, Ridgeland, MS.

Colleges Where Values Are Particularly Important

As a result of the atmosphere created by the faculty and the administration, students at these schools are encouraged to feel that such values as integrity and kindness are important. Colleges with a religious tradition, listed under "Religious Life" in this section, provide additional value-oriented schools.

Agnes Scott C (GA)
Allentown C (PA)
Alma C (MI)
Baylor U (TX)
Berea C (KY)
Biola U (CA)
Brigham Young U (UT)
Calvin C (MI)
Catholic U (DC)
Cedar Crest C (PA)
Central C (IA)
Centre C (KY)
Converse C (SC)
Cottey C (MO)
Creighton U (NE)
Dallas, U of (TX)
Erskine C (SC)
Evangel C (MO)
Fisk U (TN)
Flagler C (FL)
Furman U (SC)
Gonzaga U (WA)
Guilford C (NC)
Haverford C (PA)
Hendrix C (AR)
High Point U (NC)
Hillsdale C (MI)
Hollins C (VA)
Hope C (MI)
Houghton C (NY)
Illinois C
Illinois Wesleyan U
Knox C (IL)
Luther C (IA)
Merrimack C (MA)
Millsaps C (MS)
Monmouth C (IL)
Moravian C (PA)
Morehouse C (GA)
Mt. St. Joseph, C of (OH)
Mt. St. Vincent, C of (NY)
Nichols C (MA)
Northwestern C (IA)
Notre Dame, U of (IN)
Oral Roberts U (OK)
Otterbein C (OH)
Ozarks, C of the (MO)
Pepperdine U (CA)
Phillips U (OK)
Presbyterian C (SC)
Providence C (RI)
Randolph-Macon Woman's C (VA)
Ripon C (WI)
St. Andrews Presbyterian C (NC)
St. Benedict, C of/St. John's U (MN)
St. Bonaventure U (NY)
St. Francis C (PA)
St. Mary of the Plains C (KS)
St. Michael's C (VT)
St. Olaf C (MN)
Salve Regina U (RI)

Seattle U (WA)
Southwestern U (TX)
Stetson U (FL)
Sweet Briar C (VA)
Trinity C (DC)
Tuskegee U (AL)
Valparaiso U (IN)
Wartburg C (IA)
Washburn U (KS)
Wells C (NY)
Whittier C (CA)
William Jewell C (MO)

POLITICAL/SOCIAL AWARENESS

Colleges for the Politically Aware

Students at these colleges are particularly concerned about and alert to national and international events.

Albion C (MI)
American U (DC)
Amherst C (MA)
Antioch C (OH)
Barnard C (NY)
Bates C (ME)
Brandeis U (MA)
Brown U (RI)
Bryn Mawr C (PA)
California, U of, Berkeley
California, U of, Los Angeles
Carleton C (MN)
Claremont McKenna C (CA)
Clark U (MA)
Colorado, U of
Columbia U (NY)
Dartmouth C (NH)
Davidson C (NC)
Drew U (NJ)
Earlham C (IN)
Fordham U (NY)
George Washington U (DC)
Georgetown U (DC)
Grinnell C (IA)
Hampshire C (MA)
Harvard U (MA)
Haverford C (PA)
Illinois, U of, Urbana
International Training, School for (VT)
Iowa, U of
Macalester C (MN)
Massachusetts, U of, Amherst
Mills C (CA)
Montana, U of
New York U
New York, State U of, Binghamton
Oberlin C (OH)
Ohio U, Athens
Oregon, U of
Pitzer C (CA)
Princeton U (NJ)
Rutgers U (NJ)
Smith C (MA)
Swarthmore C (PA)
Vassar C (NY)
Washington, U of

Wellesley C (MA)
Wesleyan U (CT)
William and Mary, C of (VA)
Wisconsin, U of, Madison
Yale U (CT)
Yeshiva U (NY)

Most Activist Campuses

TOP TEN

1. Wisconsin, U of, Madison
2. Mt. Holyoke C (MA)
3. Massachusetts, U of, Amherst
4. Minnesota, U of, Morris
5. Stanford U (CA)
6. New York, State U of, Binghamton
7. New School for Social Research (NY)
8. Illinois, U of, Urbana
9. North Carolina, U of, Chapel Hill
10. Howard U (DC)

HONORABLE MENTIONS

Boston U (MA)
California, U of, Berkeley
District of Columbia, U of the

Source: Reprinted with permission from *Mother Jones* magazine, © 1998, Foundation for National Progress.

Colleges Where Students Are Politically and Socially Active

More than eighty colleges were surveyed, and the following are those where students are making a difference in terms of community service and political/social activism, both on campus and in the surrounding community.

Antioch C (OH)
Berea C (KY)
California State U, Humboldt
Cornell U (NY)
DePauw U (IN)
Hampshire C (MA)
James Madison U (VA)
Marquette U (WI)
Michigan, U of
North Carolina, U of, Chapel Hill
Ohio Wesleyan U
Rochester, U of (NY)
Walla Walla C (WA)
Warren Wilson C (NC)
Wesleyan U (CT)

Source: *Who Cares?*, The Magazine for People Who Do, Fall 1996.

Schools with Active College Democrats

Brandeis U (MA)
California, U of, Berkeley
California, U of, Los Angeles
Colby C (ME)
Colorado, U of
George Washington U (DC)
Georgetown U (DC)
Harvard U (MA)
Johns Hopkins U (MD)
Kent State U (OH)
Louisiana State U, Baton Rouge
Mankato State U (MN)
Michigan, U of, Ann Arbor
Minnesota, U of, Twin Cities
Montana, U of
Mt. Holyoke C (MA)
New York, State U of, C at Geneseo
North Carolina, U of, Chapel Hill
Oberlin C (OH)
Oregon, U of
St. Mary's C (MD)
Southern Illinois U, Carbondale
Southern U (LA)
Spelman C (GA)
Trinity C (CT)
Wisconsin, U of, Madison

Schools with Active College Republicans

Angelo State U (TX)
Ball State U (IN)
Boston C (MA)
California, U of, Berkeley
California, U of, Los Angeles
Carroll C (WI)
Catholic U (DC)
Colgate U (NY)
Cornell U (NY)
Dallas, U of (TX)
Florida Institute of Technology
Florida, U of
Marquette U (WI)
Mississippi State U
Mississippi, U of
Missouri, U of, Columbia
New Orleans, U of (LA)
Northeast Missouri State U
Oklahoma, U of
Pennsylvania State U, University Park
St. Bonaventure U (NY)
St. Joseph's U (PA)
South Florida, U of
Southern California, U of
Texas A&M U
Texas, U of, Austin
Villanova U (PA)
West Virginia U
Wisconsin, U of, Milwaukee
Wisconsin, U of, Whitewater

The Experts' Choice: Colleges for the Politically Conservative

The following schools were ranked highest as appropriate for the conservative student.

Auburn U (AL)
Babson C (MA)
Baylor U (TX)
Boston C (MA)
Brigham Young U (UT)
Bucknell U (PA)
Creighton U (NE)
Dartmouth C (NH)
Davidson C (NC)
Denison U (OH)
DePauw U (IN)
Fairfield U (CT)
Florida Southern C
Furman U (SC)
Georgetown U (DC)
Hamilton C (NY)
Hampden-Sydney C (VA)
Hillsdale C (MI)
Hobart C/William Smith C (NY)
Holy Cross, C of the (MA)
Middlebury C (VT)
Notre Dame, U of (IN)
Pennsylvania, U of
Pepperdine U (CA)
Princeton U (NJ)
Purdue U (IN)
Richmond, U of (VA)
St. Lawrence U (NY)
Southern Methodist U (TX)
Stetson U (FL)
U.S. Air Force Academy (CO)
U.S. Military Academy (NY)
U.S. Naval Academy (MD)
Vanderbilt U (TN)
Wake Forest U (NC)
Washington and Lee U (VA)
William and Mary, C of (VA)
Williams C (MA)

Colleges with Prominent Conservative Newspapers

Based on reputation and/or circulation, these are prominent conservative campus publications.

California, U of, Berkeley	*Berkeley Review*
Columbia U (NY)	*Federalist Paper*
Dartmouth C (NH)	*Dartmouth Review*
Duke U (NC)	*Duke Review*
Harvard U (MA)	*Harvard Salient*
Kenyon C (OH)	*Kenyon Observer*
Massachusetts Institute of Technology/ Wellesley C (MA)	*Counterpoint*
Michigan, U of, Ann Arbor	*The Michigan Review*
Princeton U (NJ)	*Princeton Sentinel*
Rice U (TX)	*The Rice Sentinel*
Stanford U (CA)	*Stanford Review*
Texas, U of, Austin	*University Review of Texas*
Vassar C (NY)	*Vassar Spectator*
Williams C (MA)	*Williams Observer*
Yale U (CT)	*Eli*

Source: The Collegiate Network, Madison Center, Washington, DC.

Colleges for the Socially Conscious Student

At these schools, students show particular sensitivity to and an inclination toward solving the problems of the world and its people.

American U (DC)
Antioch C (OH)
Beloit C (WI)
Bennington C (VT)
Berea C (KY)
Boston U (MA)
Brandeis U (MA)
Brown U (RI)
California State U, Humboldt
California, U of, Berkeley
California, U of, Santa Cruz
Carleton C (MN)
Centre C (KY)
Clark U (MA)
Columbia U (NY)
Cornell U (NY)
DePauw U (IN)
Earlham C (IN)
Eastern Mennonite C (VA)
Evergreen State C (WA)
George Washington U (DC)
Goucher C (MD)
Grinnell C (IA)
Hampshire C (MA)
Harvard U (MA)
Iowa, U of
James Madison U (VA)
Judaism, U of (CA)
Lesley C (MA)
Lewis and Clark C (OR)
Long Island U, Southampton (NY)
Macalester C (MN)
Marlboro C (VT)
Marquette U (WI)
Montana, U of
New York U
New York, State U of, Binghamton
North Carolina, U of, Chapel Hill
Oberlin C (OH)
Occidental C (CA)
Ohio Wesleyan U
Oregon, U of
Prescott C (AZ)
Presidio World C (CA)
Princeton U (NJ)
Rutgers U (NJ)
Smith C (MA)
Swarthmore C (PA)
Trinity C (CT)
Vassar C (NY)
Walla Walla C (WA)
Warren Wilson C (NC)
Washington, U of
Wellesley C (MA)
Wesleyan U (CT)
Wisconsin, U of, Madison
Yale U (CT)

Colleges with Notable Alternative/Progressive Newspapers

Brandeis U (MA)	*Watch*
California, U of, Davis	*Third World Forum*
California, U of, San Diego	*New Indicator*
Dartmouth C (NH)	*The Bug*
Evergreen State C (WA)	*Evergreen Free Press*
Kansas, U of	*Take This!*
Massachusetts Institute of Technology	*The Thistle*
Oregon, U of	*Student Insurgent*
Syracuse U (NY)	*The Alternative Orange*
Texas, U of, Austin	*The Other Texan*

Colleges with Many Opportunities for Volunteerism

Large clubs or organizations providing community service opportunities are found at these colleges.

Albion C (MI) (Gerald Ford Institute)
Alma C (MI)
Berea C (KY)
Birmingham-Southern C (AL)
Brevard C (NC) (Project Inside Out)
Cabrini C (PA) (community service is part of curriculum)
Davis and Elkins C (WV)
Dayton, U of (OH)
DePauw U (IN)
Earlham C (IN)
Emory U (GA) (Volunteer Emory)
Fordham U (NY)
Goucher C (MD)
Haverford C (PA) (The 8th Dimension)
Holy Cross, C of the (MA) (Student Program for Urban Development)
Howard U (DC)
Lawrence U (WI)
Marquette U (WI)
Middlebury C (VT)
Minnesota, U of, Twin Cities (Into the Streets)
North Park C (IL) (urban outreach program)
Princeton U (NJ)
Reed C (OR)
Rhodes C (TN)
Rochester, U of (NY)
Rutgers U (NJ)
St. Benedict, C of/St. John's U (MN) (VISTO Program)
St. Michael's C (VT)
Santa Clara U (CA)
Susquehanna U (PA)
Vassar C (NY)
Wittenberg U (OH) (requires community service activity)
Yale U (CT)

Colleges Offering Community Service Scholarships

Entering first-year students, active in high school community service projects, are eligible to be Bonner Scholars at these colleges. Sponsored by the Bonner Foundation, the program offers scholarships in exchange for community service work.

Antioch C (OH)
Berry C (GA)
Carson-Newman C (TN)
Concord C (WV)

Davidson C (NC)
DePauw U (IN)
Earlham C (IN)
Emory and Henry C (VA)
Ferrum C (VA)
Guilford C (NC)
Hood C (MD)
Mars Hill C (NC)
Maryville C (TN)
Morehouse C (GA)
Oberlin C (OH)
Ozarks, C of the (MO)
Rhodes C (TN)
Richmond, U of (VA)
Spelman C (GA)
Waynesburg C (PA)
West Virginia Wesleyan C
Wofford C (SC)

Source: Bonner Scholars Program, Princeton, NJ.

Colleges with Large Model United Nations Programs

Model UN offers high school and college students the opportunity to study world diplomacy issues by participating in simulations of world organizations such as the United Nations, the North Atlantic Treaty Organization, and the Organization of African Unity. The following schools have large campus programs and/or sponsor programs for high school students.

Americas, Universidad de las Puebla (Mexico)
Auburn U (AL)
California, U of, Riverside
Chicago, U of (IL)
Georgetown U (DC)
Georgia State U
Harvard U (MA)
Hope C (MI)
Howard U (DC)
Old Dominion U (VA)
Pennsylvania, U of

RESIDENCE HALLS AND FOOD SERVICE

Colleges with the Most Residence Hall Rooms

Boston U (MA)
Connecticut, U of
Eastern Kentucky U
Illinois, U of, Urbana
Indiana U, Bloomington
Iowa State U
Massachusetts, U of, Amherst C (MA)
Michigan State U
Michigan, U of, Ann Arbor
Ohio State U, Columbus
Pennsylvania State U, University Park
Purdue U (IN)
Texas A&M U
Virginia Polytechnic Institute and State U
Washington State U

Colleges with a Housing Shortage

Securing a room in a residence hall can be a problem for some students during some years at these colleges.

Arizona State U
Arizona, U of
Auburn U (AL)
Baylor U (TX)
Boston C (MA)
Boston U (MA)
California, U of, Berkeley
California, U of, Irvine
California, U of, Los Angeles
California, U of, Riverside
California, U of, San Diego
California, U of, Santa Barbara
Clemson U (SC)
Cincinnati, U of (OH)
Cornell U (NY)
DePaul U (IL)
Drexel U (PA)
Eugene Lang C (NY)
Florida, U of
Georgetown U (DC)
Georgia Institute of Technology
Hawaii, U of, Manoa
Hofstra U (NY)
Indiana U, Bloomington
Johns Hopkins U (MD)
Kentucky, U of
Maryland, U of, College Park
McGill U (Canada)
Miami U (OH)
Michigan, U of, Ann Arbor
Minnesota, U of, Twin Cities
New Mexico State U
New York, State U of, Stony Brook
North Carolina State U
North Carolina, U of, Wilmington
Northeastern U (MA)
Ohio State U, Columbus
Pennsylvania State U, University Park
Pittsburgh, U of (PA)
Puget Sound, U of (WA)
Purdue U (IN)
Reed C (OR)
Rhode Island, U of
Rutgers U (NJ)
Stanford U (CA)
Temple U (PA)
Texas A&M U
Texas, U of, Austin
Trenton State C (NJ)
Villanova U (PA)
Wisconsin, U of, Madison

Colleges with Great Dorms

These colleges have either unusually attractive residence halls or especially strong residence hall programs for students.

Agnes Scott C (GA)
Alfred U (NY)
Bates C (ME)
Bowdoin C (ME)
Bryn Mawr (PA)
Bucknell U (PA)
California State U, Sonoma
California, U of, Davis
Central Michigan U
Christopher Newport U (VA)
Colby C (ME)
Connecticut C
Cottey C (MO)
Dayton, U of (OH)
Delaware, U of
Earlham C (IN)
Fairfield U (CT)
Florida State U
Franklin and Marshall C (PA)
Georgia Institute of Technology
Georgia State U
Grinnell C (IA)
Hamilton C (NY)
Hampden-Sydney C (VA)
Harvey Mudd C (CA)
Haverford C (PA)
Hollins C (VA)
Iowa State U
Knox C (IL)
Miami U (OH)
Michigan State U
Michigan, U of, Ann Arbor
Mills C (CA)
Mt. Holyoke C (MA)
Northwood U (FL)
Oral Roberts U (OK)
Pacific, U of the (CA)
Pitzer C (CA)
Princeton U (NJ)
Quinnipiac C (CT)
Randolph-Macon Woman's C (VA)
Richmond, U of (VA)
St. Lawrence U (NY)
Scripps C (CA)
Skidmore C (NY)
Smith C (MA)
Southern Methodist U (TX)
Stanford U (CA)
Susquehanna U (PA)
Sweet Briar C (VA)
Trinity U (TX)
Vassar C (NY)
Wellesley C (MA)
Wheaton C (MA)
Williams C (MA)
Wofford C (SC)
Wooster, C of (OH)

Colleges with Comprehensive Residential Hall Systems

These schools offer comprehensive living-learning centers, which provide a place to live, as well as a focal point for dining, interacting with faculty, and participating in athletics and government. Some of these systems are modeled on the one used at Oxford University in England.

California, U of, San Diego
California, U of, Santa Cruz
Harvard U (MA)
Pennsylvania State U, University Park
Rice U (TX)
Smith C (MA)
Yale U (CT)

Colleges with Wellness Residence Halls

Residence halls at these schools are designed to foster a healthy lifestyle. They may have quiet hours, no-drinking or no-smoking policies, exercise equipment, or special counseling.

Aurora U (IL)
Austin Peay State U (TN)
Ball State U (IN)
Boston U (MA)
Brown U (RI)
Bucknell U (PA)
California, U of, Berkeley
California, U of, Irvine
Cincinnati, U of (OH)
Colorado State U
Elon C (NC)
Emporia State U (KS)
Evergreen State C (WA)
Framingham State C (MA)
Illinois State U
Kansas State U
Keene State C (NH)
Lehigh U (PA)
Louisiana State U, Baton Rouge
Louisville, U of (KY)
Montana State U
Mt. Holyoke C (MA)
New Hampshire, U of
New Hampshire, U of, Manchester
New Mexico, U of, Albuquerque
New York, State U of, Buffalo
New York, State U of, C at Potsdam
North Carolina, U of, Wilmington
North Iowa Area Community C
Northern Arizona U

Colleges with Wellness Residence Halls (continued)

Northern Colorado, U of
Northern Iowa, U of
Northern Michigan U
Oakland U (MI)
Oklahoma State U
Ottawa, U of (Canada)
Pacific U (OR)
Paris Junior C (TX)
Pennsylvania State U, University Park
Plymouth State C (NH)
Rutgers U (NJ)
St. Francis, C of (IL)
Salisbury State U (MD)
San Jacinto C (TX)
Shippensburg U (PA)
Slippery Rock U (PA)
Southern Connecticut State U
Southern Illinois U, Edwardsville
Stetson U (FL)
U.S. Air Force Academy (CO)
Vanderbilt U (TN)
Vermont, U of
Vincennes U (IN)
Washington State U
Western Illinois U
West Texas State U
Wisconsin, U of, Stevens Point

Source: *National Wellness Information Resource Center, 1991–92 Directory* (Muncie, IN: Institute for Wellness, Ball State U, 1991), 130.

Best College Food

1. Atlantic, C of the (ME)
2. Bowdoin C (ME)
3. Cornell U (NY)
4. Dartmouth C (NH)
5. Sweet Briar C (VA)
6. Randolph-Macon Woman's C (VA)
7. Dickinson C (PA)
8. Bennington C (VT)
9. Colby C (ME)
10. Gettysburg C (PA)

Source: TPR student survey, Time/The Princeton Review, *The Best College for You*, 1998.

Worst College Food

1. St. John's C (MD)
2. Tuskegee U (AL)
3. Oglethorpe U (GA)
4. Fisk U (TN)
5. New Mexico Institute of Mining and Technology

6. New York, State U of, Albany
7. Worchester Polytechnic Institute (MA)
8. New College (FL)
9. Hampton U (VA)
10. Catawba C (NC)

Source: TPR student survey, Time/The Princeton Review, *The Best College for You*, 1998.

Colleges Rated by Availability of Health Food

These colleges were ranked from highest to lowest for daily availability of varied, low-fat, cholesterol-free, and vegetarian foods.

1. Duke U (NC)
2. Pennsylvania, U of
3. Notre Dame, U of (IN)
4. Columbia U (NY)
5. Brown U (RI)
6. Stanford U (CA)
7. Kentucky, U of
8. Amherst C (MA)
9. Minnesota, U of, Twin Cities
10. Smith C (MA)
11. Howard U (DC)
12. Arizona State U
13. California Institute of Technology
14. Georgetown U (DC)
15. Pomona C (CA)
16. Wellesley C (MA)
17. Harvard U (MA)
18. Rice U (TX)
19. Southern Methodist U (TX)
20. Yale U (CT)
21. Dartmouth C (MA)
22. Massachusetts Institute of Technology
23. Bryn Mawr C (PA)
*24. Haverford C (PA)
25. Case Western Reserve U (OH)
26. Bowdoin C (ME)
27. California, U of, Los Angeles
28. Houston, U of
29. Illinois, U of, Chicago
30. Florida State University
31. Emory U (GA)
32. Miami, U of (FL)
33. Washington, U of
34. Williams C (MA)
35. Johns Hopkins U (MD)
36. U.S. Air Force Academy (CO)
37. U.S. Naval Academy (MD)
38. U.S. Military Academy (NY)

*See Author's Note, p. xxv.

Source: Physicians Committee for Responsible Medicine, Washington, DC, October 1996.

RELIGIOUS LIFE

Coalition for Christian Colleges and Universities

The following are members of the Coalition for Christian Colleges and Universities, an association of Christian colleges that are "committed to Christ as the center of campus life."

Abilene Christian U (TX)
Anderson U (IN)
Asbury C (KY)
Azusa Pacific U (CA)
Bartlesville Wesleyan C (OK)
Belhaven C (MS)
Bethel C (IN)
Bethel C (KS)
Bethel C (MN)
Biola U (CA)
Bluffton C (OH)
Bryan C (TN)
California Baptist C
Calvin C (MI)
Campbell U (NC)
Campbellsville C (KY)
Cedarville C (OH)
Colorado Christian U
Cornerstone C (MI)
Covenant C (GA)
Dallas Baptist U (TX)
Dordt C (IA)
East Texas Baptist U (TX)
Eastern C (PA)
Eastern Mennonite C (VA)
Eastern Nazarene C (MA)
Erskine C (SC)
Evangel C (MO)
Fresno Pacific C (CA)
Geneva C (PA)
George Fox C (OR)
Gordon C (MA)
Goshen C (IN)
Grace C (IN)
Grand Canyon U (AZ)
Greenville C (IL)
Hope International U (CA)
Houghton C (NY)
Huntington C (IN)
Indiana Wesleyan U
John Brown U (AR)
Judson C (IL)
King C (TN)
King's C, The (Canada)

Lee U (TN)
LeTourneau U (TX)
Malone C (OH)
Master's C, The (CA)
Messiah C (PA)
MidAmerica Nazarene C (KS)
Milligan C (TN)
Montreat C (NC)
Mt. Vernon Nazarene C (OH)
North Park C (IL)
Northwest C (WA)
Northwest Christian C (OR)
Northwest Nazarene C (ID)
Northwestern C (IA)
Northwestern C (MN)
Nyack C (NY)
Oklahoma Baptist U
Olivet Nazarene U (IL)
Oral Roberts U (OK)
Ozarks, C of the (MO)
Palm Beach Atlantic C (FL)
Point Loma Nazarene C (CA)
Redeemer C (Canada)
Roberts Wesleyan C (NY)
Seattle Pacific U (WA)
Simpson C (CA)
Sioux Falls, U of (SD)
Southern California C
Southern Nazarene U (OK)
Southern Wesleyan U (SC)
Southwest Baptist U (MO)
Spring Arbor C (MI)
Sterling C (KS)
Tabor C (KS)
Taylor U (IN)
Trevecca Nazarene C (TN)
Trinity Christian C (IL)
Trinity International U (IL)
Trinity Western U (Canada)
Union U (TN)
Warner Pacific C (OR)
Warner Southern C (FL)
Western Baptist C (OR)
Westmont C (CA)
Wheaton C (IL)
Whitworth C (WA)
Williams Baptist C (AR)

Christian College Consortium

This is a group of outstanding evangelical liberal arts schools.

Asbury C (KY)
Bethel C (MN)
George Fox C (OR)
Gordon C (MA)
Greenville C (IL)
Houghton C (NY)
Malone C (OH)
Messiah C (PA)
Seattle Pacific U (WA)
Taylor U (IN)
Trinity C (IL)
Westmont C (CA)
Wheaton C (IL)

The Ten Best Christian Colleges

1. Wheaton C (IL)
2. Westmont C (CA)
3. Taylor U (IN)
4. Notre Dame, U of (IN)
5. Gordon C (MA)
6. Messiah C (PA)
7. Calvin C (MI)
8. Earlham C (IN)
9. Valparaiso U (IN)
10. Houghton C (NY)

Source: "The 10 Best Christian Colleges," *Parents of Teenagers* (October/November 1990): 8–9.

Bible Colleges

These colleges, accredited by the American Association of Bible Colleges, "assist men and women in the development of a biblical worldview, with a special emphasis upon preparation for church-related vocations."

Alaska Bible C
American Baptist C (TN)
Appalachian Bible C (WV)
Arizona C of the Bible
Arlington Baptist C (TX)
Baptist Bible C (MO)
Baptist Bible C (PA)
Barclay C (KS)
Bethany Bible C (Canada)
Boise Bible C (ID)
Briercrest Bible C (Canada)
Calvary Bible C (MO)
Canadian Bible C (Canada)
Central Bible C (MO)
Central Christian C of the Bible (MO)
Central Pentecostal C (Canada)
Cincinnati Bible C (OH)
Circleville Bible C (OH)
Clear Creek Baptist Bible C (KY)
Colegio Biblico Pentecostal (Puerto Rico)
Colorado Christian U
Columbia Bible C (Canada)
Columbia International C (SC)
Crown C (MN)
Dallas Christian C (TX)
East Coast Bible C (NC)
Eastern Pentecostal Bible C (Canada)
Emmanuel Bible C (Canada)
Emmaus Bible C (IA)
Eugene Bible C (OR)
Faith Baptist Bible C (IA)
Florida Christian C
Free Will Baptist Bible C (TN)
God's Bible School and C (OH)
Grace Bible C (MI)
Grace U (NE)
Great Lakes Christian C (MI)
Heritage Baptist C (Canada)
Hillcrest Christian C (Canada)
Hobe Sound Bible C (FL)
International Bible C (AL)
John Wesley C (NC)
Johnson Bible C (TN)
Kentucky Christian C
Kentucky Mountain Bible C
Lancaster Bible C (PA)
LIFE Bible C (CA)
Lincoln Christian C (IL)
Magnolia Bible C (MS)
Manhattan Christian C (KS)
Mid-America Bible C (OK)
Minnesota Bible C
Moody Bible Institute (IL)
Multnomah Bible C (OR)
Nazarene Bible C (CO)
Nebraska Christian C
North American Baptist C (Canada)
Northwest Baptist Theological C (Canada)
Oak Hills Bible C (MN)
Ontario Bible C (Canada)
Ozark Christian C (MO)

Bible Colleges (continued)

Philadelphia C of Bible (PA)
Piedmont Bible C (NC)
Practical Bible C (NY)
Providence C (Canada)
Puget Sound Christian C (WA)
Reformed Bible C (MI)
Roanoke Bible C (NC)
Rocky Mountain College (Canada)
St. Louis Christian C (MO)
San Jose Christian C (CA)
Southeastern Baptist C (MS)
Southeastern Bible C (AL)
Southeastern C of the Assemblies of God (FL)
Southwestern Assemblies of God U (TX)
Southwestern C (AZ)
Steinbach Bible C (Canada)
Tennessee Temple U
Toccoa Falls C (GA)
Trinity C (FL)
Valley Forge Christian C (PA)
Vennard C (IA)
Washington Bible C (MD)
Wesley C (MS)
Western Pentecostal Bible C (Canada)

Source: American Association of Bible Colleges, Fayetteville, AR.

Ten Schools with Active Participation in Campus Crusade for Christ

Auburn U (AL)
Bowling Green State U (OH)
California, U of, Santa Barbara
Indiana U, Bloomington
Miami U (OH)
Oklahoma Baptist U
Pennsylvania State U, University Park
Texas A&M U
Texas, U of, Austin
Washington, U of

Colleges with Active Participation in Intervarsity Christian Fellowship

Over 650 colleges participate in Intervarsity Christian Fellowship. These are some of the more active campus programs in recent years.

Appalachian State U (NC)
California Polytechnic State U, San Luis Obispo
California, U of, Berkeley
California, U of, San Diego
Delaware, U of
Furman U (SC) (large Fellowship of Christian Athletes group)
Illinois, U of, Chicago
Illinois, U of, Urbana
Minnesota, U of, Twin Cities
North Carolina State U
North Carolina, U of, Chapel Hill
Northwestern U (IL)
Occidental C (CA)
Randolph-Macon Woman's C (VA)
Wayne State U (MI)
William and Mary, C of (VA)
Wisconsin, U of, Madison

Catholic Colleges

These colleges are members of the Catholic College Admission Association.

Albertus Magnus C (CT)
Allentown C (PA)
Alvernia C (PA)
Anna Maria C (MA)
Aquinas C (TN)
Assumption C (MA)
Avila C (MO)
Barat C (IL)
Barry U (FL)
Bellarmine C (KY)
Belmont Abbey C (NC)
Benedictine C (KS)
Benedictine U (IL)
Boston C (MA)
Brescia C (KY)
Briar Cliff C (IA)
Cabrini C (PA)
Canisius C (NY)
Cardinal Stritch C (WI)
Carlow C (PA)
Carroll C (MT)
Catholic U (DC)
Chaminade U (HI)
Chestnut Hill C (PA)
Christian Brothers U (TN)
Christiandom C (VA)
Creighton U (NE)
Dallas, U of (TX)
Dayton, U of (OH)
DePaul U (IL)
Detroit Mercy, U of (MI)
Dominican C of Blauvelt (NY)
Dominican C of San Rafael (CA)
Dominican U (IL)
Duquesne U (PA)
D'Youville C (NY)
Elms C (MA)
Emmanuel C (MA)
Fairfield U (CT)
Fontbonne C (MO)
Fordham U (NY)
Franciscan U (OH)
Gannon U (PA)
Georgian Court C (NJ)
Gonzaga U (WA)
Great Falls, U of (MT)
Gwynedd-Mercy C (PA)
Holy Cross C (IN)
Holy Cross, C of the (MA)
Holy Family C (PA)
Holy Names C (CA)
Immaculata C (PA)
Incarnate Word, U of (TX)
Iona C (NY)
John Carroll U (OH)
Kansas Newman C
King's C (PA)
La Roche C (PA)
La Salle U (PA)
Le Moyne C (NY)
Lewis U (IL)
Loras C (IA)
Loyola C (MD)
Loyola Marymount U (CA)
Loyola U (IL)
Loyola U (LA)
Manhattan C (NY)
Marquette U (WI)
Mary, U of (ND)
Marygrove C (MI)
Marymount C (CA)

Marymount U (VA)
Marywood C (PA)
Mater Dei C (NY)
Mercy C (OH)
Mercyhurst C (PA)
Merrimack C (MA)
Misericordia C (PA)
Molloy C (NY)
Mt. Aloysius C (PA)
Mt. Marty C (SD)
Mt. Mary C (SD)
Mt. Mary C (WI)
Mt. Mercy C (IA)
Mt. St. Joseph, C of (OH)
Mt. St. Mary's C (CA)
Mt. St. Mary's C (MD)
Mt. St. Vincent, C of (NY)
Nazareth C (NY)
Neumann C (PA)
New Rochelle, C of (NY)
Niagara U (NY)
Notre Dame C (NH)
Notre Dame C (OH)
Notre Dame, C of (CA)
Notre Dame of Maryland, C of
Notre Dame, U of (IN)
Ohio Dominican C
Our Lady of Holy Cross C (LA)
Our Lady of the Lake U (TX)
Portland, U of (OR)
Providence C (RI)
Quincy U (IL)
Regis C (MA)
Regis U (CO)
Rivier C (NH)
Rockhurst C (MO)
Rosemont C (PA)
Sacred Heart U (CT)
St. Ambrose U (IA)
St. Benedict, C of (MN)
St. Bonaventure U (NY)
St. Catherine, C of (MN)
St. Edward's U (TX)
St. Elizabeth, C of (NJ)
St. Francis C (NY)
St. Francis C (PA)
St. John Fisher C (NY)
St. John's U (MN)
St. Joseph C (CT)
St. Joseph's C (ME)
St. Joseph's U (PA)
St. Leo C (FL)
St. Louis U (MO)
St. Martin's C (WA)
St. Mary, C of (NE)
St. Mary-of-the-Woods C (IN)
St. Mary's C (CA)
St. Mary's C (IN)
St. Mary's C (MI)
St. Mary's U (MN)
St. Mary's U (TX)
St. Michael's C (VT)
St. Norbert C (WI)
St. Peter's C (NJ)
St. Rose, C of (NY)
St. Thomas, U of (MN)
St. Thomas U (FL)
St. Vincent C (PA)
Salve Regina U (RI)
San Diego, U of (CA)
San Francisco, U of (CA)
Santa Clara U (CA)
Santa Fe, C of (NM)
Scranton, U of (PA)
Seattle U (WA)
Seton Hall U (NJ)
Seton Hill C (PA)
Siena C (NY)
Siena Heights C (MI)
Spalding U (KY)
Spring Hill C (AL)

Catholic Colleges (continued)

Stonehill C (MA)
Thomas More C (KY)
Trinity C (DC)
Trinity C (VT)
Ursuline C (OH)
Villanova U (PA)
Viterbo C (WI)
Walsh U (OH)
Wheeling Jesuit C (WV)
Xavier U (LA)
Xavier U (OH)

The Jesuit Colleges

The Jesuits, an order of Roman Catholic clergy, are known for their influence on and interest in education.

Boston C (MA)
Canisius C (NY)
Creighton U (NE)
Detroit Mercy, U of (MI)
Fairfield U (CT)
Fordham U (NY)
Georgetown U (DC)
Gonzaga U (WA)
Holy Cross, C of the (MA)
John Carroll U (OH)
Le Moyne C (NY)
Loyola C (MD)
Loyola Marymount U (CA)
Loyola U (IL)
Loyola U (LA)
Marquette U (WI)
Regis U (CO)
Rockhurst C (MO)
St. Joseph's U (PA)
St. Louis U (MO)
St. Peter's C (NJ)
San Francisco, U of (CA)
Santa Clara U (CA)
Scranton, U of (PA)
Seattle U (WA)
Spring Hill C (AL)
Wheeling Jesuit C (WV)
Xavier U (OH)

Percentage of Catholic Students at Well-Known Roman Catholic Institutions

These percentages of undergraduate students are approximate.

	PERCENT
Boston C (MA)	70
Catholic U (DC)	90
Creighton U (NE)	70
Dallas, U of (TX)	65
Dayton, U of (OH)	75
Fairfield U (CT)	90
Georgetown U (DC)	60
Gonzaga U (WA)	60
La Salle U (PA)	75
Loras C (IA)	85
Loyola C (MD)	70
Loyola Marymount U (CA)	70

Percentage of Catholic Students at Well-Known Roman Catholic Institutions (continued)

	PERCENT
Loyola U (IL)	70
Loyola U (LA)	70
Marquette U (WI)	80
Notre Dame, U of (IN)	88
Portland, U of (OR)	50
Providence C (RI)	85
St. John's U (NY)	60
San Diego, U of (CA)	65
Santa Clara U (CA)	65
Villanova U (PA)	85
Xavier U (OH)	80

Christian Brothers Colleges

A Roman Catholic order, Christian Brothers devote themselves exclusively to Christian education.

Christian Brothers U (TN)
La Salle U (PA)
Lewis U (IL)
Manhattan C (NY)
St. Mary's C (CA)
St. Mary's C (MN)
Santa Fe, C of (NM)

Episcopal Colleges

These are members of the Association of Episcopal Colleges.

Bard C (NY)
Clarkson C (NE)
Cuttington U C (Liberia)
Hobart C (NY)
Kenyon C (OH)
St. Augustine C (IL)
St. Augustine C (NC)
St. Paul's C (VA)
South, U of the (TN)
Trinity C (Philippines)
Voorhees C (SC)

Lutheran Colleges

Augsburg C (MN)
Augustana C (IL)
Augustana C (SD)
Augustana University C (Canada)
Bethany C (KS)
Bethany Lutheran C (MN)
California Lutheran U (CA)
Capital U (OH)
Carthage C (WI)
Concordia C (AL)
Concordia C (Canada)
Concordia C (MI)
Concordia C, Moorhead (MN)
Concordia C, St. Paul (MN)
Concordia C (NE)
Concordia C (NY)
Concordia C (OR)
Concordia Lutheran C (TX)
Concordia U (CA)
Concordia U (IL)
Concordia U (WI)
Dana C (NE)
Gettysburg C (PA)
Grand View C (IA)
Gustavus Adolphus C (MN)
Immanuel Lutheran C (WI)
Lenoir-Rhyne C (NC)
Luther C (IA)
Luther C, U of Regina (Canada)
Lutheran Bible Institute (WA)
Martin Luther C (MN)
Midland Lutheran C (NE)
Muhlenberg C (PA)
Newberry C (SC)
Northwestern C (WI)
Pacific Lutheran U (WA)
Roanoke C (VA)
St. Olaf C (MN)
Suomi C (MI)
Susquehanna U (PA)
Texas Lutheran C
Thiel C (PA)
Upsala C (NJ)
Valparaiso U (IN)
Wagner C (NY)
Waldorf C (IA)
Wartburg C (IA)
Wisconsin Lutheran C
Wittenberg U (OH)

Methodist Colleges

Adrian C (MI)
Alaska Pacific U
Albion C (MI)
Albright C (PA)
Allegheny C (PA)
American U (DC)
Andrew C (GA)
Baker U (KS)
Baldwin-Wallace C (OH)
Bennett C (NC)
Bethune-Cookman C (FL)
Birmingham-Southern C (AL)
Boston U (MA)
Brevard C (NC)
Centenary C (LA)
Centenary C (NJ)
Central Methodist C (MO)
Claflin C (SC)
Clark Atlanta U (GA)
Columbia C (SC)
Cornell C (IA)
Dakota Wesleyan U (SD)
Denver, U of (CO)
DePauw U (IN)
Dickinson C (PA)
Dillard U (LA)
Drew U (NJ)
Duke U (NC)
Emory and Henry C (VA)
Emory U (GA)
Emory U, Oxford C (GA)
Evansville, U of (IN)
Ferrum C (VA)
Florida Southern C
Green Mountain C (VT)
Greensboro C (NC)
Hamline U (MN)
Hendrix C (AR)
High Point U (NC)
Hiwassee C (TN)
Huntingdon C (AL)
Huston-Tillotson C (TX)
Illinois Wesleyan U
Indianapolis, U of (IN)
Iowa Wesleyan C
Kansas Wesleyan U
Kendall C (IL)
Kentucky Wesleyan C
LaGrange C (GA)
Lambuth U (TN)
Lebanon Valley C (PA)
Lindsey Wilson C (KY)
Lon Morris C (TX)
Louisburg C (NC)
Lycoming C (PA)
MacMurray C (IL)
Martin Methodist C (TN)
McKendree C (IL)
McMurry U (TX)
Methodist C (NC)
Millsaps C (MS)
Morningside C (IA)
Mt. Union C (OH)
Nebraska Wesleyan U
North Carolina Wesleyan C
North Central C (IL)
Ohio Northern U
Ohio Wesleyan U
Oklahoma City U
Otterbein C (OH)
Pacific, U of the (CA)
Paine C (GA)
Pfeiffer C (NC)
Philander Smith C (AR)
Puget Sound, U of (WA)
Randolph-Macon C (VA)
Randolph-Macon Woman's C (VA)

Reinhardt C (GA)
Rocky Mountain C (MT)
Rust C (MS)
Shenandoah U (Va)
Simpson C (IA)
Southern Methodist U (TX)
Southwestern C (KS)
Southwestern U (TX)
Spartanburg Methodist C (SC)
Sue Bennett C (KY)
Syracuse U (NY)
Tennessee Wesleyan C
Texas Wesleyan U
Union C (KY)
Virginia Wesleyan C
Wesley C (DE)
Wesleyan C (GA)
West Virginia Wesleyan C
Wiley C (TX)
Willamette U (OR)
Wofford C (SC)
Wood Junior C (MS)
Young Harris C (GA)

Presbyterian Colleges

These are members of the Association of Presbyterian Colleges and Universities.

Agnes Scott C (GA)
Albertson C (ID)
Alma C (MI)
Arkansas C
Austin C (TX)
Barber-Scotia C (NC)
Beaver C (PA)
Belhaven C (MS)
Blackburn C (IL)
Bloomfield C (NJ)
Buena Vista C (IA)
Carroll C (WI)
Centre C (KY)
Coe C (IA)
Davidson C (NC)
Davis and Elkins C (WV)
Dubuque, U of (IA)
Eckerd C (FL)
Erskine C (SC) (a member of ACPU, but not related to the Presbyterian Church)
Grove City C (PA)
Hampden-Sydney C (VA)
Hanover C (IN)
Hastings C (NE)
Illinois C
Jamestown C (ND)
Johnson C. Smith U (NC)
King C (TN)
Knoxville C (TN)
Lafayette C (PA)
Lake Forest C (IL)
Lees C (KY)
Lees-McRae C (NC)
Lewis and Clark C (OR)
Lindenwood C (MO)
Lyon C (AR)
Macalester C (MN)

Presbyterian Colleges (continued)

Mary Baldwin C (VA)
Mary Holmes C (MS)
Maryville C (TN)
Millikin U (IL)
Missouri Valley C (MO)
Monmouth C (IL)
Montreat C (NC)
Muskingum C (OH)
Occidental C (CA)
Ozarks, C of the (MO)
Ozarks, U of the (AR)
Peace C (NC)
Pikeville C (KY)
Presbyterian C (SC)
Queens C (NC)
Rhodes C (TN)
Rocky Mountain C (MT)
St. Andrews Presbyterian C (NC)
Schreiner C (TX)
Sheldon Jackson C (AK)
Sterling C (KS)
Stillman C (AL)
Trinity U (TX)
Tulsa, U of (OK)
Tusculum C (TN)
Warren Wilson C (NC)
Waynesburg C (PA)
Westminster C (MO)
Westminster C (PA)
Westminster C (UT)
Whitworth C (WA)
Wilson C (PA)
Wooster, C of (OH)

Quaker (Religious Society of Friends) Colleges

The Quaker tradition stresses such values as self-examination, diversity, community involvement, tolerance, and social justice.

Barclay C (KS)
Bryn Mawr C (PA)
Earlham C (IN)
Earlham School of Religion (IN)
Friends U (KS)
George Fox C (OR)
Guilford C (NC)
Haverford C (PA)
Houston Graduate School of Theology (TX)
Malone C (OH)
Swarthmore C (PA)
Whittier C (CA)
William Penn C (IA)
Wilmington C (OH)

Southern Baptist Colleges

Anderson C (SC)
Averett C (VA)
Baylor U (TX)
Belmont U (TN)
Blue Mountain C (MS)
Bluefield C (VA)
Brewton-Parker C (GA)
California Baptist C
Campbell U (NC)
Campbellsville U (KY)
Carson-Newman C (TN)
Charleston Southern U (SC)
Chowan C (NC)
Clear Creek Baptist Bible C (KY)
Cumberland C (KY)
Dallas Baptist U (TX)
East Texas Baptist U
Florida Baptist Theological C
Furman U (SC)
Gardner-Webb C (NC)
Georgetown C (KY)
Grand Canyon U (AZ)
Hannibal-LaGrange C (MO)
Hardin-Simmons U (TX)
Houston Baptist U (TX)
Howard Payne U (TX)
Judson C (AL)
Louisiana C
Mars Hill C (NC)
Mary Hardin-Baylor, U of (TX)
Mercer U (GA)
Meredith C (NC)
Mississippi C
Missouri Baptist C
Mobile C (AL)
North Greenville C (SC)
Oklahoma Baptist U
Ouachita Baptist U (AR)
Palm Beach Atlantic C (FL)
Richmond, U of (VA)
Samford U (AL)
Shorter C (GA)
Southwest Baptist U (MO)
Stetson U (FL)
Truett-McConnell C (GA)
Union U (TN)
Virginia Intermount C
Wake Forest U (NC)
Wayland Baptist U (TX)
William Carey C (MS)
William Jewell C (MO)
Williams Baptist C (AR)
Wingate C (NC)

Colleges with a High Proportion of Mormon Students

Brigham Young U (HI)
Brigham Young U (UT)
Latter-Day Saints Business C (UT)
Ricks C (ID)
Salt Lake Community C (UT)
Utah State U
Utah, U of

Colleges with a Supportive Jewish Community

Adelphi U (NY)
Alfred U (NY)
American U (DC)
Amherst C (MA)
Arizona, U of
Babson C (MA)
Barnard C (NY)
Bates C (ME)
Boston U (MA)
Brandeis U (MA)
Brown U (RI)
Bryn Mawr C (PA)
California Institute of Technology
California State U, Fullerton
California State U, Northridge
California, U of, Berkeley
California, U of, Los Angeles
California, U of, San Diego
California, U of, Santa Cruz
Carnegie Mellon U (PA)
Chicago, U of (IL)
Cincinnati, U of (OH)
Claremont McKenna C (CA)
Clark U (MA)
Colgate U (NY)
Columbia U (NY)
Connecticut C
Cornell U (NY)
Curry C (MA)
Denver, U of (CO)
Dickinson C (PA)
Drexel U (PA)
Duke U (NC)
Emerson C (MA)
Emory U (GA)
Franklin and Marshall C (PA)
Georgetown U (DC)
George Washington U (DC)
Goucher C (MD)
Grinnell C (IA)
Hartford, U of (CT)
Harvard U (MA)
Harvey Mudd C (CA)
Haverford C (PA)
Hobart C/William Smith C (NY)
Hofstra U (NY)
Ithaca C (NY)
Johns Hopkins U (MD)
Judaism, U of (CA)
Lehigh U (PA)
Lesley C (MA)
List C of Jewish Studies (NY)
Long Island U, C. W. Post (NY)
Lynn U (FL)
Maryland, U of, College Park
Massachusetts Institute of Technology
Miami, U of (FL)
Michigan, U of, Ann Arbor
Muhlenberg C (PA)
New York, City U of, Brooklyn C
New York, City U of, Queens C
New York, State U of, Albany
New York, State U of, Binghamton
New York, State U of, C at Oneonta
New York, State U of, Stony Brook
New York U
Northwestern U (IL)
Oberlin C (OH)

Pennsylvania, U of
Pitzer C (CA)
Pomona C (CA)
Rochester, U of (NY)
Rutgers U (NJ)
Sarah Lawrence C (NY)
Scripps C (CA)
Skidmore C (NY)
Simmons C (MA)
Stanford U (CA)
Swathmore C (PA)
Syracuse U (NY)
Temple U (PA)
Tufts U (MA)
Tulane U (LA)
Union C (NY)
Vassar C (NY)
Washington U (MO)
Wesleyan U (CT)
Yale U (CT)
Yeshiva U (NY)

Colleges with Kosher Kitchens

These colleges offer either kosher meal plans, lunches or dinners provided by a Jewish organization, frozen meals, or cooperative food buying plans.

Adelphi U (NY)
Arizona, U of
Bates C (ME)
Beaver C (PA)
Boston U (MA)
Brandeis U (MA)
Bridgeport, U of (CT)
Brown U (RI)
Bryn Mawr C (PA)
Carleton C (MN)
Carnegie Mellon U (PA)
Case Western Reserve U (OH)
Claremont McKenna C (CA)
Clark U (MA)
Colby C (ME)
Columbia U (NY)
Connecticut, U of
Cornell U (NY)
Dickinson C (PA)
Drexel U (PA)
Duke U (NC)
Duquesne U (PA)
Emerson C (MA)
Emory U (GA)
Fairleigh Dickinson U (NJ)
Florida, U of
Georgetown U (DC)
George Washington U (DC)
Gettysburg C (PA)
Goucher C (MD)
Gratz C (PA)
Hamilton C (NY)
Hartford, U of (CT)
Harvard U (MA)
Haverford C (PA)
Hofstra U (NY)
Illinois, U of, Chicago
Ithaca C (NY)
Johns Hopkins U (MD)
Judaism, U of (CA)

Colleges with Kosher Kitchens (continued)

La Salle U (PA)
Loyola U (IL)
Macalester C (MN)
Maryland, U of, College Park
Massachusetts Institute of Technology
Massachusetts, U of, Amherst
Miami U (OH)
Michigan State U
Michigan, U of, Ann Arbor
Middlebury C (VT)
Millersville U (PA)
Minnesota, U of, Twin Cities
Mt. Holyoke C (MA)
Muhlenberg C (PA)
Nevada, U of, Las Vegas
New York, City U of Brooklyn C
New York, City U of, City C
New York, State U of, Albany
New York, State U of, Binghamton
New York, State U of, Buffalo
New York, State U of, C at Buffalo
New York, State U of, C at Oswego
New York, State U of, Stony Brook
New York U
Northeastern U (MA)
Oberlin C (OH)
Ohio State U, Columbus
Pennsylvania State U, University Park
Pennsylvania, U of
Pittsburgh, U of (PA)
Princeton U (NJ)
Rensselaer Polytechnic Institute (NY)
Rhode Island, U of
Rochester, U of (NY)
Rowan C (NJ)
Rutgers U (NJ)
St. Lawrence U (NY)
Simmons C (MA)
Smith C (MA)
Stanford U (CA)
Stevens Institute of Technology (NJ)
Syracuse U (NY)
Temple U (PA)
Towson State U (MD)
Tufts U (MA)
Union C (NY)
U.S. Military Academy (NY)
Vassar C (NY)
Washington U (MO)
Wayne State U (MI)
Wesleyan U (CT)
Westfield State C (MA)
William Paterson C (NJ)
Williams C (MA)
Wisconsin, U of, Madison
Yale U (CT)
Yeshiva U (NY)

SPECIAL NEEDS FACILITIES

Four-Year Colleges Geared for the Physically Handicapped Student

These schools enroll a high percentage of disabled students and provide specially equipped residence hall spaces.

California Polytechnic State U, San Luis Obispo
California State U, San Bernardino
California State U, San Francisco
California, U of, Davis
Central Oklahoma, U of
Ferris State U (MI)
Florida A&M U
Florida State U
Florida, U of
Gallaudet U (DC) (specializes in teaching hearing-impaired students)
Hofstra U (NY)
Houston, U of (TX)
Illinois, U of, Urbana
Kentucky, U of
Long Island U, Brooklyn (NY)
Madonna U (MI)
Massachusetts, U of, Amherst
McNeese State U (LA)
Minnesota, U of, Duluth
Missouri Southern State C
Montclair State C (NJ)
Morehead State U (KY)
Mt. Aloysius C (PA)
New York, State U of, Albany
New York, State U of, Buffalo
New York, State U of, C of Technology, Alfred
North Carolina A&T State U
Northern Kentucky U
Rhode Island, U of
St. Andrews Presbyterian C (NC)
South Carolina, U of, Columbia
Southern Illinois U, Carbondale
Southern Methodist U (TX)
Southwest State U (MN)

Four-Year Colleges Geared for the Physically Handicapped Student (continued)

Texas, U of, Austin
Utah, U of
Wayne State U (MI)
Wisconsin, U of, Whitewater
Wright State U (OH)

Two-Year Colleges Geared for the Physically Handicapped Student

These schools enroll a high percentage of disabled students and provide specially equipped residence hall spaces.

Central Community C (NE)
Delgado Community C (LA)
Ellsworth Community C (IA)
Floyd C (GA)
Iowa Western Community C
North Central Technical C (OH)
Paris Junior C (TX)
Seattle Central Community C (WA)
Texas State Technical C, Amarillo
Texas State Technical C, Waco
University C, Bangor (ME)
Waubonsee Community C (IL)

Colleges Highly Rated for the Hearing-Impaired Student

In a survey of students with severe or profound hearing losses, these schools were cited for their special support services. The list does not include institutions specially designed for the hearing impaired.

Bloomsburg U (PA)
Boston U (MA)
Brigham Young U (UT)
Bryant C (RI)
California State U, Northridge
California, U of, Berkeley
California, U of, Davis
California, U of, Los Angeles
Champlain C (VT)
Clemson U (SC)
Cornell U (NY)
Eastern Kentucky U
Harvard U (MA)
Hebrew Union C (CA)
Jacksonville State U (AL)
Lenoir-Rhyne C (NC)
Madonna C (MI)
Maryland, U of, Baltimore County
Massachusetts Institute of Technology
Massachusetts, U of, Amherst
Mercer U (GA)
Miami U (OH)
Michigan, U of, Dearborn
Mt. Holyoke C (MA)
New York, State U of, Binghamton
North Carolina, U of, Chapel Hill
Northeastern U (MA)
Northern Colorado, U of
Ohio State U, Columbus
Oregon, U of
Ottawa, U of (Canada)
Pennsylvania State U, Beaver
Pennsylvania State U, University Park
Purdue U (IN)
Saskatchewan, U of (Canada)
Skidmore C (NY)
Southwestern Louisiana, U of
Stanford U (CA)
Syracuse U (NY)
Texas A&M U
Tufts U (MA)
Utah, U of
Vanier C (Canada)
Virginia Polytechnic Institute and State U
Virginia, U of
Waterloo, U of (Canada)
William and Mary, C of (VA)
Wisconsin, U of, Milwaukee

Source: Data compiled from information in Ellen Plotkin, *A Guide to Mainstreamed College Programs for Hearing Impaired Students* (Washington, DC: Alexander Graham Bell Association, 1989).

CAMPUS MEDIA

Outstanding College Newspapers

These colleges won awards at the National Scholastic Press Association/Associated Collegiate Press Conventions in San Francisco in February/March 1998 and in Chicago in November 1997.

FOUR-YEAR COLLEGES

Arizona, U of	*Arizona Daily Wildcat*
Art Institute of Chicago, School of the (IL)	*F*
Babson C (MA)	*The Babson Free Press*
Ball State U (IN)	*The Ball State Daily News*
California State U, Chico	*The Orion*
California State U, Fullerton	*The Daily Titan*
Clemson U (SC)	*The Tiger*
East Carolina U (NC)	*The East Carolinian*
Indiana U–Purdue U, Indianapolis	*The Sagamore*
Kansas State U	*Kansas State Collegian*
Kansas, U of	*University Daily Kansan*
Loyola Marymount U (CA)	*Los Angeles Loyolan*
Marquette U (WI)	*Marquette Tribune*
Missouri Southern State C	*The Chart*
Missouri, U of, Columbia	*The Maneater*
Nebraska, U of, Lincoln	*Daily Nebraskan*
North Dakota, U of	*Dakota Student*
Northern Illinois U	*Northern Star*
Oklahoma, U of	*Oklahoma Daily*
Oregon, U of	*Oregon Daily Emerald*

Pacific U (OR)	*Pacific University Index*
Pennsylvania, U of	*The Daily Pennsylvanian*
Pepperdine U (CA)	*The Graphic*
Principia C (IL)	*The Principia Pilot*
San Francisco State U (CA)	*Golden Gater*
San Francisco, U of (CA)	*The Foghorn*
South Dakota, U of	*Volante*
Washington, U of	*The Daily*
William and Mary, C of (VA)	*The Flat Hat*

TWO-YEAR COLLEGES

Chabot C (CA)	*Chabot Spectator*
Contra Costa C (CA)	*The Advocate*
Daytona Beach Community C (FL)	*In Motion*
Diablo Valley C (CA)	*The Inquirer*
Eastfield C (TX)	*Et Cetera*
El Camino C (CA)	*The Union*
Irvine Valley C (CA)	*The Voice*
Mesa Community C (CO)	*Mesa Legend*
North Idaho C	*The Sentinel*
Santa Ana C (CA)	*El Don*
Utah Valley State C	*The College Times*
Waldorf C (IA)	*The Lobbyist*

Source: National Scholastic Press Association.

Outstanding College Yearbooks

These colleges won awards at the National Scholastic Press Association/Associated Collegiate Press National Media Convention in Chicago, Illinois, in November 1997.

Azusa Pacific U (CA)	*Tavaleph*
Culver-Stockton C (MO)	*Dome*
Idaho, U of	*Gem of the Mountains*
Indiana U, Bloomington	*Arbutus*
Kansas State U	*Royal Purple*
Missouri Western State C	*Griffon*
Ouachita Baptist U (AR)	*Ouachitonian*

Outstanding College Yearbooks (continued)

Texas Tech U	*La Ventana*
U.S. Air Force Academy (CO)	*Polaris*
Vanderbilt U (TN)	*The Commodore*

Source: National Scholastic Press Association.

Outstanding College Literary Magazines

These colleges won awards at the National Scholastic Press Association/Associated Collegiate Press National Convention in Chicago, Illinois, in November 1997.

Arapahoe Community C (CO)	*Progenitor*
South Carolina, U of, Coastal	*Archarios*
Louisiana State U, Baton Rouge	*Legacy*
North Carolina, U of, Charlotte	*Sanskrit*
Tallahassee Community C (FL)	*The Eyrie*

Source: National Scholastic Press Association.

Outstanding College Magazines

These colleges won awards for feature magazines at the National Scholastic Press Association/Associated Collegiate Press National Media Convention in Chicago, Illinois, in November 1997.

El Camino C (CA)	*Warrior Life*
Indiana U, Bloomington	*Lux*
Missouri, U of, Columbia	*Stir Magazine*
Rochester Institute of Technology (NY)	*Reporter Magazine*
Santa Ana C (CA)	*West 17th*

Source: National Scholastic Press Association.

Award-Winning College Television Stations

These schools won the 1996 National Association of College Broadcasters programming awards.

Arkansas, U of	UATV
California U (PA)	CUTV
Colorado State U	CTV
DePauw U (IN)	CCM
Duke U (NC)	Cable 13
Dutchess Community C (NY)	Channel 42
Emerson C (MA)	EIV
Fort Valley State U (GA)	FVSC
Ithaca C (NY)	ICTV
Kansas, U of	K14HY-TV
Michigan State U	MSU
Mississippi State U	Television Center
New York, State U of, C at Geneseo	GSTV
New York, State U of, Fredonia	WNYF-TV
New York U	NYU-TV
North Dakota, U of	Studio One
Norwich U (VT)	NUTV
Oklahoma, U of	OUTV
Robert Morris C (PA)	RMC-TV
Texas, U of, Austin	KVR9
Towson State U (MD)	WMJF-LP

Award-Winning College Radio Stations

These stations won the 1996 National Association of College Broadcasters awards.

Alabama, U of	WVUA
Burlington County C (NJ)	WBZC
California, U of, Berkeley	KALX
Colby Community C (KS)	KTCC
Georgia, U of	WUOG
Hobart C/William Smith C (NY)	WEOS
Hofstra U (NY)	WRHU-FM

Award-Winning College Radio Stations (continued)

Iowa, U of	KRUI
Kansas, U of	HJHK-FM
LaVerne, U of (CA)	KULV
Luzerne County Community C (PA)	WSFX
Manchester C (IN)	WBKE
Marshall U (WV)	WMUL
Mississippi State U	WMSV
New York, State U of, C at Brockport	WBSU
New York U	WNYU-FM
North Central C (IL)	WONC
Northeastern U (MA)	WRBB
Northwest Missouri State U	KDLX
Palomar C (CA)	KKSM-AM
Rowan C (NJ) (Station of the Year Award)	WGLS-FM
Syracuse U (NY)	WJPZ
West Texas A&M U	KWTS
Wisconsin, U of, Stevens Point	WWSP-FM

CAMPUS SAFETY

There are no lists of colleges included here because data concerning crime on campus is deceptive and ambiguous: Campus safety is a matter of common sense, not statistics. Clearly, crime is a reality in our society, and campuses are not immune from that influence. Prospective students should speak to college officials and current students to determine both the reality of crime as well as the perception of safety at chosen campuses.

According to *USA Today*, the safest colleges are those with 10,000 to 20,000 students in a city with a population of under 100,000 persons. The colleges most prone to violent crime are those with fewer than 10,000 students in cities of more than 500,000 persons. The size of the town or city is the best predictor of violent crime on campus. Campus crime statistics can be misleading because colleges report data in different ways and because crime patterns vary at different times of the year. Also, since offenses are not always reported on a per student basis, larger schools often show higher crime incidences. Since the Student Right to Know and Campus Security Act of 1990 requires colleges to report information on crime, the latest facts on campus safety are available from each college.

SOCIAL POTPOURRI

Colleges with Active Honor Codes

These schools have active honor codes or systems specifying campus norms and ethical behavior. The colleges hold students responsible for their behavior and allow for academic freedoms such as self-scheduled examinations.

Agnes Scott C (GA)
Allegheny C (PA)
Birmingham-Southern C (AL)
Brigham Young U (UT)
Bryn Mawr C (PA)
Bowdoin C (ME)
California Institute of Technology
Connecticut C
Davidson C (NC)
Earlham C (IN)
Gettysburg C (PA)
Hamilton C (NY)
Hampden-Sydney C (VA)
Harvey Mudd C (CA)
Haverford C (PA)
Hollins C (VA)
Hood C (MD)
Knox C (IL)
Lawrence U (WI)
Mt. Holyoke C (MA)
Oberlin C (OH)
Oral Roberts U (OK)
Princeton U (NJ)
Randolph-Macon Woman's C (VA)
Rhodes C (TN)
Rice U (TX)
Skidmore C (NY)
Smith C (MA)
South, U of the (TN)
Sweet Briar C (VA)
Trinity C (DC)
U.S. Military Academies
Valparaiso U (IN)
Vanderbilt U (TN)
Virginia, U of
Wake Forest U (NC)
Washington and Lee U (VA)
Wellesley C (MA)
Wells C (NY)
William and Mary, C of (VA)

Colleges with Dress and/or Hair Codes

Specifications about student clothing may range from a military uniform to "modest" dress. "Modest" dress may include requirements for skirts and dresses or suits and ties as classroom attire; no shorts may be allowed in class; there may be prohibitions against jewelry and skintight garments. Hair codes range from regulation military cuts to a prohibition against mohawks.

Abilene Christian U (TX) (dress code)
Bob Jones U (SC)
Brigham Young U (UT)
Cedarville C (OH)
Champlain C (VT) (dress code)
Citadel, The (SC)
Evangel C (MO)
Grand Canyon U (AZ) (dress code)
Indiana Wesleyan U (dress code)
LeTourneau U (TX)
Liberty U (VA)
Maharishi International U (IA)
Northwestern C (MN)
Nyack C (NY) (dress code)
Oral Roberts U (OK)
South, U of the (TN) (dress code by tradition, not regulation)
Thomas Aquinas C (CA) (dress code)
Thomas More C (NH) (dress code)
Walla Walla C (WA) (dress code)

Colleges with a Winning Tradition in Debate

These schools have winning debate teams or a long-standing reputation for excellent programs in debate.

Alabama, U of, Tuscaloosa
Bates C (ME)
Baylor U (TX)
Bob Jones U (SC)
Carroll C (MT)
Dartmouth C (NH)
Hampden-Sydney C (VA) (200-year-old debating society)
Harvard U (MA)
Hillsdale C (MI)
Illinois State U
Mississippi, U of
Northwestern U (IL)
Princeton U (NJ)
Sacred Heart U (CT)
St. Olaf C (MN)
Southern Illinois U
Texas Southern U

Colleges with Comprehensive Debate Programs

These schools have extensive programs including two major types of collegiate debate: cross-examination and national debate topic.

Alabama, U of, Tuscaloosa
Arkansas, U of, Monticello
Augustana C (SD)
California State U, Fresno
California State U, Northridge
California State U, San Diego
Cameron U (OK)
Central Missouri State U
Colorado C
Colorado, U of
Cypress C (CA)
Eastern New Mexico U
Emory U (GA)
Florida State U
Fort Hays State U (KS)
Georgia State U
Johnson County Community C (KS)
Kansas City Kansas Community C
Kansas, U of
Louisiana State U, Shreveport
Macalester C (MN)
Miami U (OH)
Miami, U of (FL)
Missouri Southern State C
Missouri, U of, Kansas City
Missouri, U of, St. Louis
Nebraska, U of, Lincoln
Nevada, U of, Las Vegas
New Mexico, U of, Albuquerque
North Dakota, U of
Northeast Missouri State U
Northern Arizona U
Northern Illinois U
Northern Iowa, U of
Odessa C (TX)
Pace U (NY)
Pittsburgh, U of (PA)
Redlands, U of (CA)
San Jacinto C (TX)
Southern Colorado, U of
Southern Utah State C
Southwest Missouri State U
Southwest State U (MN)
Southwest Texas State U
Texas Southern U
Utah, U of
Washburn U (KS)
Weber State U (UT)
Wichita State U (KS)
Wisconsin, U of, River Falls
Wyoming, U of

Military Colleges

This list does not include major U.S. military academies.

Citadel, The (SC)
Georgia Military C (two-year college)
Kemper Military School and C (MO) (two-year college)
Maine Maritime Academy
Marion Military Institute (AL) (two-year college)
New Mexico Military Institute (NM) (two-year college)
North Georgia C
Norwich U (VT)
Valley Forge Military C (PA) (two-year college)
Virginia Military Institute
Wentworth Military Academy (MO) (two-year college)

Colleges with Strong ROTC Programs

Alabama, U of, Tuscaloosa
Auburn U (AL)
California State U, San Diego
Fordham U (NY)
Jacksonville U (FL)
Kentucky, U of
Michigan State U
Michigan, U of, Ann Arbor
Montana State U
Notre Dame, U of (IN)
Oklahoma, U of
Oregon State U
San Diego, U of (CA)
Texas A&M U
Villanova U (PA)
Virginia Polytechnic Institute and State U
Western Illinois U

The Top Ten Extracurricular Activities

Academic group or club
Band, orchestra, or choir
Drama or theater group
Intramurals
Public interest group
Religious group
Sorority or fraternity
Student government
Varsity or junior varsity sports
Volunteer work

Colleges with Excellent Film Series

California, U of Los Angeles
Chicago, U of (IL)
Cornell U (NY)
Dartmouth C (NH)
Duke U (NC)
Georgia, U of
Harvard U/Radcliffe C (MA)
Iowa, U of
Rutgers U (NJ)
Texas, U of, Austin
Vanderbilt U (TN)
Vassar C (NY)
Wesleyan U (CT)
Wisconsin, U of, Madison

Colleges That Attract Popular Bands and Celebrities

Arizona State U
Boise State U (ID)
Idaho State U
Johnson and Wales U (RI) (known for production of comedy shows)
Nevada, U of, Las Vegas
New Mexico State U, Las Cruces
Pennsylvania State U, University Park
South Florida, U of
Syracuse U (NY)
Virginia Polytechnic Institute and State U
Washington State U

INTERNATIONALISM

STUDY ABROAD

Colleges with Strong Foreign Study Programs

These schools offer extensive study options in other countries.

American U (DC)
Beaver C (PA)
Boston U (MA)
Carleton C (MN)
Central C (IA) (over half the student body studies abroad)
Clark U (MA)
Colby C (ME) (over half the student body studies abroad)
Colgate U (NY)
Connecticut C
Dallas, U of (TX) (almost all sophomores study at the Rome campus)
Dartmouth C (NH)
Davidson C (NC)
Dickinson C (PA)
Earlham C (IN)
Georgetown U (DC)
Goshen C (IN) (study service team)
Guilford C (NC)
Hiram C (OH) (half the student body studies abroad)
Hollins C (VA)
Kalamazoo C (MI)
Lawrence U (WI)
Lewis and Clark C (OR)
Long Island U, Southampton (NY) (Friends World Program)
Macalester C (MN)
Michigan State U
Middlebury C (VT)
Northeastern U (MA)
Oberlin C (OH)
Pacific U (OR)
Pitzer C (CA)
Pomona C (CA)
Queens C (NC) (International Experience Program)
Randolph-Macon Woman's C (VA)
St. Benedict, C of/St. John's U (MN)
St. Lawrence U (NY)
St. Norbert C (WI)
St. Olaf C (MN) (about half the student body studies abroad)
Scripps C (CA)

Colleges with Strong Foreign Study Programs (continued)

Smith C (MA)
Sweet Briar C (VA)
Taylor U (IN)
Thomas More C (NH)
Tufts U (MA)
Union C (NY)
U.S. International U (CA)
Webster U (MO)
Wells C (NY)
Whitman C (WA)

American Colleges with International Campuses

These are schools with foreign campuses. The location of the campus is specified.

Dallas, U of (TX): Rome, Italy
Emerson C (MA): Kasteel Well and Maastricht, The Netherlands
Evansville, U of (IN): Harlaxton, England
Ithaca C (NY): London, England
Loyola U (IL): Rome, Italy
Maryland, U of, University C: Schwäbisch Gmünd, Germany
New York U: Florence, Italy
Rockford C (IL): relationship with Regents C, London
St. Louis U (MO): Madrid, Spain
Syracuse U (NY): Florence, Italy; Madrid, Spain; Strasbourg, France; London, England; Harare, Zimbabwe; Hong Kong, China
Temple U (PA): Rome, Italy; Tokyo, Japan; London, England
Trinity C (CT): Rome, Italy
Webster U (MO): Vienna, Austria; Leiden, The Netherlands; London, England; Geneva, Switzerland

Members of the American Collegiate Consortium for East-West Cultural and Academic Exchange

The member colleges of the consortium offer students opportunities to study in the former Soviet Union; in turn, universities in the new independent states and the Baltic countries send students to study at the American schools.

Alabama, U of, Tuscaloosa
Allegheny C (PA)
Amherst C (MA)
Bates C (ME)
Baylor U (TX)
Beloit C (WI)
Bowdoin C (ME)
Colby C (ME)
Colgate U (NY)
Connecticut C
Davidson C (NC)
Dickinson C (PA)
Hamilton C (NY)
Haverford C (PA)
Illinois, U of, Urbana
Illinois Wesleyan U
Kenyon C (OH)
Lafayette C (PA)
Lehigh U (PA)
Michigan, U of, Ann Arbor
Middlebury C (VT)
Missouri, U of, Columbia
Mt. Holyoke C (MA)
Norwich U (VT)
Oberlin C (OH)
Occidental C (CA)
Ohio Wesleyan U
Rhodes C (TN)
St. Lawrence U (NY)
Sarah Lawrence C (NY)
Skidmore C (NY)
Smith C (MA)
Susquehanna U (PA)
Swarthmore C (PA)
Trinity C (CT)
Tulsa, U of (OK)
Union C (NY)
Vassar C (NY)
Vermont, U of
Washington and Lee U (VA)
Wellesley C (MA)
Wesleyan U (CT)
Wheaton C (MA)
Williams C (MA)
Wittenberg U (OH)

Members of the Intercollegiate Center for Classical Studies in Rome

Located in downtown Rome, the center offers students opportunities to study Greek and Latin literature, ancient world history, archeology, and art.

Amherst C (MA)
Barnard C (NY)
Beloit C (WI)
Birmingham-Southern C (AL)
Boston U (MA)
Bowdoin C (ME)
Brown U (RI)
Bryn Mawr C (PA)
Carleton C (MN)
Centenary C (LA)
Centre C (KY)
Claremont McKenna C (CA)
Clark U (MA)
Colgate U (NY)
Colorado, U of
Cornell U (NY)
Dickinson C (PA)
Duke U (NC)
Fordham U (NY)
Grinnell C (IA)
Hamilton C (NY)
Hampden-Sydney C (VA)
Harvard U (MA)
Hobart C/William Smith C (NY)
Hollins C (VA)
Holy Cross, C of the (MA)
Indiana U, Bloomington
Johns Hopkins U (MD)
Lawrence U (WI)
Lehigh U (PA)
Mary Washington C (VA)
Maryland, U of, College Park
Massachusetts, U of, Amherst
Millsaps C (MS)
Minnesota, U of, Twin Cities
Mt. Holyoke C (MA)
North Carolina, U of, Chapel Hill
Northwestern U (IL)
Oberlin C (OH)
Ohio State U, Columbus
Pennsylvania, U of
Pitzer C (CA)
Pomona C (CA)
Princeton U (NJ)
Reed C (OR)
Rice U (TX)
Rutgers U (NJ)
Scripps C (CA)
Skidmore C (NY)
Smith C (MA)
Southern California, U of
Randolph-Macon C (VA)
Randolph-Macon Woman's C (VA)
Rhodes C (TN)
St. John's U (NY)
South, U of the (TN)
Stanford U (CA)
Swarthmore C (PA)
Sweet Briar C (VA)
Trinity C (CT)
Trinity U (TX)
Union C (NY)
Vanderbilt U (TN)

Vassar C (NY)
Wabash C (IN)
Washington and Lee U (VA)
Wellesley C (MA)
Wesleyan U (CT)
Williams C (MA)
Yale U (CT)

Colleges in the Associated Kyoto Program

These schools are members of a consortium that sponsors students for study in Japan for one year.

Amherst C (MA)
Bucknell U (PA)
Carleton C (MN)
Colby C (ME)
Connecticut C
Middlebury C (VT)
Mt. Holyoke C (MA)
Oberlin C (OH)
Pomona C (CA)
Smith C (MA)
Wesleyan U (CT)
Whitman C (WA)
Williams C (MA)

BRITISH AND CANADIAN UNIVERSITIES

The Ten Largest British Universities

Birmingham, U of (UK)
Cambridge U (UK)
Edinburgh, U of (UK)
Glasgow, U of (UK)
Leeds, U of (UK)
Newcastle Upon Tyne, U of (UK)
Oxford U (UK)
Sheffield, U of (UK)
Ulster (UK)
Victoria U of Manchester (UK)

The Ten Largest British University Libraries

Birmingham, U of (UK)
Cambridge U (UK)
Edinburgh, U of (UK)
Glasgow, U of (UK)
Leeds, U of (UK)
London School of Economics (UK)
Manchester Institute of Science and Technology, U of (UK)
Oxford U (UK)
University C, London (UK)
Victoria U of Manchester (UK)

Residential Canadian Universities

While many Canadian universities are commuter schools, these colleges have housing available to students.

Acadia U
Alberta, U of
Bishop's U
Brandon U
British Columbia, U of
Camrose Lutheran University C
Dalhousie U
Guelph, U of
Lakehead U
McGill U
McMaster U
Mt. St. Vincent U
New Brunswick, U of
Queen's U
St. Francis Xavier U
St. Mary's U
Toronto, U of
Trent U
Trinity Western U
Waterloo, U of
Western Ontario, U of

INTERNATIONAL POTPOURRI

Colleges That Promote Internationalism

These schools show interest in international, interdisciplinary scholarship, particularly in contemporary European and American social science issues.

Akron, U of (OH)
American C (Switzerland)
Amherst C (MA)
Arizona State U
Beloit C (WI)
Boston U (MA)
Brandeis U (MA)
Brown U (RI)
Bryn Mawr C (PA)
California, U of, Berkeley
California, U of, Los Angeles
California, U of, San Diego
California, U of, Santa Barbara
California, U of, Santa Cruz
Chicago, U of (IL)
Clemson U (SC)
Colorado, U of
Columbia U (NY)
Connecticut C
Connecticut, U of
Cornell U (NY)
Dallas, U of (TX)
Dayton, U of (OH)
Delaware, U of
Dickinson C (PA)
Duke U (NC)
Europe, C of, Bruges (Belgium)
Florida, U of
Fordham U (NY)
George Mason U (VA)
Georgetown U (DC)
German Historical Institute (DC)
Hamline U (MN)
Harvard U (MA)
Illinois, U of, Urbana
Indiana U, Bloomington
Johns Hopkins U (MD)
Kalamazoo C (MI)
Kansas, U of
Kenyon C (OH)
Maryland, U of, Baltimore County
Maryland, U of, College Park
Massachusetts Institute of Technology

Massachusetts, U of, Amherst
McMaster U (Canada)
Michigan, U of, Ann Arbor
Minnesota, U of, Twin Cities
Nevada, U of, Reno
New Hampshire, U of
New Mexico, U of, Albuquerque
New School for Social Research (NY)
New York, City U of, Baruch C
New York, City U of, Graduate Center
New York, State U of, Albany
New York, State U of, Buffalo
New York, State U of, Stony Brook
New York U
North Carolina, U of, Chapel Hill
Northeastern U (MA)
Northwestern U (IL)
Notre Dame, U of (IN)
Ohio Wesleyan U
Oregon, U of
Pennsylvania, U of
Pittsburgh, U of (PA)
Polytechnic U (NY)
Princeton U (NJ)
Purdue U (IN)
Rochester Institute of Technology (NY)
Rochester, U of (NY)
Rutgers U (NJ)
St. Lawrence U (NY)
St. Norbert C (WI)
School for International Training (VT)
Skidmore C (NY)
Stanford U (CA)
Swarthmore C (PA)
Syracuse U (NY)
Texas, U of, Austin
Trinity U (TX)
Tufts U (MA)
U.S. International U (CA)
Vanderbilt U (TN)
Virginia Polytechnic Institute and State U
Washington U (MO)
Washington, U of
Wisconsin, U of, Madison
Wesley C (DE)
Wesleyan U (CT)
Wooster, C of (OH)
Yale U (CT)

Source: Council for European Studies, Columbia U, NY.

Colleges That Prepare Students to Think Internationally

These schools graduate a disproportionate number of students who pursue work in international affairs within government or academe. In addition, undergraduates at these colleges are more likely to study foreign languages and/or be involved in foreign study programs.

Agnes Scott C (GA)
Amherst C (MA)
Austin C (TX)
Barnard C (NY)
Bates C (ME)
Beloit C (WI)
Bennington C (VT)
Bowdoin C (ME)
Bryn Mawr C (PA)
Carleton C (MN)
Colby C (ME)
Colorado C
Connecticut C
Davidson C (NC)
Denison U (OH)
Dickinson C (PA)
Earlham C (IN)
Eckerd C (FL)
Goshen C (IN)
Goucher C (MD)
Grinnell C (IA)
Hamilton C (NY)
Hampshire C (MA)
Haverford C (PA)
Kalamazoo C (MI)
Kenyon C (OH)
Knox C (IL)
Lawrence U (WI)
Macalester C (MN)
Middlebury C (VT)
Mills C (CA)
Mt. Holyoke C (MA)
Oberlin C (OH)
Occidental C (CA)
Pitzer C (CA)
Pomona C (CA)
Principia C (IL)
Randolph-Macon Woman's C (VA)
Reed C (OR)
St. Olaf C (MN)
Sarah Lawrence C (NY)
Scripps C (CA)
Smith C (MA)
Swarthmore C (PA)
Sweet Briar C (VA)
Union C (NY)
Vassar C (NY)
Wellesley C (MA)
Wells C (NY)
Wesleyan U (CT)
Williams C (MA)
Wooster, C of (OH)

Source: David C. Engerman and Parker G. Marden, *In the International Interest: The Contributions and Needs of America's International Liberal Arts Colleges* (Beloit, WI: The International Liberal Arts Colleges, 1992).

Popular American Universities Abroad

These colleges and universities award American degrees. Course work, grading, and instruction are similar to those found at U.S. schools.

American C in Oxford (UK)
American C in Oxford, Warnborough C (UK)
American C of Paris (France)
American C (Switzerland)
American U of Paris (France)
American U of Rome (Italy)
Franklin C (Switzerland)
John Cabot International C, Rome (Italy)
Regents C, London (UK)
Richmond C (UK)
U.S. International U (Mexico City, Mexico)
U.S. International U (Nairobi, Africa)

The Top Foreign Business Schools

IMD (International Institute for Management Development) (Switzerland)
INSEAD (European Institute of Business Administration) (France)
London Business School (UK)
Manchester, U of (UK)
McGill U (Canada)
Stockholm School of Economics (Sweden)
Tokyo, U of (Japan)
Western Ontario, U of (Canada)

The Top Ten U.S. Colleges in Foreign Student Enrollment

The colleges are followed by the number of foreign students on the campus. Data is based on the academic year 1996–97.

1. Boston U (MA)	4,657
2. New York U	4,491

The Top Ten U.S. Colleges in Foreign Student Enrollment (continued)

3. Southern California, U of	4,183
4. Wisconsin, U of, Madison	3,886
5. Columbia U (NY)	3,807
6. Ohio State U, Columbus	3,772
7. Texas, U of, Austin	3,403
8. Harvard U (MA)	3,238
9. Illinois, U of, Urbana	3,194
*10. Michigan, U of, Ann Arbor	3,194

*See Author's Note, p. xxv.

Source: Institute of International Education, New York, NY.

U.S. Colleges with a Large Number of Foreign Students

American U (DC)
Andrews U (MI)
Bard C (NY)
Beloit C (WI)
Bennington C (VT)
Boston U (MA)
Clark U (MA)
Columbia U (NY)
Drexel U (PA)
Eckerd C (FL)
Florida Institute of Technology
George Washington U (DC)
Georgetown U (DC)
Harvard U (MA)
Hawaii Pacific U
Illinois Institute of Technology
Macalester C (MN)
Massachusetts Institute of Technology
Miami, U of (FL)
Mt. Holyoke C (MA)
New Jersey Institute of Technology
New School for Social Research (NY)
Nova Southeastern U (FL)
Oklahoma City U
Pennsylvania, U of
Rochester, U of (NY)
Southern California, U of
Stanford U (CA)
Thomas Aquinas C (CA)
Tufts U (MA)
Tulsa, U of (OK)
U.S. International U (CA)

Country Origins of Foreign Students Who Study in the U.S.

Data is based on the year 1996–97.

	Country	Students
1.	Japan	46,292
2.	China	42,503
3.	Republic of Korea	37,130
4.	India	30,641
5.	Taiwan	30,487
6.	Canada	22,984
7.	Malaysia	14,527
8.	Thailand	13,481
9.	Indonesia	12,461
10.	Hong Kong	10,942
11.	Germany	8,990
12.	Mexico	8,975
13.	Turkey	8,194
14.	United Kingdom	7,357
15.	Russia	6,199
16.	Brazil	6,168
17.	Pakistan	6,095
18.	France	5,692
19.	Spain	4,673
20.	Venezuela	4,590

Source: Institute of International Education, New York, NY.

States Where the Largest Numbers of Foreign Students Are Enrolled in Colleges

Data is based on the year 1996–97.

1.	California	57,017
2.	New York	46,076
3.	Texas	28,686
4.	Massachusetts	26,568
5.	Florida	20,307
6.	Illinois	19,626
7.	Pennsylvania	18,110
8.	Michigan	17,319
9.	Ohio	16,763
10.	Washington	10,959

Source: Institute of International Education, New York, NY.

CAREERS

MEDICAL SCHOOL

The "I Want to Be a Doctor" List

These colleges allow well-qualified students guaranteed medical school admission when they apply as freshmen or early in their college studies. Some schools combine undergraduate studies and medical school in six or seven years (instead of eight years).

Akron, U of (OH)
Boston U (MA)
Brown U (RI)
California, U of, Los Angeles
California, U of, Riverside
Case Western Reserve U (OH)
Drew U (NJ)
East Tennessee State U
Fisk U (TN)
George Washington U (DC)
Howard U (DC)
Illinois Institute of Technology
Kent State U (OH)
Lehigh U (PA)
Miami, U of (FL)
Michigan State U
Michigan, U of, Ann Arbor
Missouri, U of, Kansas City
Montclair State U (NJ)
New Jersey Institute of Technology
New York, City U of, Brooklyn C
New York, State U of, Binghamton
New York U
Northwestern U (IL)
Pennsylvania State U, University Park
Rensselaer Polytechnic Institute (NY)
Rice U (TX)
Richard Stockton C (NJ)
Rochester, U of (NY)
Rutgers U (NJ)
Siena C (NY)
Sophie Davis School of Biomedical Education (NY)

The "I Want to Be a Doctor" List (continued)

South Alabama, U of
Southern California, U of
Stevens Institute of Technology (NJ)
Trenton State C (NJ)
Union C (NY)
Villanova U (PA)
Wisconsin, U of, Madison (for in-state residents)
Youngstown State U (OH)

Source: Association of American Medical Colleges, Washington, DC.

Postgraduate, Premed Colleges

Some students decide late in their college studies to enter the field of medicine; others do not have the grades or the prerequisite courses to compete successfully. These schools offer programs to college graduates who wish to take preparatory courses for medical school.

Bennington C (VT) (Postbaccalaureate Certificate Program)
Boston U, School of Medicine (MA) (aimed at underrepresented minorities/disadvantaged)
Bowman Gray School of Medicine (NC) (interested in attracting minority applicants)
Bryn Mawr C (PA) (Postbaccalaureate Premedical Program)
California, U of, Davis, School of Medicine (aimed at underrepresented minorities/disadvantaged)
California, U of, Irvine, College of Medicine (aimed at underrepresented minorities/disadvantaged)
California, U of, San Diego (aimed at underrepresented minorities/disadvantaged)
Columbia U, School of General Studies (NY) (Postbaccalaureate Premedical Program)
Connecticut, U of, Farmington (Postbaccalaureate Program)
Creighton U, School of Medicine (NE) (aimed at underrepresented minorities/disadvantaged)
Duquesne U (PA) (Postbaccalaureate Premedical Program)
Goucher C (MD) (Postbaccalaureate Premedical Program)
Hahnemann U, School of Medicine (PA) (Medical Science Track Program)
Harvard U (MA) (Extension School)
Kansas, U of, Kansas City (aimed at underrepresented minorities/disadvantaged)
Miami, U of, College of Arts and Sciences (FL) (Premedical Postbaccalaureate Program)
Michigan State U, College of Human Medicine (aimed at underrepresented minorities/disadvantaged)
Michigan, U of, Ann Arbor (aimed at underrepresented minorities/disadvantaged)
Mills C (CA) (Postbaccalaureate Medical Program)
New C (CA) (Science Institute)
New York, State U of, Buffalo, School of Medicine (aimed at underrepresented minorities/disadvantaged)

Postgraduate, Premed Colleges (continued)

New York U, College of Arts and Sciences (Postbaccalaureate Program)

Ohio State U, Columbus, College of Medicine (interested in attracting minority applicants)

Pennsylvania, U of, College of General Studies (aimed at underrepresented groups and those willing to work in underserved areas)

Scripps C (CA) (Postbaccalaureate Premedical Certificate Program)

Southern Illinois U, Carbondale, School of Medicine (aimed at minority, rural, low-income students)

Texas, U of, Galveston (aimed at underrepresented minorities/disadvantaged)

Towson State U, Department of Biological Sciences (MD) (Postbaccalaureate Premedical/Predental Program)

Virginia, U of, School of Medicine (aimed at underrepresented minorities/disadvantaged)

Wayne State U, School of Medicine (MI) (aimed at underrepresented minorities/disadvantaged and Michigan residents)

LAW SCHOOL

The "I Want to Be a Lawyer" List

These colleges offer students the opportunity to be considered for law school admission after three years of undergraduate study. Students must meet the normal requirements of admission at the cooperating law school. A double asterisk sign (**) indicates that the school participates in the Accelerated Interdisciplinary Legal Education Program at Columbia University Law School, New York. Outstanding students may be nominated by their college for admission consideration at Columbia Law. If accepted by Columbia, students begin law studies following their third year as an undergraduate.

Barnard C (NY)**
Bowdoin C (ME)**
Brandeis U (MA)**
Carleton C (MN)**
Claremont McKenna C (CA)**
Colgate U (NY)**
Colorado C**
Columbia U (NY)**
Davidson C (NC)**
Duquesne U (PA)
Grinnell C (IA)**
Hamilton C (NY)**
Hampshire C (MA)**
Hartwick C (NY)
Johns Hopkins U (MD)**
Knox C (IL)**
Macalester C (MN)**
Miami, U of (FL)
Missouri, U of, Columbia
Mt. Holyoke C (MA)**
New York, City U of, City C
New York, State U of, Albany
Occidental C (CA)**
Princeton U (NJ)**
Reed C (OR)**
Rensselaer Polytechnic Institute (NY)**
Rice U (TX)**
Richmond, U of (VA)
Rochester, U of (NY)**
St. Olaf C (MN)**

The "I Want to Be a Lawyer" List (continued)

Stevens Institute of Technology (NJ)
Union C (NY)
Wabash C (IN)**
Whitman C (WA)**
William Woods C (MO)
Wooster, C of (OH)**

Most Satisfied Students in Law School

At these law schools, students are most satisfied.

1. Washington and Lee U (VA)
2. Washburn U (KS)
3. Western New England U (MA)
4. William and Mary, C of (VA)
5. Southern California, U of
6. Seton Hall U (NJ)
7. Notre Dame, U of (IN)
8. Northeastern U (MA)
9. Virginia, U of
10. Georgetown U (DC)
11. Brigham Young U (UT)
12. Cincinnati, U of (OH)
13. Vanderbilt U (TN)
14. Richmond, U of (VA)
15. South Texas C of Law
16. Yale U (CT)
17. Washington, U of
18. Arkansas, U of, Little Rock
19. Montana, U of
20. Missouri, U of, Columbia

Source: *The National Jurist*, April/May 1996, 1-800-296-9656.

Colleges with the Highest Percentage of Graduates Going to Law School

		PERCENT
1.	Washington and Jefferson C (PA)	18
2.	Brandeis U (MA)	17
*3.	Emory U (GA)	17
4.	Chicago, U of (IL)	16
5.	South, U of the (TN)	15
*6.	Trinity C (DC)	15
7.	Davidson C (NC)	14
8.	New York U	13
9.	Transylvania U (KY)	12
*10.	Wabash C (IN)	12

*See Author's Note, p. xxv.

Source: Copyright 1992, Orchard House, Inc., Concord, MA.

COLLEGES AWARDING THE MOST DOCTORAL DEGREES

Colleges in this section award the most doctoral degrees. These colleges have the resources (faculty, libraries, research opportunities, etc.) needed to sustain a large graduate enrollment. Students preparing for undergraduate study should weigh the advantages with the disadvantages of a college that emphasizes graduate student preparation. For example, because they are larger, colleges focusing on graduate education may not offer the support and personal attention that colleges more oriented toward undergraduate students provide. An emphasis, then, on graduate studies may offer either a boost or a deterrent to undergraduate students.

Twenty-five Schools Granting the Most Doctorates

These are the colleges that gave research doctorates (Ph.D.'s and similar degrees) to the most students from July 1995 to June 1996.

1. California, U of, Berkeley	768
2. Wisconsin, U of, Madison	752
3. Texas, U of, Austin	744
4. Minnesota, U of, Twin Cities	724
5. Ohio State U, Columbus	708
6. Illinois, U of, Urbana	699
7. Michigan, U of, Ann Arbor	685
8. California, U of, Los Angeles	606
9. Texas A&M U	569

10.	Stanford U (CA)	565
11.	Massachusetts Institute of Technology	553
12.	Harvard U (MA)	527
*13.	Pennsylvania State U, University Park	527
14.	Cornell U (NY)	516
15.	Purdue U (IN)	507
16.	Washington, U of	495
17.	Michigan State U	479
18.	Maryland, U of, College Park	463
19.	Pennsylvania, U of	452
20.	Southern California, U of	445
21.	Columbia U (NY)	429
22.	Nova Southeastern U (FL)	420
23.	Florida, U of	418
24.	Indiana U, Bloomington	407
25.	California, U of, Davis	397

*See Author's Note, p. xxv.

Source: Data compiled from information in *1996 Survey of Earned Doctorates*, National Research Council, Washington, DC.

Colleges Granting the Most Doctorates in the Humanities

These are the colleges that awarded the most research doctorates from July 1995 to June 1996 in these fields: English and American language, foreign languages and literature, and other humanities.

1.	Texas, U of, Austin	108
2.	Yale U (CT)	105
3.	Michigan, U of, Ann Arbor	104
4.	California, U of, Los Angeles	103
5.	Indiana U, Bloomington	90
6.	Harvard U (MA)	88
*7.	New York U	88
8.	California, U of, Berkeley	87
9.	Columbia U (NY)	82
10.	Minnesota, U of, Twin Cities	77

Colleges Granting the Most Doctorates in the Humanities (continued)

11.	Chicago, U of (IL)	70
*12.	Southern California, U of	70
*13.	Washington, U of	70
14.	Wisconsin, U of, Madison	68
15.	New York, City U of, Graduate School, U Center	66
16.	Pennsylvania, U of	62
17.	Princeton U (NJ)	61
18.	Cornell U (NY)	60
*19.	Iowa, U of	60
20.	North Carolina, U of, Chapel Hill	59
*21.	Rutgers U (NJ)	59
22.	Illinois, U of, Urbana	56
23.	New York, State U of, Stony Brook	55
24.	Ohio State U	53
*25.	Stanford, U of (CA)	53
26.	Florida State U	52
27.	Boston U (MA)	51
28.	Maryland, U of, College Park	50
*29.	Pennsylvania State U, University Park	50
*30.	Temple U (PA)	50

*See Author's Note, p. xxv.

Source: Data compiled from information in *1996 Survey of Earned Doctorates*, National Research Council, Washington, DC.

Colleges Granting the Most Doctorates in the Social Sciences

These are the colleges that awarded the most research doctorates from July 1995 to June 1996 in these fields: psychology, economics and econometrics, anthropology and sociology, political science and international relations, and other social sciences.

1.	Chicago, U of (IL)	128
2.	Michigan, U of, Ann Arbor	108
3.	Wisconsin, U of, Madison	105
4.	Illinois, U of, Urbana	101
5.	Pennsylvania, U of	99

6.	Minnesota, U of, Twin Cities	98
7.	New York, City U of, Graduate School, U Center	96
8.	California, U of, Berkeley	95
9.	Ohio State U, Columbus	93
10.	Maryland, U of, College Park	86
*11.	Michigan State U	86
12.	California, U of, Los Angeles	84
*13.	Columbia U (NY)	84
14.	Texas, U of, Austin	83
15.	Cornell U (NY)	80
16.	Indiana U, Bloomington	77
17.	Texas A&M U	83
18.	California School of Professional Psychology, San Diego	72
19.	Harvard U (MA)	71
20.	Yale U (CT)	69
21.	Temple U (PA)	68
22.	Stanford U (CA)	63
23.	Southern California, U of	62
*24.	Virginia, U of	62
*25.	Washington, U of	62
26.	North Carolina, U of, Chapel Hill	61
27.	California School of Professional Psychology, Alameda	59
*28.	Kansas, U of	59
29.	New York U	58
*30.	Northwestern U (IL)	58

*See Author's Note, p. xxv.

Source: Data compiled from information in *1996 Survey of Earned Doctorates*, National Research Council, Washington, DC.

Colleges Granting the Most Doctorates in History

These are the colleges that awarded the most research doctorates from July 1995 to June 1996 in history.

1.	Wisconsin, U of, Madison	36
2.	Yale U (CT)	33

Colleges Granting the Most Doctorates in History (continued)

3.	California, U of, Los Angeles	32
*4.	Harvard U (MA)	32
5.	Chicago, U of (IL)	27
6.	Columbia U (NY)	24
7.	Indiana U, Bloomington	23
8.	California, U of, Berkeley	22
9.	Minnesota, U of, Twin Cities	20
10.	Michigan, U of, Ann Arbor	16
*11.	Pennsylvania, U of	16
*12.	Stanford U (CA)	16
13.	Florida State U	15
*14.	Rutgers U (NJ)	15
*15.	Virginia, U of	15
16.	Princeton U (NJ)	14
17.	Cornell U (NY)	13
18.	North Carolina, U of, Chapel Hill	12
*19.	Ohio State U, Columbus	12
20.	Iowa, U of	11
21.	Illinois, U of, Urbana	10
*22.	Texas, U of, Austin	10

*See Author's Note, p. xxv.

Source: Data compiled from information in *1996 Survey of Earned Doctorates*, National Research Council, Washington, DC.

Colleges Awarding the Most Doctorates in the Life Sciences

These are colleges that awarded the most research doctorates from July 1995 to June 1996 in these fields: biological sciences (including biochemistry), health sciences, and agricultural sciences.

1.	California, U of, Davis	179
*2.	Minnesota, U of, Twin Cities	179
3.	Wisconsin, U of, Madison	171
4.	California, U of, Berkeley	161
5.	Cornell U (NY)	160

6.	Johns Hopkins U (MD)	154
7.	Harvard U (MA)	145
8.	Ohio State U, Columbus	143
9.	Texas A&M U	141
10.	Florida, U of	130
11.	Illinois, U of, Urbana	128
12.	North Carolina, U of, Chapel Hill	124
13.	Michigan State U	122
14.	California, U of, Los Angeles	118
15.	Purdue U (IN)	116
16.	Washington, U of	113
17.	Georgia, U of	112
18.	Michigan, U of, Ann Arbor	108
19.	Houston, U of, System	98
*20.	North Carolina State U	98
21.	Oregon State U	96
22.	Iowa State U	95
23.	Iowa, U of	91
24.	Texas, U of, Austin	87
25.	Pennsylvania State U, University Park	83
26.	Yale U (CT)	81
27.	Alabama, U of, Tuscaloosa	79
28.	Columbia U (NY)	77
29.	Kentucky, U of	76
*30.	Pennsylvania, U of	76
*31.	Rutgers U (NJ)	76

*See Author's Note, p. xxv.

Source: Data compiled from information in *1996 Survey of Earned Doctorates*, National Research Council, Washington, DC.

Colleges Granting the Most Doctorates in the Physical Sciences

These are the colleges that awarded the most research doctorates from July 1995 to June 1996 in these fields: physics and astronomy; chemistry; earth, atmospheric, and marine sciences; mathematics; and computer sciences.

1.	California, U of, Berkeley	159
2.	Massachusetts Institute of Technology	150
3.	Illinois, U of, Urbana	140
4.	Wisconsin, U of, Madison	122
5.	Stanford U (CA)	121
6.	Texas, U of, Austin	119
7.	Purdue U (IN)	108
*8.	Texas A&M U	108
9.	California, U of, Los Angeles	105
*10.	Maryland, U of, College Park	105
11.	Cornell U (NY)	101
12.	Minnesota, U of, Twin Cities	100
13.	Washington, U of	97
14.	Michigan, U of, Ann Arbor	94
15.	Arizona, U of	92
16.	Colorado, U of	86
17.	Columbia U (NY)	82
*18.	Princeton U (NJ)	82
19.	Michigan State U	81
20.	New York, State U of, Stony Brook	80
21.	Rutgers U (NJ)	79
22.	Pennsylvania, U of	78
23.	Chicago, U of (IL)	77
24.	California Institute of Technology	75
25.	Harvard U (MA)	73
26.	California, U of, San Diego	70
27.	Rochester, U of (NY)	68
28.	Florida, U of	66
*29.	Northwestern U (IL)	66
30.	California, U of, Davis	65

*See Author's Note, p. xxv.

Source: Data compiled from information in *1996 Survey of Earned Doctorates*, National Research Council, Washington, DC.

Colleges Granting the Most Doctorates in Engineering

These are colleges that awarded the most research doctorates from July 1995 to June 1996 in the field of engineering.

1.	Massachusetts Institute of Technology	234
2.	Stanford U (CA)	193
3.	Michigan, U of, Ann Arbor	189
4.	California, U of, Berkeley	182
5.	Texas, U of, Austin	181
6.	Georgia Institute of Technology	167
7.	Purdue U (IN)	158
8.	Illinois, U of, Urbana	148
9.	Pennsylvania State U, University Park	144
10.	Texas A&M U	142
11.	Minnesota, U of, Twin Cities	118
12.	Wisconsin, U of, Madison	112
13.	Ohio State U, Columbus	111
14.	North Carolina State U	109
15.	Virginia Polytechnic Institute and State U	96
16.	Carnegie Mellon U (PA)	91
*17.	Cornell U (NY)	91
*18.	Northwestern U (IL)	91
19.	Washington, U of	90
20.	Rensselaer Polytechnic Institute (NY)	85
21.	Maryland, U of, College Park	83
22.	Colorado, U of	78
*23.	Southern California, U of	78
24.	California, U of, Davis	76
*25.	Florida, U of	76
26.	Rutgers U (NJ)	73
27.	Arizona State U	65
*28.	Arizona, U of	65
29.	California, U of, Los Angeles	64
30.	California Institute of Technology	62
*31.	Iowa State U	62

*See Author's Note, p. xxv.

Source: Data compiled from information in *1996 Survey of Earned Doctorates*, National Research Council, Washington, DC.

THE BUSINESS WORLD

Schools from which Top Business Executives Received Their Degrees

These are the undergraduate institutions that have graduated the largest number of business executives, such as presidents, vice presidents, and directors of the nation's leading corporations.

1. New York, City U of
2. Yale U (CT)
3. Harvard U (MA)
4. Wisconsin, U of, Madison
5. California, U of (no specific campus listed)
6. Princeton U (NJ)
7. Pennsylvania, U of
8. Michigan, U of, Ann Arbor
9. Illinois, U of, Urbana
10. New York U
11. Cornell U (NY)
12. Minnesota, U of, Twin Cities

Source: *Standard & Poor's Executive/College Survey* (New York: The Standard & Poor's Register of Corporations, Directors, and Executives and Compmark Data Services, 1990), 5.

Top Colleges Attended by Business Leaders

The following is a ranking of schools based on the number of present and past chief executive officers of Fortune 500 and Service 500 companies who graduated from these institutions. Over 1,500 executives were surveyed.

1.	Yale U (CT)	43
2.	Princeton U (NJ)	32
3.	Harvard U (MA)	25
4.	Northwestern U (IL)	19
5.	Cornell U (NY)	17
6.	Columbia U (NY)	15
*7.	Stanford U (CA)	15
8.	Michigan, U of, Ann Arbor	13
9.	Dartmouth C (NH)	12
10.	Illinois, U of, Urbana	11
*11.	Missouri, U of, Columbia	11
*12.	Texas, U of, Austin	11
13.	Purdue U (IN)	10
14.	Massachusetts Institute of Technology	9
*15.	Wisconsin, U of, Madison	9
16.	Ohio State U, Columbus	8
*17.	Pennsylvania, U of	8
18.	Auburn U (AL)	7
*19.	Duke U (NC)	7
*20.	New York, City U of, City C	7
*21.	Virginia, U of	7

*See Author's Note, p. xxv.

Source: Susan Caminiti, "Where the CEOs Went to College," *Fortune*, June 18, 1990,

Top Twenty Colleges Attended by Business Leaders (Based on Size of College)

The list ranks schools based on the number of present and past CEOs who graduated from a particular institution compared to the size of that school. Over 1,500 executives from Fortune 500 and Service 500 companies were surveyed.

1. Yale U (CT)
2. Princeton U (NJ)
3. Washington and Lee U (VA)
4. Harvard U (MA)
5. Dartmouth C (NH)
6. Northwestern U (IL)
7. Davidson C (NC)
8. Wesleyan U (CT)
9. Amherst C (MA)
10. Columbia U (NY)
11. DePauw U (IN)
12. Holy Cross, C of the (MA)
13. Williams C (MA)
14. Rice U (TX)
15. Stanford U (CA)
16. Massachusetts Institute of Technology
17. Xavier U (OH)
18. Cornell U (NY)
19. Duke U (NC)
20. Colgate U (NY)

Source: Susan Caminiti, "Where the CEOs Went to College," *Fortune*, June 18, 1990,

CAREER POTPOURRI

Colleges That Offer a Fast Track to a Career

These schools have either many career-oriented majors or a particularly career-focused student body.

Alaska, U of, Anchorage
Albion C (MI)
Alfred U (NY)
Alma C (MI)
Aquinas C (MI)
Auburn U (AL)
Babson C (MA)
Boise State U (ID)
Bradford C (MA)
Bradley U (IL)
Brandeis U (MA)
Bucknell U (PA)
Catholic U (DC)
Carnegie Mellon U (PA)
Centenary C (NJ)
Cincinnati, U of (OH)
Claremont McKenna C (CA)
Clarkson C (NE)
Cornell U (NY)
Davidson C (NC)
DePauw U (IN)
Drexel U (PA)
Elizabethtown C (PA)
Emory U (GA)
Endicott C (MA)
Fairleigh Dickinson U (NJ)
Florida State U
Fordham U (NY)
George Washington U (DC)
Hawaii Pacific U
Hofstra U (NY)
Idaho State U
Ithaca C (NY)
Johns Hopkins U (MD)
Manhattanville C (NY)
Marquette U (WI)
Merrimack C (MA)
Mt. St. Mary's C (CA)
Muhlenberg C (PA)
Nebraska, U of, Lincoln
New York Institute of Technology
Notre Dame, U of (IN)
Ohio Wesleyan U
Otterbein C (OH)
Pacific U (OR)
Pennsylvania, U of
Pine Manor C (MA)

Colleges That Offer a Fast Track to a Career (continued)

Quinnipiac C (CT)
Rochester Institute of Technology (NY)
Russell Sage C (NY)
Simmons C (MA)
Spelman C (GA)
Union C (NY)
Wabash C (IN)
Washington and Jefferson C (PA)
Widener U (PA)
Wisconsin, U of, Stout

The Experts' Choice: Career-Oriented Colleges

Babson C (MA)
Bentley C (MA)
Boston U (MA)
Carnegie Mellon U (PA)
Cornell U (NY)
Denver, U of (CO)
Drexel U (PA)
Embry-Riddle Aeronautical U (FL)
Fashion Institute of Technology (NY)
Franklin and Marshall C (PA)
Georgia Institute of Technology
Goucher C (MD)
Hollins C (VA)
Ithaca C (NY)
Johnson and Wales U (RI)
Northeastern U (MA)
Simmons C (MA)
Syracuse U (NY)

Outstanding Culinary Programs

Academy of Culinary Arts (NJ)
Baltimore International Culinary C (MD)
California Culinary Institute
Cooking School of the Rockies (CO)
Culinary Institute of America (NY)
Florida Culinary Institute
French Culinary Institute (NY)
Johnson and Wales U (RI)
Kendall C (IL)
L'Académie de Cuisine (MD)
New England Culinary Institute (VT)
New York City Technical C
New York Institute of Technology
New York Restaurant School
Paul Smith's C (NY)
Pennsylvania Institute of Culinary Arts

The Best Schools for Golf-Related Careers

These colleges have programs that prepare students to be golf professionals, to run a golf pro shop or country club, and related careers.

Ferris State U (MI)
Golf Academy of the South (Orlando, FL)
Mississippi State U
National Institute of Golf Management (Wheeling, WV)
New Mexico State U
Pennsylvania State U, University Park
Professional Golfers Career C (Temecula, CA)
San Diego Golf Academy (CA)

ATHLETICS

MAJOR ATHLETIC CONFERENCES

The Atlantic Coast Conference

Clemson U (SC)
Duke U (NC)
Florida State U
Georgia Institute of Technology
Maryland, U of, College Park
North Carolina State U
North Carolina, U of, Chapel Hill
Virginia, U of
Wake Forest U (NC)

Atlantic 10

Boston U (MA)
Connecticut, U of (football only)
Delaware, U of
James Madison U (VA)
Maine, U of
Massachusetts, U of, Amherst
New Hampshire, U of
Northeastern U (MA)
Richmond, U of (VA)
Rhode Island, U of
Villanova U (PA)
William and Mary, C of (VA)

The Big East

Boston C (MA)
Connecticut, U of
Georgetown U (DC)
Miami, U of (FL)
Pittsburgh, U of (PA)
Providence C (RI)
Rutgers U (NJ) (football only)
St. John's U (NY)
Seton Hall U (NJ)
Syracuse U (NY)
Temple U (PA) (football only)

The Big East (continued)

Villanova U (PA)
Virginia Tech
(football only)
West Virginia U
(football only)

Big Sky

California State U, Northridge
California State U, Sacramento
Eastern Washington U
Idaho State U
Montana State U
Montana, U of
Northern Arizona U
Portland State U (OR)
Weber State U (UT)

The Big Ten

Illinois, U of, Urbana
Indiana U, Bloomington
Iowa, U of
Michigan State U
Michigan, U of, Ann Arbor
Minnesota, U of, Twin Cities
Northwestern U (IL)
Ohio State U, Columbus
Pennsylvania State U,
University Park
Purdue U (IN)
Wisconsin, U of, Madison

Big 12

Baylor U (TX)
Colorado, U of
Iowa State U
Kansas State U
Kansas, U of
Missouri, U of, Columbia
Nebraska, U of, Lincoln
Oklahoma State U
Oklahoma U of
Texas A&M U
Texas Tech U
Texas, U of, Austin

Conference USA

Cincinnati, U of (OH)
East Carolina U (NC)
Houston, U of (TX)
Louisville, U of (KY)
Memphis, U of (TN)
Southern Mississippi, U of
Tulane U (LA)

The Ivy League

Brown U (RI)
Columbia U (NY)
Cornell U (NY)
Dartmouth C (NH)
Harvard U (MA)
Pennsylvania, U of
Princeton U (NJ)
Yale U (CT)

Mid-American Conference

Akron, U of (OH)
Ball State U (IN)
Bowling Green State U (OH)
Central Michigan U
Eastern Michigan U
Kent State U (OH)
Marshall U (WV)
Miami U (OH)
Northern Illinois U
Ohio U
Toledo, U of (OH)
Western Michigan U

The Pacific-10

Arizona State U
Arizona, U of
California, U of, Berkeley
California, U of, Los Angeles
Oregon State U
Oregon, U of
Southern California, U of
Stanford U (CA)
Washington State U
Washington, U of

Patriot League

Bucknell U (PA)
Colgate U (NY)
Fordham U (NY)
Holy Cross, C of the (MA)
Lafayette C (PA)
Lehigh U (PA)
Towson State U (MD)

The Southeastern Conference

Alabama, U of, Tuscaloosa
Arkansas, U of, Fayetteville
Auburn U (AL)
Florida, U of
Georgia, U of
Kentucky, U of
Louisiana State U, Baton Rouge
Mississippi State U
Mississippi, U of
South Carolina, U of, Columbia
Tennessee, U of, Knoxville
Vanderbilt U (TN)

Southwestern Athletic Conference

Alabama State U
Alcorn State U (MS)
Arkansas, U of, Pine Bluff
Grambling State U (LA)
Jackson State U (MS)
Mississippi Valley State U
Prairie View A&M U (TX)
Southern U A&M (LA)
Texas Southern U

Western Athletic Conference

Brigham Young U (UT)
California State U, Fresno
California State U, San Diego
California State U, San Jose
Colorado State U
Hawaii, U of
Nevada, U of, Las Vegas
New Mexico, U of
Rice U (TX)
Southern Methodist U (TX)
Texas Christian U
Texas, U of, El Paso
Tulsa, U of (OK)
U.S. Air Force Academy (CO)
Utah, U of
Wyoming, U of

Major Independents

Alabama, U of, Birmingham
Arkansas State U
Central Florida U
Louisiana Tech U
Notre Dame, U of (IN)
Northeast Louisiana State U
Southwestern Louisiana, U of
U.S. Military Academy (NY)
U.S. Naval Academy (MD)

THE BEST IN SPORTS

Listed in this section are schools with (1) a recent championship season (within the last five years or so) or (2) a strong team or program (including overall strength, particularly outstanding players, a winning coach, or a high level of funding). Colleges listed are from all levels of play (from club to varsity) and from a number of conferences (such as the National Collegiate Athletic Association, the National Association of Intercollegiate Athletics, and the National Christian College Athletic Association).

"Strong" teams are inherently changeable depending on current players, the coach, and financial support from the college or university.

Colleges listed under "Recent Championships" for a particular sport are not repeated in the "Strong Program" section.

ARCHERY

Colleges with Strong Archery Programs

Arizona State U
James Madison U (VA)
Miami U (OH)
Purdue U (IN)
Texas A&M U

BADMINTON

Colleges with Strong Badminton Programs

Academy of the New Church (PA)
Alaska, U of, Fairbanks
Arizona State U
California State U, Long Beach
California State U, San Diego
California State U, San Jose
California, U of, Berkeley
California, U of, Davis
California, U of, Los Angeles
Duke U (NC)
George Mason U (VA)
George Washington U (DC)
Howard U (DC)
Northern Michigan U
Princeton U (NJ)
Southern California, U of
Swarthmore C (PA)
Texas A&M

BASEBALL (MEN)

College Baseball Title Holders

The schools are ranked by the number of times they won the College World Series.

Southern California, U of	11
Arizona State U	5
Louisiana State U, Baton Rouge	4
Texas, U of, Austin	4
Minnesota, U of, Twin Cities	3

Source: National Collegiate Athletic Association, Overland Park, KS.

Colleges with Recent Baseball Championships

Anderson C (SC)
Bellevue C (NE)
Brewton-Parker C (GA)
California State U, Chico
California State U, Fullerton
Central Missouri State U
Florida Southern U
Kennesaw State C (GA)
La Verne, U of (CA)
Lewis and Clark C (OR)
Louisiana State U, Baton Rouge
Montclair State U (NJ)
Mt. Vernon Nazarene C (OH)
Oklahoma, U of
St. Francis C (IN)
Southern Maine, U of
Spring Arbor C (MI)
Tampa, U of (FL)
William Paterson C (NJ)
Wisconsin, U of, Oshkosh

Colleges with Strong Baseball Programs

Amherst C (MA)
Arizona State U
Arizona, U of
Arkansas, U of
Auburn U (AL)
Birmingham-Southern C (AL)
California State U, Fresno
California State U, Fullerton
California State U, Long Beach
Clemson U (SC)
Creighton U (NE)
Florida State U (FL)
Florida, U of
Georgia Institute of Technology
Indiana State U
John A. Logan C (IL)
Loyola Marymount U (CA)
Miami U (OH)
Miami, U of (FL)
Michigan, U of, Ann Arbor
North Carolina State U
North Carolina, U of, Chapel Hill
Oklahoma City U
Oklahoma State U
Oklahoma, U of
Pepperdine U (CA)
Ramapo C (NJ)
Richmond, U of (VA)
St. Olaf C (MN)
South Alabama, U of
Southern California, U of
Southern U (LA)
Stanford U (CA)
Texas A&M U
Texas, U of, Arlington
Texas, U of, Austin
Washington State U
Western Arizona U
Wichita State U (KS)

BASKETBALL

All Time Top Ten Men's College Basketball Teams

Consists of the composite Associated Press Top 20 teams, seasons 1948–49 to 1995–96, based on final rankings for each year.

1. Kentucky, U of
2. North Carolina, U of, Chapel Hill
3. California, U of, Los Angeles
4. Duke U (NC)
5. Indiana U
6. Kansas, U of
7. Louisville, U of (KY)
8. Notre Dame, U of (IN)
9. Michigan, U of, Ann Arbor
10. Cincinnati, U of (OH)

Source: *1998 ESPN Information Please® Almanac*, copyright © 1998 Information Please LLC. All rights reserved.

Top Ten Men's Basketball Teams in Tournament Appearances

Number of appearances (through 1996) listed after the name of the university.

1.	Kentucky, U of	38
2.	California, U of, Los Angeles	32
3.	North Carolina, U of, Chapel Hill	30
4.	Louisville, U of (KY)	26
5.	Indiana U, Bloomington	25
*6.	Kansas, U of	25
7.	Notre Dame, U of (IN)	24
8.	St. John's U (NY)	23
*9.	Syracuse U (NY)	23
*10.	Villanova U (PA)	23

*See Author's Note, p. xxv.

Source: *1998 ESPN Information Please® Almanac*, copyright © 1998 Information Please LLC. All rights reserved.

Ten Most Winning Division I Women's College Basketball Teams

Consists of teams with highest percentages of winning games through the 1996 season.

1. Louisiana Tech U
2. Tennessee, U of, Knoxville
3. Texas, U of, Austin
4. Mt. St. Mary's C (MD)
5. Montana, U of
6. Stephen F. Austin State U (TX)
7. California State U, Long Beach
8. Mississippi, U of
9. North Carolina State U
10. Virginia, U of

Source: *1998 ESPN Information Please® Almanac*, copyright © 1998 Information Please LLC. All rights reserved.

Colleges with Recent Basketball Championships

Arizona, U of (men)
Arkansas Tech U (women)
Arkansas, U of (men)
Bethel C (KS) (men)
Birmingham-Southern U (AL) (men)
California State, U, Bakersfield (men)
California, U of, Los Angeles (men)
Capital U (OH) (women)
Central Bible C (MO) (men)
Central C (IA) (women)
Christian Heritage C (CA) (men)
Connecticut, U of (women)
Fort Hays State U (KS) (men)
Hawaii Pacific U (men)
Illinois Wesleyan U (men)
Indiana Wesleyan U (men)
Kentucky Christian C (men)
Kentucky, U of (men)
Lebanon Valley C (PA) (men)
Lee C (TX) (men)
LIFE U (GA) (men)
Malone C (OH) (men)
Montana State U, Northern (women)
New York U (women)
North Carolina, U of, Chapel Hill (men, women)
North Dakota State U (women)
Northern State U (SD) (women)
Northwest Nazarene C (ID) (women)
Ohio Northern U (men)
Oklahoma City C (men)
Rowan C (NJ) (men)
Southern Indiana, U of (men)
Southern Nazarene U (OK) (women)
Tennessee, U of, Knoxville (women)
Texas Tech U (women)
Western Oregon U (women)
Wisconsin, U of, Platteville (men, women)

Colleges with Strong Basketball Programs

Alabama, U of, Tuscaloosa (women)
Allegheny C (PA) (women)
Arizona, U of (men)
Arkansas, U of, Fayetteville (men, women)
Auburn U (AL) (men, women)
Baptist Bible C (MO) (men)
Birmingham-Southern C (AL) (men)
Bucknell U (PA) (men)
California State U, Fresno (men)
California State U, Stanislaus (women)
California, U of, Berkeley (men)
California, U of, Los Angeles (men, women)
California, U of, San Diego (men)
Charleston, C of (SC) (men)
Christian Heritage C (CA) (men)
Cincinnati, U of (OH) (men)
Clark U (MA) (men)
Clemson U (SC) (men)
Colorado, U of (women)
Connecticut, U of (men, women)
Creighton U (NE) (men, women)
Dartmouth C (NH) (women)
DePaul U (IL) (women)
Duke U (NC) (men, women)
Eastern Michigan U (men)
Florida State U (men)
Florida, U of (men, women)
Franklin and Marshall C (PA) (men)
George Washington U (DC) (men, women)
Georgia Institute of Technology (men)
Georgia, U of (men, women)
Gonzaga U (WA) (men)
Guilford C (NC) (men)
Hamilton C (NY) (men)
Hollins C (VA) (women)
Illinois, U of, Urbana (men)
Indiana, U of, Bloomington (men)
Iowa State U (men)
Iowa, U of (men, women)
James Madison U (VA) (men, women)
Kansas, U of (men, women)
Kentucky, U of (men)
Loras C (IA) (men)
Louisiana State U, Baton Rouge (women)
Louisiana Tech U (women)
Maine, U of, Orono (women)
Marquette U (WI) (men)
Maryland, U of, College Park (men, women)
Massachusetts, U of, Amherst (men)
Memphis, U of (TN) (men)
Miami, U of (FL) (women)
Michigan State U (men)
Minnesota, U of, Twin Cities (men)
Mississippi State U (men)
Mississippi, U of (men, women)
Missouri, U of, Columbia (men, women)
Montana, U of (men, women)
Nevada, U of, Las Vegas (men)
New Mexico, U of (men)
North Carolina State U (men)
North Carolina, U of, Chapel Hill (men, women)

Colleges with Strong Basketball Programs (continued)

North Carolina, U of, Charlotte (men)
Northeastern U (MA) (men)
Notre Dame, U of (IN) (women)
Ohio State U, Columbus (men, women)
Ohio U (men)
Oklahoma State U (men)
Oklahoma, U of (men)
Old Dominion U (VA) (women)
Oregon, U of (men)
Pennsylvania State U, University Park (women)
Pennsylvania, U of (men)
Pine Manor C (MA) (women)
Princeton U (NJ) (men)
Purdue U (IN) (men, women)
Randolph-Macon C (VA) (men)
Rhode Island, U of (men, women)
Rollins C (FL) (men)
Rutgers U (NJ) (women)
St. Joseph's U (PA) (men)
Santa Clara U (CA) (women)
Slippery Rock U (PA) (women)
South Carolina, U of, Coastal (men)
Southern California, U of (women)
Southwest Missouri State U (women)
Stanford U (CA) (men, women)
Stephen F. Austin State U (TX)(women)
Syracuse U (NY) (men)
Temple U (PA) (men)
Tennessee, U of (women)
Texas Tech U (men, women)
Texas, U of, Austin (men, women)
Texas, U of, El Paso (men)
Transylvania U (KY) (men)
Trinity C (CT) (men)
Tulane U (LA) (men)
Utah, U of (men)
Vanderbilt U (TN) (men, women)
Vermont, U of (women)
Villanova U (PA) (men)
Virginia State U (women)
Virginia, U of (women)
Wake Forest U (NC) (men)
Washington, U of (women)
Western Kentucky U (women)
Whitman C (WA) (women)
Wisconsin, U of, Green Bay (men)
Wittenberg U (OH) (men)
Xavier U (OH) (men)

BOWLING

Colleges with Strong Bowling Programs

Arizona State U (men)
California State U, Fresno (women)
California State U, Sacramento (women)
California State U, San Jose (men)
Cincinnati, U of (OH) (men)
Coppin State C (MD) (men, women)
Erie Community C (NY) (women)
Florida, U of (men, women)
Illinois State U (women)
Michigan State U (women)
Nebraska, U of, Lincoln (men, women)
Ohio State U, Columbus (men, women)
Sacred Heart U (CT) (men, women)
Saginaw Valley State U (MI) (men)
Southwest Missouri State U (women)
Vincennes U (IN) (men)
West Texas State U (men, women)
West Virginia U (men)
Wichita State U (KS) (men, women)
William Paterson C (NJ) (men, women)

BOXING

Colleges with Strong Boxing Programs

Arizona, U of
Boston C (MA)
California, U of, Berkeley
Central Connecticut State U
Citadel, The (SC)
Iowa State U
Kentucky, U of
Lock Haven U (PA)
Massachusetts Institute of Technology
Nevada, U of, Reno
Ohio U, Athens
Pennsylvania State U
Santa Clara U (CA)
Shippensburg U (PA)
U.S. Air Force Academy (CO)
U.S. Military Academy (NY)
U.S. Naval Academy (MD)
Virginia Military Institute
Westchester Community C (NY)
Westfield State C (MA)
Xavier U (OH)

CANOE

Colleges with Strong Canoe Programs

California State U, Humboldt
Dartmouth C (NH)
Goddard C (VT)
Grinnell C (IA)
South, U of the (TN)
Warren Wilson C (NC)
Western Piedmont Community C (NC)

CREW

Colleges with Strong Crew Programs

Boston U (MA) (women)
Brown U (RI) (men, women)
California, U of, Berkeley (men)
California, U of, Davis (women)
California, U of, Santa Barbara (men, women)
Connecticut C (men, women)
Cornell U (NY) (men, women)
Dartmouth C (NH) (men)
Florida Institute of Technology (men)
Georgetown U (DC) (women)
Harvard U (MA) (men)
Iowa, U of (women)
LaSalle U (PA) (men)
Marietta C (OH) (men)
Massachusetts, U of, Amherst (men)
Mills C (CA) (women)
Northeastern U (MA) (men)
Pennsylvania, U of (men)
Princeton U (NJ) (men, women)
Santa Clara U (CA) (women)
Skidmore C (NY) (women)
Smith C (MA) (women)
Stanford U (CA) (men, women)
Temple U (PA) (men, women)
U.S. Coast Guard Academy (CT) (men)
U.S. Naval Academy (MD) (men, women)
Virginia, U of (men, women)
Washington, U of (men, women)
Wesleyan U (CT) (men, women)
Williams C (MA) (men)
Wisconsin, U of, Madison (men, women)
Yale U (CT) (men, women)

CROSS-COUNTRY

Colleges with Recent Cross-Country Championships

Adams State C (CO) (men, women)
Arkansas, U of, Fayetteville (men)
California Polytechnic State U, San Luis Obispo (women)
Edinboro U (PA) (men)
Iowa State U (men)
Lubbock Christian U (TX) (men)
Malone C (OH) (men, women)
Massachusetts, U of, Lowell (men)
Michigan State U (men)
New York, State U of, C at Cortland (women)
North Central C (IL) (men)
Puget Sound, U of (WA) (women)
Rochester, U of (NY) (men)
Simon Fraser U (Canada) (women)
South Dakota State U (men)
Texas, U of, El Paso (men)
Villanova U (PA) (women)
Vincennes U (IN) (women)
Western State C (CO) (women)
Wisconsin, U of, Madison (men)
Wisconsin, U of, Oshkosh (men, women)

Colleges with Strong Cross-Country Programs

Adams State C (CO) (men, women)
Arizona, U of (men)
Arkansas, U of (women)
Bowling Green State U (OH) (men, women)
Brevard C (NC) (men)
Brigham Young U (UT) (men)
Bucknell U (PA) (men, women)
Colorado, U of (men)
Eastern Michigan U (men, women)
Illinois State U (men, women)
Indiana U, Bloomington (men)
Iowa State U (men)
Lehigh U (PA) (men, women)
Malone C (OH) (women)
Marshall U (WV) (men, women)
Minnesota, U of, Twin Cities (men, women)
North Carolina State U (men, women)
Oberlin C (OH) (women)
Ohio U (women)
Oregon, U of (men, women)

Colleges with Strong Cross-Country Programs (continued)

Pennsylvania State U, University Park (men)
Smith C (MA) (women)
South Florida, U of (men, women)
Southern Illinois U, Carbondale (men, women)
Stanford U (CA) (men, women)
Texas, U of, Austin (women)
Villanova U (PA) (men, women)
Wake Forest U (NC) (men)
West Virginia, U of (men, women)
William and Mary, C of (VA) (women)
Williams C (MA) (men)
Wisconsin, U of, La Crosse (men, women)

EQUESTRIENNE/EQUESTRIAN

Colleges with Strong Equestrienne/Equestrian Programs

Alfred U (NY)
Averett C (VA)
Boston U (MA)
California Polytechnic State U, Pomona
California Polytechnic State U, San Luis Obispo
California, U of, Davis
Cazenovia C (NY)
Centenary C (NJ)
Colorado State U
Fairleigh Dickinson U (NJ)
Ferrum C (VA)
Findlay, U of (OH)
Georgia, U of
Goucher C (MD)
Harcum C (PA)
Hartwick C (NY)
Hollins C (VA)
Johnson and Wales U (RI)
Kansas State U
Lafayette C (PA)
Mary Washington C (VA)
Marymount C (NY)
Massachusetts, U of, Amherst
Midway C (KY)
Morehead State U (KY)
Mt. Holyoke C (MA)
Mt. Ida C (MA)
New York, State U of, C at Cobleskill
New York, State U of, C at Morrisville
Otterbein C (OH)
Pace U (NY)
Randolph-Macon Woman's C (VA)
Roger Williams C (RI)
St. Andrews Presbyterian C (NC)
St. Lawrence U (NY)
St. Mary-of-the-Woods C (IN)
Skidmore C (NY)
Smith C (MA)
South, U of the (TN)
Southern Illinois U, Carbondale
Stephens C (MO)
Sweet Briar C (VA)
Teikyo Post U (CT)
Truman State U (MO)
Virginia Intermont C
Wesleyan C (GA)
William Woods C (MO)
Wilson C (PA)

FENCING

Colleges with Strong Fencing Programs

California State U, Long Beach (men, women)
Cleveland State U (OH) (men, women)
Columbia U/Barnard C (NY) (men, women)
Cornell U (NY) (men, women)
Detroit Mercy, U of (MI) (men, women)
Duke U (NC) (men, women)
Fairleigh Dickinson U (NJ) (men, women)
Ferris State U (MI) (men, women)
Hollins C (VA) (women)
Illinois, U of, Urbana (men, women)
Johns Hopkins U (MD) (women)
Lawrence U (WI) (men, women)
Massachusetts Institute of Technology (men)
Michigan State U (men, women)
Michigan, U of, Ann Arbor (men, women)
Minnesota, U of, Twin Cities (men, women)
New York U (women)
North Carolina, U of, Chapel Hill (men, women)
Northwestern U (IL) (men, women)
Notre Dame, U of (IN) (men, women)
Ohio State U, Columbus (men, women)
Pennsylvania State U, University Park (men, women)
Purdue U (IN) (men, women)
Stanford U (CA) (men, women)
Temple U (PA) (women)
Tri-State U (IN) (men, women)
Wayne State U (MI) (men, women)

FIELD HOCKEY (WOMEN)

Colleges with Recent Field Hockey Championships

James Madison U (VA)
Lock Haven U (PA)
Maryland U of, College Park
New Jersey, C of
New York, State U of, C at Cortland
North Carolina, U of, Chapel Hill
Old Dominion U (VA)
Trenton State C (NJ)

Colleges with Strong Field Hockey Programs

Bloomsburg U (PA)
Bowdoin C (ME)
Bridgewater C (VA)
Bridgewater State C (MA)
Clark U (MA)
Colgate U (NY)
Connecticut, U of
Delaware, U of
Denison U (OH)
Denver, U of (CO)
Dickinson C (PA)
Drew U (NJ)
Elizabethtown C (PA)
Franklin and Marshall C (PA)
Gettysburg C (PA)
Iowa State U
Iowa, U of
Ithaca C (NY)
Johns Hopkins U (MD)
Keene State C (NH)
Lafayette C (PA)
Lehigh U (PA)
Lynchburg C (VA)
Massachusetts, U of, Amherst
Messiah C (PA)
Muhlenberg C (PA)
New Hampshire, U of
North Carolina, U of, Chapel Hill
Northwestern U (IL)
Pennsylvania State U, University Park
Pennsylvania, U of
Plymouth State C (NH)
Salem State C (MA)
Salisbury State U (MD)
Southern Maine, U of
Temple U (PA)
Trinity C (CT)
Ursinus C (PA)
Virginia, U of
William Smith C (NY)

FOOTBALL (MEN)

Ten All-Time Most Winning College Football Teams

This list includes colleges in Division I-A, through the 1996 season, and including bowl games.

1. Notre Dame, U of (IN)
2. Michigan, U of, Ann Arbor
3. Alabama, U of, Tuscaloosa
4. Oklahoma, U of
5. Texas, U of, Austin
6. Ohio State U, Columbus
7. Southern California, U of
8. Nebraska, U of, Lincoln
9. Pennsylvania State U, University Park
10. Tennessee, U of

Source: *1998 ESPN Information Please® Almanac*, copyright © 1998 Information Please LLC. All rights reserved.

The Longest Football Winning Streaks

This is a list of number of wins (including bowl games) for colleges in NCAA Division I.

1.	Oklahoma, U of	47
2.	Washington, U of	39
3.	Yale U (CT) (two separate streaks of 37 games each)	37
4.	Toledo, U of (OH)	35
5.	Pennsylvania, U of	34
6.	Oklahoma, U of	31
*7.	Pennsylvania, U of	31
*8.	Pittsburgh, U of (PA)	31
9.	Texas, U of, Austin	30
10.	Miami, U of (FL)	29
*11.	Michigan, U of, Ann Arbor	29
12.	Alabama, U of, Tuscaloosa	28
*13.	Michigan State U	28
*14.	Oklahoma, U of	28

*See Author's Note, p. xxv.

Source: *1998 ESPN Information Please® Almanac*, copyright © 1998 Information Please LLC.

The Five Longest Football Losing Streaks

This list includes only NCAA Division I schools.

1.	Columbia U (NY)	44
2.	Northwestern U (IL)	34
3.	Kansas State U	28
*4.	Virginia, U of	28
5.	Eastern Michigan U	27

*See Author's Note, p. xxv.

Source: *1998 ESPN Information Please® Almanac*, copyright © 1998 Information Please LLC. All rights reserved.

The Twenty-five Longest College Football Rivalries

Number of games in the series is listed after the names of the colleges through the 1995 season.

1.	Lafayette C (PA) vs. Lehigh U (PA)	131
2.	Princeton U (NJ) vs. Yale U (CT)	118
3.	Harvard U (MA) vs. Yale U (CT)	112
4.	Minnesota, U of, Twin Cities, vs. Wisconsin, U of, Madison	105
*5.	Richmond U of (VA) vs. William and Mary, C of (VA)	105
6.	Kansas, U of, vs. Missouri, U of, Columbia	104
7.	Baylor U (TX) vs. Texas Christian U	102
*8.	Texas, U of, Austin, vs. Texas A&M U	102
9.	Cincinnati, U of (OH) vs. Miami U (OH)	100
10.	Auburn U (AL) vs. Georgia, U of	99
*11.	Oregon, U of, vs. Oregon State U	99
12.	California, U of, Berkeley, vs. Stanford U (CA)	98
*13.	Indiana U, Bloomington, vs. Purdue U (IN)	98
14.	U.S. Military Academy (NY) vs. U.S. Naval Academy (MD)	96
15.	Clemson U (SC) vs. South Carolina, U of, Columbia	93
*16.	Kansas, U of, vs. Kansas State U	93

*17.	Utah, U of, vs. Utah State U	93
18.	Louisiana State U, Baton Rouge, vs. Tulane U (LA)	92
*19.	Michigan, U of, Ann Arbor, vs. Ohio State U, Columbus	92
*20.	Mississippi, U of, vs. Mississippi State U	92
*21.	Pennsylvania State U, University Park, vs. Pittsburgh, U of (PA)	92
22.	Kentucky, U of, vs. Tennessee, U of, Knoxville	91
23.	Georgia, U of, vs. Georgia Institute of Technology	90
*24.	Oklahoma, U of, vs. Oklahoma State U	90
*25.	Oklahoma, U of, vs. Texas, U of Austin	90

*See Author's Note, p. xxv.

Source: *1998 ESPN Information Please® Almanac*, copyright © 1998 Information Please LLC. All rights reserved.

Colleges with Recent Football Championships

Albion C (MI)
Central State U (OH)
Florida State U
Florida, U of
Marshall U (WV)
Montana, U of
Mt. Union C (NY)
Nebraska, U of, Lincoln
North Alabama U
Northern Colorado, U of
Wisconsin, U of, La Crosse
Youngstown State U (OH)

Colleges with Strong Football Programs

Alabama State U
Alabama, U of, Tuscaloosa
Alfred U (NY)
Arizona State U
Arizona, U of
Auburn U (AL)
Augustana C (IL)
Baldwin-Wallace C (OH)
Ball State U (IN)
Boise State U (ID)
Boston C (MA)
Brigham Young U (UT)
California State U, Fresno
California State U, San Diego
California State U, San Jose
California, U of, Berkeley
California, U of, Los Angeles
Carson-Newman C (TN)
Clemson U (SC)
Colorado State U
Colorado, U of
Delaware State C
Delaware, U of
DePauw U (IN)
Dickinson C (PA)
East Carolina U (NC)
East Texas State U
Eastern Washington U
Florida State U
Gardner-Webb C (NC)
Georgia, U of
Gettysburg C (PA)
Grambling State U (LA)
Gustavus Adolphus C (MN)
Hampden-Sydney C (VA)
Hanover C (IN)
Holy Cross, C of the (MA)
Houston, U of (TX)
Idaho, U of
Iowa, U of
James Madison U (VA)
Kansas State U
Lafayette C (PA)
Linfield C (OR)
Louisiana State U, Baton Rouge
Lycoming C (PA)
Maryland, U of, College Park
Miami, U of (OH)
Michigan State U
Michigan, U of, Ann Arbor
Middle Tennessee State U
Mississippi State U
Montana, U of
Nassau Community C (NY)
North Carolina, U of, Chapel Hill
Northeastern Oklahoma A&M U
Northern Arizona U
Northern Iowa U
Northwest Mississippi Community C
Northwestern U (IL)
Notre Dame, U of (IN)
Occidental C (CA)
Ohio State U, Columbus
Oklahoma State U
Oklahoma, U of
Oregon, U of
Pasadena City C (CA)
Pennsylvania State U, University Park
Pennsylvania, U of
Pittsburgh, U of (PA)
Portland State U (OR)
Purdue U (IN)
Rice U (TX)
Richmond, U of (VA)

Ricks C (ID)
Saddleback C (CA)
St. John's U (MN)
Samford U (AL)
Simpson C (IA)
South Carolina, U of, Columbia
Southern California, U of
Southern Mississippi, U of
Stanford U (CA)
Susquehanna U (PA)
Syracuse U (NY)
Tennessee, U of, Knoxville
Texas A&M U
Texas Tech U
Texas, U of, Austin
Toledo, U of (OH)
U.S. Air Force Academy (CO)
Utah, U of
Virginia Polytechnic Institute and State U
Wabash C (IN)
Washington and Jefferson C (PA)
Washington State U
Washington, U of
William and Mary, C of (VA)
Wittenberg U (OH)
Worcester Polytechnic Institute (MA)

Golf

Colleges with Recent Golf Championships

Arizona State U (women)
Arizona, U of (men)
California State U, San Diego (men)
Columbus C (GA) (men)
Florida Southern C (men)
Florida, U of (men)
Lynn U (FL) (women)
Methodist C (NC) (men)
Oklahoma State U (men)
Pepperdine U (CA) (men)
Spring Arbor C (MI) (men)
Stanford U (CA) (men)
Tri-State U (IN) (women)

Colleges with Strong Golf Programs

Abilene Christian U (TX) (men)
Amherst C (MA) (men, women)
Arizona, U of (women)
Arkansas, U of, Fayetteville (men)
California State U, Fresno (men)
Central C (IA) (men, women)
Clemson U (SC) (men)
Colgate U (NY) (men)
Duke U (NC) (men, women)
Florida State U (men)
Florida, U of (women)
Franklin and Marshall C (PA) (men, women)
Furman U (SC) (women)
Georgia, U of (men, women)
Indianapolis, U of (IN) (men)
Kentucky, U of (women)
Knox C (IL) (men)
Loras C (IA) (women)
Miami U (OH) (men)
Mississippi State U (men, women)
Muskingum C (OH) (men)
New Mexico State U (men, women)
New Mexico, U of, Albuquerque (men, women)
Nevada, U of, Las Vegas (men)
North Carolina, U of, Chapel Hill (men, women)
Ohio State U, Columbus (men)
Oklahoma State U (women)
Pepperdine U (CA) (men)
Ramapo C (NJ) (men)
Richmond, U of (VA) (men)
St. John's U (NY) (men)
Skidmore C (NY) (men)
Slippery Rock U (PA) (men)
South Carolina, U of, Columbia (men)
Southern California, U of (men, women)
Southern Methodist U (TX) (men, women)
Stanford U (CA) (men, women)
Texas, U of, Austin (men, women)
Tulsa, U of (OK) (men, women)
Wake Forest U (NC) (men)

(See Best Schools for Golf-Related Careers, page 285.)

GYMNASTICS

Colleges with Recent Gymnastics Championships

Alabama, U of, Tuscaloosa (women)
California, U of, Berkeley (men)
California, U of, Los Angeles (women)
Georgia, U of (men, women)
Nebraska, U of, Lincoln (men)
Ohio State U (men)
Oklahoma, U of (men)
Stanford U (CA) (men)
Utah, U of (women)

Colleges with Strong Gymnastics Programs

Arizona State U (men, women)
Brigham Young U (UT) (men, women)
California State U, Fullerton (women)
California State U, San Jose (men, women)
California, U of, Berkeley (men)
California, U of, Los Angeles (women)
California, U of, Santa Barbara (men, women)
Denver, U of (CO) (women)
Florida, U of (women)
Iowa, U of (men)
Michigan, U of, Ann Arbor (women)
Minnesota, U of, Twin Cities (men, women)
Nebraska, U of, Lincoln (men)
New Mexico, U of, Albuquerque (men)
Ohio State U, Columbus (men, women)
Oklahoma, U of (women)
Oregon State U (women)
Oregon, U of (women)
Pennsylvania State U, University Park (women)
Stanford U (CA) (women)
Towson State U (MD) (women)

HANDBALL

Colleges with Strong Handball Programs

Arizona, U of
California, U of, Berkeley
Chabot C (CA)
Cincinnati, U of (OH)
Lake Forest C (IL)
Memphis State U (TN)
Montana, U of
Pacific U (OR)
Pennsylvania State U, University Park
Slippery Rock U (PA)
Southwest Missouri State U
Texas A&M U
Texas, U of, Austin
U.S. Air Force Academy (CO)
U.S. Military Academy (NY)

ICE HOCKEY (MEN)

Colleges with the Most Division I Ice Hockey Championships

1.	Michigan, U of, Ann Arbor	8
2.	North Dakota, U of	6
3.	Denver, U of (CO)	5
*4.	Wisconsin, U of, Madison	5

*See Author's Note, p. xxv.

Source: National Collegiate Athletic Association, Overland Park, KS.

Colleges with Recent Ice Hockey Championships

Alabama, U of, Huntsville
Bemidji State U (MN)
Boston U (MA)
Lake Superior State U (MI)
Maine, U of, Orono
Michigan, U of, Ann Arbor
Middlebury C (VT)
North Dakota, U of
Wisconsin, U of, River Falls
Wisconsin, U of, Stevens Point

Colleges with Strong Ice Hockey Programs

Alaska, U of, Anchorage
Amherst C (MA)
Boston C (MA)
Boston U (MA)
Bowdoin C (ME)
Bowling Green State U (OH)
Brown U (RI)
Clarkson U (NY)
Colgate U (NY)
Colorado C
Connecticut, U of
Cornell U (NY)
Denver, U of (CO)
Ferris State U (MN)
Harvard U (MA)
Hobart C (NY)
Kalamazoo C (MI)
Maine, U of, Orono
Massachusetts, U of, Lowell
Merrimack C (MA)
Miami U (OH)
Michigan State U
Michigan Technological U
Minnesota, U of, Duluth
Minnesota, U of, Twin Cities
New England C (NH)
New Hampshire, U of
North Dakota, U of
Northeastern U (MA)
Princeton U (NJ)
Rensselaer Polytechnic Institute (NY)
Rochester Institute of Technology (NY)
St. Cloud State U (MN)
St. Lawrence U (NY)
Trinity C (CT)
Union C (NY)
Wisconsin, U of, Superior

JUDO

Colleges with Strong Judo Programs

California State U, Fresno
California State U, San Jose
California, U of, Berkeley
Hawaii, U of, Manoa
Los Angeles City C (CA)
Miami-Dade Community C, North Campus (FL)
Michigan State U
U.S. Military Academy (NY)
U.S. Naval Academy (MD)

LACROSSE

Colleges with Recent Lacrosse Championships

Adelphi U (NY) (men)
Harvard U (MA) (women)
Hobart C (NY) (men)
Long Island U, C. W. Post (NY) (men)
Loyola C (MD) (men)
Maryland, U of, College Park (women)
Nazareth C (NY) (men)
New York Institute of Technology (men)
Pennsylvania State U, University Park (women)
Princeton U (NJ) (men, women)
Salisbury State U (MD) (men)
Springfield C (MA) (men)
Syracuse U (NY) (men)
Trenton State C (NJ) (women)
Ursinus C (PA) (women)
Virginia, U of (women)

Colleges with Strong Lacrosse Programs

Adelphi U (NY) (men)
Alfred U (NY) (men)
Amherst C (MA) (men, women)
Bowdoin C (ME) (men)
Brown U (RI) (men)
California, U of, Santa Barbara (men)
Cornell U (NY) (men)
Delaware, U of (women)
Denison U (OH) (men, women)
Drew U (NJ) (men, women)
Duke U (NC) (men, women)
Franklin and Marshall C (PA) (men)
Gettysburg C (PA) (men)
Harvard U (MA) (men, women)
Hofstra U (NY) (men)
Hollins C (VA) (women)
James Madison U (VA) (men, women)
Johns Hopkins U (MD) (men, women)
Lafayette C (PA) (women)
Loyola C (MD) (women)
Maryland, U of, College Park (men)
Massachusetts, U of, Amherst (men)
Michigan State U (men)
Middlebury C (VT) (men)
Muhlenberg C (PA) (men)
New Hampshire, U of (men, women)
North Carolina, U of, Chapel Hill (men)
Notre Dame, U of (IN) (men)
Pennsylvania, U of (men, women)
Princeton U (NJ) (women)
Roanoke C (VA) (men, women)
Rutgers U (NJ) (men)
Salisbury State U (MD) (men)
Slippery Rock U (PA) (men)
Sweet Briar C (VA) (women)
Temple U (PA) (women)
Towson State U (MD) (men, women)
Ursinus C (PA) (women)
U.S. Military Academy (NY) (men)
U.S. Naval Academy (MD) (men)
Virginia, U of (men)
Washington and Lee U (VA) (men, women)
Whittier C (CA) (men)
William Smith C (NY) (women)
Yale U (CT) (men)

POLO

Colleges with Strong Polo Programs

California Polytechnic State U, San Luis Obispo
California, U of, Davis
California, U of, Los Angeles
Colorado State U
Connecticut, U of
Cornell U (NY)
Florida Atlantic U
Georgia, U of
Harvard U (MA)
Kentucky, U of
Oklahoma, U of
Princeton U (NJ)
Skidmore C (NY)
Southern California, U of
Stanford U (CA)
Texas A&M U
Texas Tech U
Texas, U of, Austin
Tulane U (LA)
Virginia, U of
Washington State U
Yale U (CT)

RACQUETBALL

Colleges with Strong Racquetball Programs

Baldwin Wallace C (OH) (women)
Brigham Young U (UT) (men, women)
California State U, Sacramento (men)
California, U of, Los Angeles (men, women)
Coastline Community C (CA) (women)
Ferris State U (MI) (men)
Kansas, U of (women)
Memphis State U (TN) (men, women)
Missouri, U of, Columbia (men)
New Mexico, U of, Albuquerque (women)
Oklahoma, U of (men)
Pennsylvania State U, University Park (men, women)
Providence C (RI) (women)
Southwest Missouri State U (men, women)
Wisconsin, U of, Eau Claire (men)

RIFLE

Colleges with Strong Rifle Programs

Alaska, U of, Fairbanks
Centenary C (LA)
Citadel, The (SC)
Duquesne U (PA)
Jacksonville State U (AL)
Kentucky, U of
Missouri, U of, Kansas City
Morehead State U (KY)
Murray State U (KY)
Norwich U (VT)
Ohio State U, Columbus
Tennessee Technological U
Tennessee, U of, Martin
Virginia Military Institute
West Virginia U
Xavier U (OH)

RODEO

Colleges with Strong Rodeo Programs

Blue Mountain Community C (OR) (men, women)
California Polytechnic State U, San Luis Obispo (men, women)
California State U, Fresno (women)
Central Arizona C (men)
Montana State U (men, women)
Nevada, U of, Las Vegas (men)
Pima Community C (AZ) (men)
Scottsdale Community C (AZ) (women)
South Dakota State U (men, women)
Southern Arkansas U (women)
Southern Idaho, C of (men)
Southwestern Oklahoma State U (men)
Texas A&M U (women)
Walla Walla Community C (WA) (women)
Washington State U (women)
Western Montana C (men, women)
West Hills C (CA) (men, women)
Wyoming, U of (men, women)

RUGBY

Colleges with Strong Rugby Programs

Amherst C (MA)
Bowling Green State U (OH)
Brown U (RI)
California State U, San Diego
California, U of, Berkeley
California, U of, Santa Barbara
Dartmouth C (NH)
Harvard U (MA)
Northeastern U (MA)
Ohio State U, Columbus
Pennsylvania State U, University Park
Providence C (RI)
U.S. Air Force Academy (CO)
U.S. Military Academy (NY)
Vermont, U of
Wesleyan U (CT)
Williams C (MA)
Wyoming, U of

SAILING

Colleges with Strong Sailing Programs

Babson C (MA)
Boston C (MA)
Boston U (MA)
Bowdoin C (ME)
Brandeis U (MA)
Brown U (RI)
Bryant C (RI)
California, U of, Los Angeles
California, U of, San Diego
California, U of, Santa Barbara
Charleston, C of (SC)
Connecticut C
Connecticut, U of
Dartmouth C (NH)
Harvard U (MA)
Hawaii, U of, Manoa
Holy Cross, C of the (MA)
Maine Maritime Academy
Massachusetts Institute of Technology
Massachusetts Maritime Academy
Michigan, U of, Ann Arbor
New York, State U of, Maritime C
Northeastern U (MA)
Norwich U (VT)
Ohio Wesleyan U
Old Dominion U (VA)
Rhode Island, U of
St. Mary's C (MD)
Salem State C (MA)
Southern California, U of
Stanford U (CA)
Stonehill C (MA)
Tufts U (MA)
Tulane U (LA)
U.S. Coast Guard Academy (CT)

U.S. Merchant Marine Academy (NY)
U.S. Naval Academy (MD)
Utah, U of
Washington, U of
Wesleyan U (CT)
Wheaton C (MA)
Williams C (MA)
Worcester Polytechnic Institute (MA)
Yale U (CT)

SKIING

Colleges with Recent Ski Championships

Colorado, U of
Utah, U of
Vermont, U of

Colleges with Strong Ski Programs

Boston C (MA)
Bowdoin C (ME)
Brigham Young U (UT)
Castleton State C (VT)
Clarkson U (NY)
Colby C (ME)
Colorado C
Colorado Mountain C
Colorado, U of
Dartmouth C (NH)
Denver, U of (CO)
Eastern Utah, C of
Fort Lewis C (CO)
Franklin Pierce C (NH)
Green Mountain C (VT)
Keene State C (NH)
Massachusetts Institute of Technology
Middlebury C (VT)
Montana State U
Nevada, U of, Reno
New England C (NH)
New Hampshire, U of
Northern Michigan U
Plymouth State C (NH)
St. Anselm C (NH)
St. Lawrence U (NY)
St. Michael's C (VT)
St. Olaf C (MN)
Sierra C (CA)
Utah, U of
Vermont, U of
Washington State U
Western State C (CO)
Williams C (MA)
Wisconsin, U of, Green Bay
Wyoming, U of

SOARING

Colleges with Strong Soaring Programs

The sport of soaring entails sailing or gliding in the air, using air currents to maneuver.

Brown U (RI)
California, U of, San Diego
Central Missouri State U
Cornell U (NY)
Daniel Webster C (NH)
Embry-Riddle Aeronautical U (FL)
Illinois, U of, Urbana
Indiana State U
Iowa State U
Kent State U (OH)
Massachusetts Institute of Technology
Michigan State U
Michigan, U of, Ann Arbor
Milwaukee School of Engineering (WI)
Mississippi State U
Nevada, U of, Reno
North Dakota, U of
Ohio State U, Columbus
Oklahoma State U
Pennsylvania State U, University Park
Princeton U (NJ)
Rensselaer Polytechnic Institute (NY)
Tennessee, U of, Space Institute
U.S. Air Force Academy (CO)

SOCCER

Colleges with Recent Soccer Championships

Baptist Bible C (PA) (men)
Barry U (FL) (women)
Belhaven C (MS) (men)
Bethany C (WV) (men)
California, U of, Los Angeles (men)
California, U of, San Diego (men, women)
Franklin Pierce C (NH) (women)
Geneva C (PA) (men)
Grand Canyon U (AZ) (men)
Kean C (NJ) (women)
Lindsey Wilson C (KY) (men)
Lynn U (FL) (women)
Masters C (CA) (men)
Moody Bible Institute (IL) (men)
New Hampshire C (men)
New Jersey, C of (men)
North Carolina, U of, Chapel Hill (women)
Northland Baptist Bible (WI) (men)
Notre Dame, U of (IN) (women)
St. John's U (NY) (men)
Sangamon State U (IL) (men)
Seattle Pacific U (WA) (men)
Simon Fraser U (Canada) (women)
Southern Connecticut State U (men)
Tampa, U of (FL) (men)
Trenton State U (NJ) (women)
Virginia, U of (men)
West Virginia Wesleyan C (men)
Western Baptist C (OR) (men)
Williams C (MA) (men)
Wisconsin, U of, Madison (men)

Colleges with Strong Soccer Programs

Adelphi U (NY) (men, women)
Akron, U of (OH) (men)
Alfred U (NY) (women)
Allegheny C (PA) (women)
American U (DC) (men)
Amherst C (MA) (men, women)
Avila C (MO) (men)
Babson C (MA) (men, women)
Bowdoin C (ME) (women)
Bowling Green State U (OH) (men)
California State U, Fullerton (men)
California State U, Los Angeles (men)
California State U, San Bernardino (men)
California State U, Sonoma (men)
Castleton State C (VT) (men)
Catawba C (NC) (men)
Claremont McKenna C (CA) (men, women)
Colorado C (women)
Connecticut C (women)
Connecticut, U of (women)
Creighton U (NE) (men, women)
Dartmouth C (NH) (men, women)
Davidson C (NC) (men)
Denison U (OH) (women)
DePauw U (IN) (men)
Drew U (NJ) (men)
Duke U (NC) (men)
Emory U (GA) (men)
Evansville, U of (IN) (men)
Florida Institute of Technology (men)
Florida, U of (women)
Franklin Pierce C (NH) (men, women)
Fresno Pacific C (CA) (men)
Frostburg State U (MD) (men)
Furman U (SC) (men)
George Washington U (DC) (men)
Gordon C (MA) (men)
Green Mountain C (VT) (women)
Hartford, U of (CT) (men, women)
Hartwick C (NY) (men, women)
Harvard U (MA) (men)
Haverford C (PA) (men)
Houghton C (NY) (men, women)
Indiana, U of, Bloomington (men)
Keene State C (NH) (men, women)
Keuka C (NY) (women)
Lafayette C (PA) (men, women)
Lock Haven U (PA) (men)
Lynchburg C (VA) (men)
Macalester C (MN) (men, women)
Maryland, U of, College Park (men)
Mary Washington C (VA) (women)

Merrimack C (MA) (women)
Messiah C (PA) (men)
Methodist C (NC) (men)
Metropolitan State C (CO) (men, women)
Middlebury C (VT) (men)
Midwestern State U (TX) (men)
Missouri, U of, St. Louis (men)
Muhlenberg C (PA) (men, women)
New Mexico, U of (men)
New York, State U of, Binghamton (men)
North Carolina State U (women)
North Carolina, U of, Charlotte (men)
North Carolina, U of, Greensboro (women)
Notre Dame, U of (IN) (women)
Oakland U (MI) (men)
Oberlin C (OH) (men, women)
Ohio Wesleyan U (men)
Old Dominion U (VA) (men)
Pennsylvania State U, University Park (men)
Philadelphia C of Textiles and Sciences (PA) (men)
Plymouth State C (NH) (men, women)
Portland, U of (OR) (women)
Randolph-Macon C (VA) (women)
Regis U (CO) (women)
Richmond, U of (VA) (men)
Rochester Institute of Technology (NY) (men)
Rochester, U of (NY) (women)
Rutgers U (NJ) (men)
St. John's U (MN) (men)
St. Louis U (MO) (men)
Salem State C (MA) (men)
San Diego, U of (CA) (men)
San Francisco, U of (CA) (men)
Santa Clara U (CA) (women)
Seattle Pacific U (WA) (men)
Seton Hall U (NJ) (men)
South Carolina, U of, Coastal (men)
South Carolina, U of, Columbia (men, women)
South Carolina, U of, Spartanburg (men)
Southern Methodist U (TX) (men)
South Florida, U of (men)
Southwest, C of the (NM) (men, women)
Stanford U (CA) (women)
Tampa, U of (FL) (men)
Transylvania U (KY) (men)
Truman State U (MO) (men)
U.S. Air Force Academy (CO) (men)
Virginia, U of (women)
Wake Forest U (NC) (men)
Washington U (MO) (men)
Western Connecticut State U (men)
Westmont C (CA) (women)
William and Mary, C of (VA) (men, women)
Williams C (MA) (men, women)

Colleges with Strong Soccer Programs (continued)

William Smith C (NY) (women)
Wisconsin, U of, Madison (women)

SOFTBALL (WOMEN)

Colleges with Recent Softball Championships

Arizona, U of
California, U of, Los Angeles
California U (PA)
Central C (IA)
Chapman U (CA)
Florida Southern U
Kennesaw State C (GA)
Merrimack C (MA)
Oklahoma City U
Simpson C (CA)
Trenton State C (NJ)

Colleges with Strong Softball Programs

Adelphi U (NY)
Akron, U of (OH)
Allegheny C (PA)
Arizona State U
Boston C (MA)
Buena Vista C (IA)
California State U, Bakersfield
California State U, Fresno
California State U, Fullerton
California State U, Long Beach
California State U, Northridge
California, U of, Berkeley
Castleton State C (VT)
Central Michigan U
Concordia U (CA)
Florida Southern C
Florida State U
Florida, U of
Georgia State U
Georgia, U of
Indiana U, Bloomington
Kansas, U of
Luther C (IA)
Massachusetts, U of, Amherst
Missouri, U of, Columbia
Muhlenberg C (PA)
Nebraska, U of, Lincoln
South Carolina, U of, Columbia
Texas A&M U
Trinity C (CT)
Ursinus C (PA)

SQUASH

Colleges with Strong Squash Programs

Amherst C (MA)
Bates C (ME)
Bowdoin C (ME)
Brown U (RI)
Colby C (ME)
Connecticut C
Cornell U (NY)
Dartmouth C (NH)
Franklin and Marshall C (PA)
Harvard U (MA)
Johns Hopkins U (MD)
Massachusetts Institute of Technology
Middlebury C (VT)
Pennsylvania, U of
Princeton U (NJ)
Smith C (MA)
Trinity C (CT)
Tufts U (MA)
U.S. Naval Academy (MD)
Vassar C (NY)
Western Ontario, U of (Canada)
Williams C (MA)
Yale U (CT)

SURFING

Colleges with Strong Surfing Programs

California State U, San Diego
California, U of, San Diego
California, U of, Santa Barbara
Florida Atlantic U
Florida Institute of Technology
Golden West C (CA)
Pepperdine U (CA)
Point Loma Nazarene C (CA)
San Diego, U of (CA)
South Florida, U of

SWIMMING

Colleges with Recent Swimming Championships

Auburn U (AL) (men)
California State U, Bakersfield (men)
California State U, Northridge (women)
Drury C (MO) (men, women)
Kenyon C (OH) (men, women)
Michigan, U of, Ann Arbor (men)
Oakland U (MI) (men, women)
Puget Sound, U of (WA) (men, women)
Simon Fraser U (Canada) (women)
Southern California, U of (women)
Stanford U (CA) (men, women)
Texas, U of, Austin (men)
U.S. Air Force Academy (CO) (women)

Colleges with Strong Swimming Programs

Arizona State U (men, women)
Arizona, U of (men, women)
Arkansas, U of, Fayetteville (men, women)
California, U of, Berkeley (men, women)
California, U of, Davis (women)
California, U of, Los Angeles (men, women)
Colgate U (NY) (men, women)
Denison U (OH) (men, women)
Denver, U of (CO) (men)
Emory U (GA) (men, women)
Florida, U of (men, women)
Georgia, U of (women)
Gettysburg C (PA) (men, women)
Indiana U, Bloomington (men, women)
Johns Hopkins U (MD) (men)
Kansas, U of (men, women)
Lake Forest C (IL) (women)
Miami U (OH) (men, women)
Michigan, U of, Ann Arbor (men, women)
North Carolina State U (men)
North Carolina, U of, Chapel Hill (men, women)
North Dakota, U of (women)
Oberlin C (OH) (men)

Ohio U, Athens (men, women)
Purdue U (IN) (men, women)
Rhode Island, U of (men)
St. Olaf C (MN) (men, women)
Smith C (MA) (women)
Southern California, U of (women)
Swarthmore C (PA) (men, women)
Tennessee, U of, Knoxville (men, women)
Texas, U of, Austin (women)
Transylvania U (KY) (men, women)
Virginia, U of (men, women)
Wesleyan U (CT) (men)
Williams C (MA) (men, women)
Wittenberg U (OH) (women)

SYNCHRONIZED SWIMMING

Colleges with Strong Synchronized Swimming Programs

Arizona, U of
California, U of, Berkeley
California, U of, Davis
Canisius C (NY)
Colorado, U of
Indiana U, Bloomington
Iowa, U of
Michigan, U of, Ann Arbor
Millersville U (PA)
Northwestern U (IL)
Ohio State U, Columbus
Pennsylvania State U, University Park
Richmond, U of (VA)
Santa Clara U (CA)
Skidmore C (NY)
Stanford U (CA)
Swarthmore C (PA)
Vassar C (NY)
Walsh C (OH)
Wheaton C (MA)

TENNIS

Colleges with Recent Tennis Championships

Armstrong U (CA) (women)
Auburn U (AL) (men)
Brigham Young U (UT) (women)
California, U of, Davis (men, women)
California, U of, San Diego (women)
California, U of, Santa Cruz (men)
Emory U (GA) (women)
Flagler C (FL) (women)
Florida, U of (women)
Georgia, U of (women)
Kalamazoo C (MI) (men)
Kenyon C (OH) (women)
Lander C (SC) (men)
Lynn C (FL) (women)
Mobile, U of, (AL) (men)
North Florida, U of (women)
Rollins C (FL) (men)
Southern California, U of (men)
Stanford U (CA) (men, women)
Swarthmore C (PA) (men)
Texas, U of, Austin (women)
Texas, U of, Tyler (men)
Washington C (MD) (men)

Colleges with Strong Tennis Programs

Abilene Christian U (TX) (women)
Adelphi U (NY) (men)
Arizona State U (men, women)
Arizona, U of (women)
Arkansas, U of, Fayetteville (men)
Ball State U (IN) (men)
Berry C (GA) (men)
Birmingham-Southern C (AL) (men)
California Polytechnic State U, San Luis Obispo (women)
California State U, Northridge (men, women)
California, U of, Berkeley (women)
California, U of, Los Angeles (women)
Cameron U (OK) (women)
Carleton C (MN) (men, women)
Carson-Newman C (TN) (women)
Cedarville C (OH) (men)
Chapman U (CA) (men)
Clemson U (SC) (men, women)
Colorado, U of (men, women)
Davidson C (NC) (women)
Duke U (NC) (men, women)
Emory U (GA) (men, women)
Franklin and Marshall C (PA) (women)
Furman U (SC) (men)
Georgia, U of (men, women)

Grand Canyon U (AZ) (women)
Hollins C (VA) (women)
Illinois, U of, Urbana (women)
Indiana U, Bloomington (men, women)
Kansas, U of (men, women)
Kentucky, U of (men, women)
Kenyon C (OH) (men, women)
Louisiana State U, Baton Rouge (women)
Miami, U of (FL) (men, women)
Michigan State U, (women)
Michigan, U of, Ann Arbor (men)
Minnesota, U of, Twin Cities (men)
New York, State U of, Binghamton (women)
North Carolina, U of, Greensboro (men, women)
Northern Colorado, U of (women)
Northwestern U (IL) (men)
Notre Dame, U of (IN) (men)
Oklahoma State U (men, women)
Pepperdine U (CA) (men, women)
Pomona C/Pitzer C (CA) (men)
Presbyterian C (SC) (men)
Redlands, U of (CA) (men)
Ripon C (WI) (men)
Schreiner C (TX) (men)
South, U of the (TN) (men)
South Carolina, U of, Columbia (men, women)
Southern California, U of (women)
Southern Illinois U, Edwardsville (men)
Southern Methodist U (TX) (men, women)
South Florida, U of (men, women)
Swarthmore C (PA) (women)
Tennessee, U of, Knoxville (women)
Texas Christian U (men)
Texas, U of, Austin (men)
Trinity U (TX) (women)
U.S. Air Force Academy (CO) (women)
Virginia, U of (women)
Washington and Lee U (VA) (men)
West Florida, U of (men)
West Virginia, U of (men)
Wichita State U (KS) (men)
William and Mary, C of (VA) (men, women)
Wittenberg U (OH) (women)

TRACK

Colleges with Recent Outdoor Track Championships

Abilene Christian U (TX) (women)
Alabama A&M U (women)
Arkansas, U of, Fayetteville (men)
Barton County Community C (KS) (women)
California Polytechnic State U, San Luis Obispo (women)
Central State U (OH) (women)
Christopher Newport U (VA) (women)
Lincoln U (PA) (men)
Louisiana State U, Baton Rouge (men, women)
St. Augustine's C (NC) (men)
Southern U (LA) (women)
Wisconsin, U of, La Crosse (men)
Wisconsin, U of, Oshkosh (women)

Colleges with Recent Indoor Track Championships

Abilene Christian U (TX) (men, women)
Adams State C (CO) (men)
Alabama A&M U (women)
Arkansas, U of, Fayetteville (men)
Blinn C (TX) (men)
Central State U (OH) (men, women)
Christopher Newport U (VA) (women)
Florida, U of (women)
Lincoln U (PA) (men, women)
Louisiana State U, Baton Rouge (women)
Lubbock Christian U (TX) (men)
New York, State U of, C at Cortland (women)
Pittsburgh, U of, Johnstown (PA) (women)
Prairie View A&M U (TX) (women)
St. Augustine's C (NC) (men)
Southern U (LA) (women)
Texas, U of, Austin (women)
Texas, U of, El Paso (men)
Wayland Baptist U (TX) (women)
Wisconsin, U of, La Crosse (men)
Wisconsin, U of, Oshkosh (women)

Colleges with Strong Track Programs

Alabama, U of, Tuscaloosa (women)
Alma C (MI) (women)
Anderson U (IN) (men)
Arizona State U (men, women)
Arizona, U of (men, women)
Baylor U (TX) (men)
Boston U (MA) (men)
Brandeis U (MA) (women)
Brigham Young U (UT) (women)
Bucknell U (PA) (men)
California, U of, Los Angeles (men, women)
Christopher Newport U (VA) (men)
Clemson U (SC) (men, women)
Cornell U (NY) (women)
Dartmouth C (NH) (men)
Denison U (OH) (men)
Eastern Kentucky U (women)
Eastern Michigan U (men)
Florida State U (men, women)
Florida, U of (men)
Frostburg State U (MD) (men)
George Mason U (VA) (men, women)
Georgetown U (DC) (men)
Georgia Institute of Technology (men)
Harvard U (MA) (women)
Houston, U of (TX) (women)
Illinois, U of, Urbana (men)
Indiana U, Bloomington (men, women)
Iowa State U (men)
Iowa, U of (women)
Kansas, U of (men)
Louisiana State U, Baton Rouge (men)
Massachusetts Institute of Technology (men)
Mt. St. Mary's C (MD) (men)
Murray State U (KY) (women)
Nebraska, U of, Lincoln (men, women)
Nebraska Wesleyan U (men)
Nevada, U of, Las Vegas (women)
New York, State U of, Binghamton (men, women)
New York, State U of, Stony Brook (men)
North Central C (IL) (men)
North Dakota State U (women)
Northeast Louisiana U (men)
Northern Arizona U (men)
Occidental C (CA) (men, women)
Ohio State U, Columbus (men)
Oregon, U of (men, women)
Pennsylvania State U, University Park (women)
Rice U (TX) (men)
St. Thomas, U of (MN) (men)
Shippensburg U (PA) (men)
Slippery Rock U (PA) (women)
Smith C (MA) (women)
South Dakota State U (men)
Southern California, U of (women)
Southern Illinois, U of, Carbondale (men)

Stanford U (CA) (women)
Tennessee, U of, Knoxville (women)
Texas A&M U (men, women)
Texas, U of, Austin (men)
U.S. Naval Academy (MD) (men)
Villanova U (PA) (men, women)
Virginia, U of (men, women)
Washington State U (men, women)
Washington, U of (men)
Wisconsin, U of, La Crosse (women)
Wisconsin, U of, Madison (men, women)

ULTIMATE FRISBEE

Colleges with Strong Ultimate Frisbee Programs

California State U, Humboldt
California, U of, Berkeley
California, U of, Santa Barbara
Carleton C (MN)
Columbia U (NY)
East Carolina U (NC)
North Carolina, U of, Wilmington
Oregon, U of
Stanford U (CA)
Wilmington C (DE)

VOLLEYBALL

Colleges with Recent Volleyball Championships

Barry U (FL) (women)
Brigham Young U (HI) (women)
California State U, Bakersfield C (women)
California State U, Long Beach (women)
California, U of, Los Angeles (men)
California, U of, San Diego (women)
Nebraska, U of, Lincoln (women)
Nebraska, U of, Omaha (women)
Northern Michigan U (women)
Pennsylvania State U, University Park (men)
Stanford U (CA) (men, women)
Texas, U of, Austin (women)
Washington U (MO) (women)
West Texas State U (women)

Colleges with Strong Volleyball Programs

Allegheny C (PA) (women)
Amherst C (MA) (women)
Arizona State U (women)
Ball State U (IN) (men)
California State U, Northridge (men, women)
California, U of, Los Angeles (women)
California, U of, Riverside (women)
California, U of, Santa Barbara (men, women)
Clark U (MA) (women)
Clemson U (SC) (women)
Colorado State U (women)
Eastern Mennonite C (VA) (men, women)
Florida State U (women)
Florida, U of (women)
Furman U (SC) (women)
Georgia, U of (women)
Gordon C (MA) (women)
Hawaii Pacific U (women)
Hawaii, U of, Manoa (women)
Illinois State U (women)
Illinois, U of, Urbana (women)
Indiana U, Bloomington (men)
Indiana U–Purdue U, Fort Wayne (men)
Juniata C (PA) (women)
La Verne, U of (CA) (women)
Louisville, U of (KY) (women)
Massachusetts Institute of Technology (women)
Miami U (OH) (women)
Montana Tech (women)
Montana, U of (women)
Nebraska, U of, Lincoln (women)
New Jersey Institute of Technology (men, women)
North Carolina State U (women)
North Carolina, U of, Chapel Hill (women)
North Dakota State U (women)
Northwestern U (IL) (women)
Ohio State U, Columbus (men)
Pacific Christian C (CA) (women)
Pacific, U of the (CA) (women)
Pennsylvania State U, University Park (men)
Pepperdine U (CA) (men, women)
Purdue U (IN) (women)
Regis U (CO) (women)
St. Benedict, C of (MN) (women)
Seton Hill C (PA) (women)
Smith C (MA) (women)
South Carolina, U of, Columbia (women)
South Dakota School of Mines and Technology (women)
Southern California, U of (men, women)
South Florida, U of (women)
Tusculum C (TN) (women)

WATER POLO

Colleges with Recent Water Polo Championships

California, U of, Berkeley
California, U of, Los Angeles
Stanford U (CA)

Colleges with Strong Water Polo Programs

Amherst C (MA)
Bowdoin C (ME)
California State U, Long Beach
California, U of, San Diego
California, U of, Santa Barbara
Claremont McKenna C (CA)
Harvey Mudd C (CA)
Johns Hopkins U (MD)
Kenyon C (OH)
Massachusetts Institute of Technology
Pepperdine U (CA)
Pomona C/Claremont McKenna C (CA)
Princeton U (NJ)
Richmond, U of (VA)
Slippery Rock U (PA)
Stanford U (CA)
U.S. Naval Academy (MD)
Williams C (MA)

WATERSKIING

Colleges with Strong Waterskiing Programs

Alabama, U of, Tuscaloosa
Auburn U (AL)
California State U, Chico
California State U, Sacramento
Central Florida, U of
Clemson U (SC)
Eckerd C (FL)
Georgia C
Michigan State U
North Carolina, U of, Chapel Hill
Northeast Louisiana U
Rollins C (FL)
Southwestern Louisiana, U of
Texas A&M U
Texas, U of, Austin
Western Michigan U

WEIGHT LIFTING

Colleges with Strong Weight Lifting Programs

Arizona State U
Austin Community C (TX) (mostly women)
Indiana U, Bloomington
Johnson County Community C (KS)
Louisiana State U, Shreveport
Louisiana Tech U
Temple U (PA)
Texas A&M U
U.S. Naval Academy (MD)

WINDSURFING

Colleges with Strong Windsurfing Programs

Cornell U (NY)
Eckerd C (FL)
Florida State U
Rhode Island, U of
St. Mary's C (MD)
Stanford U (CA)
U.S. Coast Guard Academy (CT)
U.S. Naval Academy (MD)
Wisconsin, U of, Madison

WRESTLING (MEN)

Colleges with Recent Wrestling Championships

Arizona State U
Augsburg C (MN)
California State U, San Francisco
Central Oklahoma, U of
Findlay, U of (OH)
Iowa, U of
Ithaca C (NY)
Lincoln C (IL)
Missouri Valley C
Nebraska U of, Omaha
New York, State U of, C at Brockport
Northern Montana C
Oklahoma State U
Pittsburgh, U of, Johnstown (PA)
Portland State U (OR)
St. Lawrence U (NY)
Simon Fraser U (Canada)
Southern Oregon State C
Wartburg C (IA)
Western Montana U

Colleges with Strong Wrestling Programs

Bloomsburg U (PA)
Buena Vista C (IA)
California State U, Fresno
Carson-Newman C (TN)
Central C (IA)
Chicago, U of (IL)
Clemson U (SC)
Cornell C (IA)
Cornell U (NY)
Edinboro U (PA)
Elizabethtown C (PA)
Franklin and Marshall C (PA)
Iowa State U
Lake Superior State U (MI)
Lehigh U (PA)
Lock Haven U (PA)
Maryland, U of, College Park
Michigan State U
Michigan, U of, Ann Arbor
Minnesota, U of, Twin Cities
Missouri, U of, Columbia
Nebraska, U of, Lincoln
New York, State U of, Binghamton
North Carolina State U
North Carolina, U of, Chapel Hill
North Dakota State U
Northern Iowa, U of
Ohio State U, Columbus
Oklahoma, U of
Oregon State U
Pennsylvania State U, University Park
Purdue U (IN)
Simpson C (IA)
Slippery Rock U (PA)
Southern Illinois U, Edwardsville
Wartburg C (IA)
Western State C (CO)
Wisconsin, U of, Madison
Wisconsin, U of, Whitewater

ATHLETIC POTPOURRI

Jock Schools

These are colleges where sports are central to campus life, a place where sports-minded students can flourish.

1. California, U of, Los Angeles
2. Notre Dame, U of (IN)
3. Stanford U (CA)
4. Texas, U of, Austin
5. Florida, U of
6. Michigan, U of, Ann Arbor
7. North Carolina, U of, Chapel Hill
8. Pennsylvania State U, University Park
9. Nebraska, U of
10. Princeton U (NJ)
11. Southern California, U of
12. Arizona, U of
13. Ohio State U, Columbus
14. Virginia, U of
15. Wisconsin, U of Madison
16. Tennessee, U of, Knoxville
17. Iowa, U of
18. California, U of, Berkeley
19. Indiana U
20. Alabama, U of, Tuscaloosa
21. Georgia, U of
22. Michigan State U
23. Brigham Young U (UT)
24. Syracuse U (NY)
25. Duke U (NY)
26. Minnesota, U of, Twin Cities
27. Washington, U of
28. Arizona State U
29. Kentucky, U of
30. Oregon, U of
31. Kansas, U of
32. North Carolina State U
33. Louisiana State U, Baton Rouge
34. Harvard U (MA)
35. Texas A&M U
36. U.S. Military Academy (NY)
37. Utah, U of
38. Clemson U (SC)
39. Colorado, U of
40. Northwestern U (IL)
41. Villanova U (PA)
42. Auburn U (AL)

Jock Schools (continued)

43. Florida State U
44. South Carolina, U of, Columbia
45. Miami, U of (FL)
46. Connecticut, U of
47. Boston C (MA)
48. U.S. Air Force Academy (CO)
49. Georgia Institute of Technology
50. West Virginia U

Source: Reprinted courtesy of *Sports Illustrated*, April 28, 1997. "America's Top 50 Jock Schools."

Bicycling Colleges

These schools have many bikers and bike paths.

Arizona, U of
Baylor U (TX)
California, U of, Davis
California, U of, Santa Barbara
California, U of, Santa Cruz
Colgate U (NY)
Colorado, U of
Cornell U (NY)
Fort Lewis C (CO)
Montana, U of
Williams C (MA)
Wisconsin, U of, Madison

Colleges with Winning Cheerleading Teams

These schools have a strong tradition in cheerleading.

Alabama, U of, Birmingham
Bossier Parish Community C (LA)
California State U, Long Beach
Carson-Newman C (TN)
Cincinnati, U of (OH)
Cumberland C (KY)
Florida, U of
George Mason U (VA)
Georgia, U of
James Madison U (VA)
Kansas, U of
Kentucky, U of
Louisiana State U, Baton Rouge
Louisville, U of (KY)
Memphis State U (TN)
Mississippi C
Moorhead State U (MN)
New Mexico State U
North Carolina State U
North Carolina, U of, Chapel Hill
North Carolina, U of, Wilmington
Ohio State U, Columbus
Oklahoma State U
Oklahoma, U of
Palomar C (CA)
Pennsylvania State U, University Park
Pittsburg State U (KS)
South Carolina, U of, Columbia
Southern California, U of
Texas, U of, Austin
Trinity Valley Community C (TX)
Tyler Junior C (TX)
Utah, U of

Excellent Flying Programs

Central Texas C
Embry-Riddle Aeronautical U (AZ)
Embry-Riddle Aeronautical U (FL)
Florida Institute of Technology
Illinois, U of, Urbana
Ohio State U, Columbus
Oklahoma State U
Mt. San Antonio C (CA)
North Dakota, U of
Southeastern Oklahoma State U
Texas State Technical C
U.S. Air Force Academy (CO)
Western Michigan U

Top College Marching Bands

Arizona State U
Florida A&M U
Florida, U of
Illinois, U of, Urbana
Iowa, U of
James Madison U (VA)
Kansas, U of
Michigan State U
Michigan, U of, Ann Arbor
Ohio State U, Columbus
Oklahoma, U of
Texas, U of, Austin

Top Ten College Golf Courses

These schools own their own golf courses.

Arizona State U
Duke U (NC)
Michigan, U of, Ann Arbor
New Mexico, U of
Ohio State U, Columbus
Oklahoma State U
Stanford U (CA)
U.S. Air Force Academy (CO)
Wisconsin, U of, Madison
Yale U (CT)

Source: Reprinted courtesy of *Sports Illustrated*, April 28, 1997. "America's Top 50 Jock Schools."

Colleges That Own Golf Courses

Alabama, U of, Tuscaloosa
Arizona State U
Bucknell U (PA)
Colgate U (NY)
Cornell U (NY)
Dartmouth C (NH)
Duke U (NC)
Ferris State U (MI)
Florida State U
Florida, U of
Furman U (SC)
Georgia U of
Hamilton C (NY)
Illinois State U
Illinois, U of, Urbana
Indiana U, Bloomington
Iowa, U of
Jacksonville U (FL)
Maryland, U of, College Park
Michigan State U
Michigan, U of, Ann Arbor
Middlebury C (VT)
Mississippi State U
Mississippi, U of
Missouri, U of, Columbia
Montana, U of
Morehead State U (KY)
New Mexico State U
New Mexico, U of, Albuquerque
North Carolina, U of, Chapel Hill
Notre Dame, U of (IN)
Ohio State U, Columbus
Ohio U, Athens
Oklahoma State U
Pacific Lutheran U (WA)
Pennsylvania State U, University Park
Phillips U (OK)
Princeton U (NJ)
Purdue U (IN)
Shippensburg U (PA)
South Florida, U of
South, U of the (TN)
Southern Mississippi, U of
Spring Hill C (AL)
Stanford U (CA)

Colleges That Own Golf Courses (continued)

Tri-State U (IN)
Troy State U (AL)
U.S. Air Force Academy (CO)
Virginia Polytechnic Institute and State U
Virginia, U of
Williams C (MA)
Wichita State U (KS)
Wisconsin, U of, Madison
Yale U (CT)

The Fifteen Best Ski Colleges

Colleges were selected on the basis of proximity to skiing areas and competitive and recreational skiing opportunities.

Boston C (MA)
Brigham Young U (UT)
Colorado C
Colorado Mountain C
Colorado, U of
Dartmouth C (NH)
Middlebury C (VT)
Nevada, U of, Reno
Northern Michigan U
St. Lawrence U (NY)
Sierra C (CA)
Utah, U of
Vermont, U of
Washington State U
Western State C (CO)

Source: Lois Friedland, "15 Great Ski Colleges," *Ski* (December 1987) pp. 51–52.

Colleges That Own Ski Areas

Dartmouth C (NH)
Middlebury C (VT)

The Ten Largest College Basketball Arenas

1. Syracuse U (NY): Carrier Dome	33,000 seats
2. Tennessee, U of: Thompson-Boling Center	24,535 seats
3. Kentucky, U of: Rupp Arena	24,000 seats
4. North Carolina, U of, Greensboro: Greensboro Coliseum	23,100 seats
5. Brigham Young U (UT): Marriott Center	22,700 seats
6. North Carolina, U of, Chapel Hill: Dean Smith Center	21,572 seats
7. Portland State U (OR): Rose Garden	21,401 seats
8. Memphis, U of (TN): The Pyramid	20,142 seats
9. Seton Hall U (NJ): Byrne Meadowlands Arena	20,029 seats (part-time)
10. St. Louis U (MO): Kiel Center	20,000 seats

Source: *1998 ESPN Information Please ® Almanac,*

The Ten Largest College Football Stadiums

1. Tennessee, U of, Knoxville: Neyland Stadium	102,544 seats
2. Michigan, U of, Ann Arbor: Michigan Stadium	102,501 seats
3. California, U of, Los Angeles: Rose Bowl	102,083 seats
4. Southern California, U of: LA Memorial Coliseum	94,159 seats
5. Pennsylvania State U, University Park: Beaver Stadium	93,967 seats
6. Ohio State U, Columbus: Ohio Stadium	89,800 seats
7. Georgia, U of, Athens: Sanford Stadium	86,117 seats
8. Stanford U (CA): Stanford Stadium	85,500 seats
9. Auburn U (AL): Jordan-Hare Stadium	85,214 seats
10. Alabama, U of, Tuscaloosa, and Alabama, U of, Birmingham: Legion Field	83,000 seats

Source: *1998 ESPN Information Please ® Almanac,*

Colleges with Interesting Team Mascots

Alaska, U of, Fairbanks	Nanooks
Amherst C (MA)	Lord Jeffs
California, U of, Irvine	Anteaters
California, U of, Santa Cruz	Banana Slugs
Campbell U (NC)	Fighting Camels
Columbia C (CA)	Claim Jumpers
Delaware, U of	Blue Hens
Evansville, U of (IN)	Purple Aces
Evergreen State U (WA)	Geoducks
Fairfield U (CT)	Stags
Heidelberg C (OH)	Student Princes
Insurance, C of (NY)	Turtles
Kent State U (OH)	Golden Flashes
Marshall U (WV)	Thundering Herd
Mary, U of (ND)	Marauders
Missouri, U of, Kansas City	Kangaroos
Ohio Wesleyan U	Battling Bishops
Rhode Island School of Design	Nads (as in "Go! Nads!")
Rowan C (NJ)	Professors
South Carolina, U of, Spartanburg	Running Rifles
Southern Arkansas U	Muleriders
Southwestern C (KS)	The Moundbuilders
Southwestern Louisiana, U of	Ragin' Cajuns
Texas Christian U	Horned Frogs
Western Illinois U	Leathernecks
Whittier C (CA)	Poets
Whitman C (WA)	The Fighting Missionaries

ENROLLMENT

COLLEGE SIZE

U.S. Colleges Grouped by Size

The list indicates the percentage of four-year colleges within each enrollment category.

PRIVATE COLLEGES/UNIVERSITIES

under 200	18.5%
200–500	19.7%
500–1,000	19.2%
1,000–2,500	26.7%
over 2,500	15.9%

PUBLIC COLLEGES/UNIVERSITIES

under 1,000	9.7%
1,000–2,500	21.6%
2,500–5,000	23.6%
5,000–10,000	23.4%
10,000–20,000	14.6%
over 20,000	7.1%

Source: Data compiled from U.S. Department of Education information.

Top Twenty Four-Year Colleges by Enrollment

These twenty colleges have the largest undergraduate enrollments as of fall 1995.

1. Minnesota, U of, Twin Cities	51,445
2. Ohio State U, Columbus	48,676
3. Texas, U of, Austin	47,905
4. Arizona State U	42,040
5. Texas A&M U	41,790
6. Michigan State U	40,647
7. Pennsylvania State U, University Park	39,646
8. Florida, U of	39,412
9. Wisconsin, U of, Madison	39,005
10. Illinois, U of, Urbana	38,420
11. Michigan, U of, Ann Arbor	36,687
12. Purdue U (IN)	36,427
13. South Florida, U of	36,142
14. New York U	35,835
15. Indiana U, Bloomington	35,063
16. Arizona, U of	34,777
17. California, U of, Los Angeles	34,713
18. Washington, U of	33,996
19. Rutgers U (NJ)	33,773
20. Maryland, U of, College Park	32,908

Source: U.S. Department of Education.

Top Five Two-Year Schools by Enrollment

These five two-year schools have the largest enrollments as of fall 1995.

1. Community C of the Air Force (AL)	69,611
2. Miami-Dade Community C (FL)	47,060
3. Houston Community C System (TX)	39,541
4. Northern Virginia Community C	37,144
5. DuPage, C of (IL)	29,888

Source: U.S. Department of Education.

Fine Small and Medium-Sized Public Universities

While many state-supported universities are large, this list consists of high-quality state schools that are smaller and provide many opportunities for teacher-student interaction. Approximate full-time undergraduate enrollment is listed.

Alabama, U of, Huntsville	4,000
Alaska, U of, Fairbanks	3,400
Appalachian State U (NC)	10,000
Arkansas, U of, Fayetteville	12,000
Bloomsburg U (PA)	6,000
California State U, Bakersfield	2,500
California State U, Humboldt	6,000
California State U, San Bernardino	6,000
California, U of, Riverside	7,000
California, U of, Santa Cruz	9,000
Charleston, C of (SC)	5,600
Clemson U (SC)	12,000
Colorado School of Mines	1,600
Evergreen State C (WA)	2,900
Florida Atlantic U	4,600
Fort Lewis C (CO)	4,000
Georgia Southern U	10,000
Idaho, U of	6,400

Fine Small and Medium-Sized Public Universities (continued)

Kean C (NJ)	6,600
Keene State C (NH)	3,250
Lyndon State C (VT)	1,100
Maine, U of, Orono	8,500
Maine, U of, Farmington	2,000
Mankato State U (MN)	11,500
Mary Washington C (VA)	3,000
Millersville U (PA)	5,400
Minnesota, U of, Morris	2,000
Mississippi, U of	8,100
Missouri, U of, Rolla	3,700
Nevada, U of, Reno	5,300
New C (FL)	525
New York, State U of, C of Environment	1,000
New York, State U of, C at Geneseo	5,000
New York, State U of, C at Oswego	6,600
New York, State U of, Purchase	2,500
North Carolina, U of, Asheville	2,000
North Carolina, U of, Greensboro	7,900
North Dakota, U of	8,600
Pennsylvania State U, Erie	2,300
Pittsburgh, U of, Bradford	1,000
Ramapo C (NJ)	2,600
Rowan C (NJ)	5,200
St. Mary's C (MD)	1,300
Salisbury State U (MD)	4,000
Shippensburg U (PA)	5,000
Sonoma State U (CA)	5,000
South Carolina, U of, Aiken	1,900
Trenton State C (NJ)	5,100
Truman State U (MO)	5,700
William and Mary, C of (VA)	5,300
Wisconsin, U of, Eau Claire	8,900
Wyoming, U of	8,000

Schools That Feel Smaller Than They Are

While these are medium- to large-sized colleges, they have relatively small classes, offer opportunities for interaction between students and professors, and promote a personalized social atmosphere.

California Polytechnic State U, San Luis Obispo
California, U of, San Diego
Central Michigan U
Colorado State U
Dayton, U of (OH)
Delaware, U of
Duke U (NC)
Illinois State U
Iowa State U
Maine, U of, Orono
Mankato State U (MN)
Michigan, U of, Ann Arbor
Missouri, U of, Columbia
New Hampshire, U of
New York, State U of, C at Oneonta
New York, State U of, Oswego
New York, State U of, Purchase
North Carolina, U of, Chapel Hill
Northwestern U (IL)
Notre Dame, U of (IN)
Ohio U, Athens
Oregon, U of
Rhode Island, U of
Southern Methodist U (TX)
Syracuse U (NY)
Tennessee, U of, Knoxville
Vermont, U of
Virginia, U of
Western Washington U

MALE/FEMALE

The first two lists in this section consist of colleges that are exclusively male or female. Such colleges are options for students who desire the educational benefits they provide. Often located near coeducational colleges, they allow for ample social opportunities.

Men's Colleges

Deep Springs C (CA)
Divine Word C (IA)
Hampden-Sydney C (VA)
Morehouse C (GA)
Wabash C (IN)

Women's Colleges

Agnes Scott C (GA)
Alverno C (WI)
Aquinas C (MA)
Barnard C (NY) (affiliated with Columbia U, NY)
Bay Path C (MA)
Bennett C (NC)
Blue Mountain C (MS)
Bryn Mawr C (PA)
Carlow C (PA)
Cedar Crest C (PA)
Chatham C (PA)
Chestnut Hill C (PA)
Columbia C (SC)
Converse C (SC)
Cottey C (MO)
Douglass C (NJ) (a division of Rutgers U, NJ)
Elms C (MA)
Emmanuel C (MA)
Georgian Court C (NJ)

Harcum C (PA)
Hartford C for Women (CT)
Hollins C (VA)
Hood C (MD)
Immaculata C (PA)
Judson C (AL)
Lesley C (MA)
Marian Court C (MA)
Mary Baldwin C (VA)
Marymount C (NY)
Marymount Manhattan C (NY)
Meredith C (NC)
Midway C (KY)
Mills C (CA)
Moore C of Art (PA)
Mt. Holyoke C (MA)
Mt. Mary C (WI)
Mt. St. Mary's C (CA)
Mt. St. Vincent, C of (Canada)
Newcomb C (LA) (coordinate arrangement with Tulane U, LA)
New Rochelle, C of (NY)
Notre Dame, C of (MD)
Notre Dame C (OH)
Peace C (NC)
Pine Manor C (MA)
Radcliffe C (MA) (coordinate arrangement with Harvard U, MA)
Randolph-Macon Woman's C (VA)
Regis C (MA)
Rosemont C (PA)
Russell Sage C (NY)
St. Benedict, C of (MN)
St. Catherine, C of (MN)
St. Elizabeth, C of (NJ)
St. Joseph C (CT)
St. Mary, C of (NE)
St. Mary-of-the-Woods C (IN)
St. Mary's C (IN)
St. Mary's C (NC)
Salem C (NC)
Scripps C (CA)
Seton Hill C (PA)
Simmons C (MA)
Smith C (MA)
Spelman C (GA)
Stephens C (MO)
Sweet Briar C (VA)
Trinity C (DC)
Trinity C (VT)
Ursuline C (OH)
Wellesley C (MA)
Wells C (NY)
Wesleyan C (GA)
Westhampton C (VA) (coordinate arrangement with Richmond, U of, VA)
William Smith C (NY) (coordinate arrangement with Hobart C, NY)
William Woods C (MO)
Wilson C (PA)

Coed but Lopsided Colleges

These schools have a disproportionate number of men or women. The percentages are approximate.

Atlantic, C of the (ME)	60% women
Austin Peay State U (TN)	60% women
Babson C (MA)	70% men
Barat C (IL)	80% women
Bennington C (VT)	65% women
Bethune-Cookman C (FL)	60% women
California Institute of Technology (CA)	80% men
Carnegie Mellon U (PA)	65% men
Case Western Reserve U (OH)	60% men
Centenary C (NJ)	85% women
Chicago, U of (IL)	60% men
Claremont McKenna C (CA)	60% men
Clarkson U (NY)	75% men
Colby-Sawyer C (NH)	85% women
Colorado School of Mines	80% men
Cooper Union (NY)	70% men
Culinary Institute of America (NY)	75% men
Drexel U (PA)	65% men
D'Youville C (NY)	80% women
Fisk U (TN)	65% women
Florida Institute of Technology	75% men
Georgia Institute of Technology	75% men
Goucher C (MD)	70% women
Grand Valley State U (MI)	65% men
Harvey Mudd C (CA)	80% men
Houghton C (NY)	60% women
Illinois Institute of Technology	80% men
Johns Hopkins U (MD)	65% men
Lehigh U (PA)	65% men
Long Island U, C. W. Post C (NY)	65% women
Lourdes C (OH)	85% women
Manhattanville C (NY)	65% women
Marygrove C (MI)	85% women
Marymount U (VA)	80% women
Marywood C (PA)	70% women
Massachusetts Institute of Technology	65% men

Mercy C (NY)	60% women
Mt. St. Vincent, C of (NY)	80% women
New Haven, U of (CT)	70% men
New York, City U of, Hunter C	70% women
North Carolina State U	65% men
North Carolina, U of, Chapel Hill	60% women
North Carolina, U of, Greensboro	65% women
Northeastern Illinois U	60% women
Notre Dame, U of (IN)	70% men
Otterbein C (OH)	60% women
Radford U (VA)	60% women
Rensselaer Polytechnic Institute (NY)	80% men
Rockford C (IL)	65% women
Rosary C (IL)	80% women
Rose-Hulman Institute of Technology (IN)	85% men
St. Scholastica, C of (MN)	75% women
Sarah Lawrence C (NY)	70% women
Southern Illinois U, Carbondale	60% men
Spalding U (KY)	90% women
Towson State U (MD)	60% women
U.S. Air Force Academy (CO)	85% men
U.S. Military Academy (NY)	90% men
U.S. Naval Academy (MD)	90% men
Washington and Lee U (VA)	65% men
Westminster C (MO)	70% men
Westmont C (CA)	60% women
Wheaton C (MA)	65% women
Wisconsin, U of, Platteville	60% men
Wofford C (SC)	60% men
Worcester Polytechnic Institute (MA)	80% men
Xavier U (LA)	70% women

The Years That Men's Colleges Became Coed

Amherst C (MA)	1976
Bowdoin C (ME)	1970
Brown U (RI) (merger with Pembroke College)	1971
Citadel, The (SC)	1996
Claremont McKenna C (CA)	1976
Colgate U (NY)	1970
Dartmouth C (NH)	1972
Davidson C (NC)	1972
Duke U (NC)	1972
Harvard U (MA) (merger with Radcliffe College)	mid-1970s
Haverford C (PA)	1980
Holy Cross, C of the (MA)	1972
Johns Hopkins U (MD)	1971
Kenyon C (OH)	1969
Lehigh U (PA)	1971
Princeton U (NJ)	1969
Trinity C (CT)	1969
U.S. Military Academy (NY)	1975
Virginia Military Institute	1996
Virginia, U of	1970
Washington and Lee U (VA)	1985
Williams C (MA)	1970
Wofford C (SC)	1975
Yale U (CT)	1969

The Years That Women's Colleges Became Coed

Bennington C (VT)	1969
Brenau U (GA)	1997
Colby-Sawyer C (NH)	1991
Connecticut C	1969
Endicott C (MA)	1997
Fisher C (MA)	1998
Goucher C (MD)	1986
Lasell C (MA)	1998
Our Lady of the Elms, C of (MA)	1998
Pitzer C (CA)	1971
Salve Regina U (RI)	1972
Sarah Lawrence C (NY)	1968
Skidmore C (NY)	1971
Vassar C (NY)	1967
Wheaton C (MA)	1990

MINORITY

Colleges with a Significant Number of Native American Students

The list indicates the approximate percentage of Native American students among the undergraduate population at these colleges.

	PERCENT
Alaska, U of, Fairbanks	10
Bacone C (OK)	45
Bemidji State U (MN)	10
Carl Albert State C (OK)	15
Central Wyoming C	10
Eastern Utah, C of	10
Flaming Rainbow U (OK)	50
Fort Lewis C (CO)	10
Heritage C (WA)	25
Huron U (SD)	15
Mt. Senario C (WI)	15
New Mexico State U, Grants	15
New Mexico, U of, Albuquerque	10
New Mexico, U of, Gallup	70
Northeastern State U (OK)	15
Northern Arizona U	5
Northland Pioneer C (AZ)	20
Pembroke State U (NC)	25
San Juan C (NM)	25
Santa Fe, C of (NM)	10
Southeastern Oklahoma State U	25

Members of the American Indian Tribal Colleges

Most of these colleges are situated on reservations in the Western and Midwestern states. Many are two-year schools.

Bay Mills Community C (MI)
Blackfeet Community C (MT)
Cheyenne River Community C (SD)
Crownpoint Institute of Technology (NM)
D-Q U (CA)
Dull Knife Memorial C (MT)
Fond Du Lac Community C (MN)
Fort Belknap Community C (MT)
Fort Berthold C (ND)
Fort Peck Community C (MT)
Haskell Indian Junior C (KS)
Institute for American Indian Arts (NM)
Lac Courte Oreilles Ojibwa Community C (WI)
Leech Lake Tribal C (MN)
Little Big Horn C (MT)
Little Hoop Community C (ND)
Menominee Nation, C of the (WI)
Navajo Community C (AZ)
Nebraska Indian Community C
Northwest Indian C (WA)
Oglala Lakota C (SD)
Salish Kootenai C (MT)
Saskatchewan Indian Federated C (Canada)
Sinte Gleska C (SD)
Sissenton-Wahpeton Community C (SD)
Southwest Indian Polytechnic Institute (NM)
Standing Rock C (ND)
Stone Child C (MT)
Turtle Mountain Community C (ND)
United Tribes Technical C (ND)

Colleges with a Significant Number of Hispanic Students

The list indicates the approximate percentage of Hispanic students among the undergraduate population at these colleges.

	PERCENT
Adams State C (CO)	20
Arizona, U of	10
Barry U (FL)	30
California State U, Bakersfield	15
California State U, Dominguez Hills	10
California State U, Fresno	30
California State U, Fullerton	10
California State U, Los Angeles	25
California State U, Northridge	25
California State U, San Bernardino	10
California State U, Stanislaus	10
California, U of, Berkeley	10
California, U of, Los Angeles	15
California, U of, Riverside	10
California, U of, San Diego	10
California, U of, Santa Barbara	10
California, U of, Santa Cruz	10
Cerritos C (CA)	25+
Columbia U (NY)	10
Cornell U (NY)	10
Dallas, U of (TX)	10
Desert, C of the (CA)	15
DeVry Institute of Technology (IL)	15
Eastern New Mexico U	20
El Camino C (CA)	15
Fashion Institute of Technology (NY)	10
Florida International U	50
Fordham U (NY)	10
Harry S. Truman C (IL)	25+
Heritage C (WA)	20
Houston, U of (TX) (downtown campus)	25
Kean C (NJ)	15
La Verne, U of (CA)	20
Loma Linda U (CA)	10

	PERCENT
Los Angeles City C (CA)	25+
Loyola Marymount U (CA)	20
Manhattanville C (NY)	10
Marymount C (NY)	10
Marymount Manhattan C (NY)	10
Massachusetts Institute of Technology	10
Miami, U of (FL)	25
Miami U (OH)	20
Miami Dade Community C (FL)	50
Mt. St. Mary's C (CA)	30
Mt. St. Vincent, C of (NY)	20
Mt. San Antonio C (CA)	25+
New Jersey Institute of Technology	10
New Mexico Highlands U	70
New Mexico Institute of Mining and Technology	15
New Mexico Military Institute	15
New Mexico State U	25
New Mexico, U of	25
New York, City U of	(varies by specific campus)
New York, City U of, Hunter C	20
New York, City U of, John Jay C	35
New York, City U of, Lehman C	45
New York School of Interior Design	20
New York, State U of, C at Old Westbury	10
Newbury C (MA)	15
Occidental C (CA)	25
Otis/Parsons School of Art and Design (CA)	10
Our Lady of the Lake U (TX)	55
Oxnard C (CA)	25+
Pitzer C (CA)	15
Pomona C (CA)	10
St. Augustine C (IL)	95
St. Edward's U (TX)	25
St. John's U (NY)	10
St. Louis U (MO)	10
St. Mary's U (TX)	60
St. Peter's U (NJ)	15
Santa Barbara Community C (CA)	15
Santa Fe, C of (NM)	25
Southern California, U of	10

Colleges with a Significant Number of Hispanic Students (continued)

	PERCENT
Southern Colorado, U of	20
Stanford U (CA)	10
Stevens Institute of Technology (NJ)	10
Syracuse U (NY)	10
Texas A&M U, Kingsville	55
Texas Lutheran U	10
Texas, U of, Austin	10
Texas, U of, El Paso	55
Texas, U of, Pan American	25+
Texas, U of, San Antonio	25+
Trinity U (TX)	10
U.S. International U (CA)	20
Western New Mexico U	40
Whittier C (CA)	25
Woodbury U (CA)	30

Predominantly Black Colleges

Alabama A&M U
Alabama State U
Albany State C (GA)
Alcorn State U (MS)
Allen U (SC)
Arkansas Baptist C
Arkansas, U of, Pine Bluff
Barber-Scotia C (NC)
Benedict C (SC)
Bennett C (NC)
Bethune-Cookman C (FL)
Bishop State Community C (AL)
Bowie State U (MD)
Bloomfield C (NJ)
Bluefield State C (WV)
Central State U (OH)
Cheyney U (PA)
Chicago State U (IL)
Claflin C (SC)
Clark Atlanta U (GA)
Coahoma Community C (MS)
Coppin State C (MD)
Delaware State C
Denmark Technical C (SC)
Dillard U (LA)
District of Columbia, U of the
Edward Waters C (FL)
Elizabeth City State U (NC)
Fayetteville State U (NC)
Fisk U (TN)
Florida A&M U
Florida Memorial C
Fort Valley State C (GA)
Grambling State U (LA)
Hampton U (VA)
Harris Stowe State C (MO)
Hinds Community C (MS)
Howard U (DC)
Howard U, School of Medicine (DC)
Human Services, C for (NY)
Huston-Tillotson C (TX)
Interdenominational Theological Center (GA)
Jackson State U (MS)
Jarvis Christian C (TX)
Johnson C. Smith U (NC)
Kentucky State U
Knoxville C (TN)
Lane C (TN)
Langston U (OK)
LeMoyne-Owen C (TN)
Lincoln U (MO)
Lincoln U (PA)
Livingstone C (NC)
Martin U (IN)
Marygrove C (MI)
Maryland, U of, Eastern Shore
Meharry Medical C (TN)
Miles C (AL)
Mississippi Valley State U
Morehouse C (GA)
Morgan State U (MD)
Morris Brown C (GA)
Morris C (SC)
New York, City U of, Medgar Evers C
Norfolk State U (VA)
North Carolina A&T State U
North Carolina Central U
Oakwood C (AL)
Paine C (GA)
Paul Quinn C (TX)
Philander Smith C (AR)
Prairie View A&M U (TX)
Rust C (MS)
St. Augustine's C (NC)

Predominantly Black Colleges (continued)

St. Paul's C (VA)
Savannah State C (GA)
Selma U (AL)
Shaw U (NC)
Shorter C (AR)
Sojourner-Douglass C (MD)
South Carolina State C
Southern U (LA)
Southern U, New Orleans (LA)
Southern U, Shreveport (LA)
Southwestern Christian C (TX)
Spelman C (GA)
Stillman C (AL)
Talladega C (AL)
Tennessee State U
Texas C
Texas Southern U
Trenholm State Technical C (AL)
Tougaloo C (MS)
Tuskegee U (AL)
Virgin Islands, U of the
Virginia Seminary and C
Virginia State U
Virginia Union U
Voorhees C (SC)
West Virginia State C
Wilberforce U (OH)
Wiley C (TX)
Winston-Salem State U (NC)
Xavier U (LA)

Colleges Particularly Supportive of Black Student Needs

These schools do not necessarily have a high percentage of black students, but they do have programs and services that support African Americans. The list does not include predominantly black colleges.

Bates C (ME)
Brown U (RI)
Bryn Mawr C (PA)
California State U, San Diego
California, U of, Berkeley
California, U of, Riverside
Carleton C (MN)
Case Western Reserve U (OH)
Chicago, U of (IL)
Columbia U (NY)
Cornell U (NY)
Davidson C (NC)
Dayton, U of (OH)
Earlham C (IN)
Grinnell C (IA)
Harvard U (MA)
Haverford C (PA)
Houston, U of (TX)
Illinois State U
Iowa, U of
Kent State U (OH)
Maryland, U of, College Park
Mt. Holyoke C (MA)
New York, State U of, Purchase
Oberlin C (OH)
Occidental C (CA)
Pennsylvania, U of
Pittsburgh, U of (PA)
Rensselaer Polytechnic Institute (NY)
St. Joseph's U (PA)
Stanford U (CA)
Swarthmore C (PA)
Tufts U (MA)
Vassar C (NY)
Wellesley C (MA)
Wesleyan U (CT)
Wisconsin, U of, Madison
Yale U (CT)

Colleges with a Significant Number of Black Students

The list indicates the approximate percentage of black students among the undergraduate population at these schools. It does not include historically black colleges.

	PERCENT
Adelphi U (NY)	10
Alverno C (WI)	15
Aurora U (IL)	10
Austin Peay State U (TN)	15
Bard C (NY)	10
Birmingham-Southern C (AL)	15
Bridgeport, U of (CT)	25
California State U, Dominguez Hills	30
California State U, Los Angeles	10
Chowan C (NC)	30
Christopher Newport U (VA)	15
Cleveland State U (OH)	15
Columbia C (IL)	25
Columbia U (NY)	10
Daemen C (NY)	15
Delta State U (MS)	25
DePaul U (IL)	10
Detroit Mercy, U of (MI)	30
DeVry Institute of Technology (OH)	20
Emmanuel C (MA)	10
Fashion Institute of Technology (NY)	20
Findlay, U of (OH)	15
Fontbonne C (MO)	15
Fordham U (NY)	10
Gardner Webb C (NC)	10
Georgetown U (DC)	10
Georgia Military C	20
Greensboro C (NC)	15
Holy Names C (CA)	30
Illinois Institute of Technology	10
Iona C (NY)	15
James Madison U (VA)	10

	PERCENT
Kansas Wesleyan U	10
Kean C (NJ)	15
Kendall C (IL)	15
Kentucky State U	50
La Verne, U of (CA)	10
Lincoln C (IL)	10
Lincoln U (MO)	25
Lindenwood C (MO)	10
Long Island U, Brooklyn	40
Loyola U (LA)	15
MacMurray C (IL)	25
Madonna C (MI)	10
Mannes School of Music (NY)	10
Maryland C of Art and Design	30
Maryland, U of, Baltimore County	15
Maryland, U of, College Park	10
Marymount C (NY)	15
Marymount Manhattan C (NY)	20
Massachusetts Institute of Technology	10
Memphis State U (TN)	20
Mercer U (GA)	15
Methodist C (NC)	15
Mills C (CA)	10
Mt. St. Mary's C (CA)	10
Mt. Vernon C (DC)	15
Mundelein C (IL)	20
New Jersey Institute of Technology	15
New Rochelle, C of (NY)	35
New York, City U of, Baruch C	25
New York, City U of, Brooklyn C	25
New York, City U of, City C	40
New York, City U of, Lehman C	30
New York, State U of, C at Old Westbury	30
Newbury C (MA)	15
North Carolina State U	10
North Carolina, U of, Chapel Hill	10
North Carolina, U of, Charlotte	10
North Carolina, U of, Greensboro	10
Oberlin C (OH)	10
Old Dominion U (VA)	10

Colleges with a Significant Number of Black Students (continued)

	PERCENT
Oral Roberts U (OK)	15
Pitzer C (CA)	10
Pratt Institute (NY)	10
Rutgers U (NJ)	25
St. Leo C (FL)	20
South Carolina, U of, Columbia	15
Southwestern Louisiana, U of	20
Stanford U (CA)	10
Syracuse U (NY)	10
Temple U (PA)	15
Texas Woman's U	15
Trinity C (DC)	40
Upsala C (NJ)	40
Virginia, U of	10
Wayne State U (MI)	25
Wesley C (DE)	10
Wesleyan C (GA)	15
Wesleyan U (CT)	10
West Alabama, U of	30
Wilmington C (DE)	15
Winthrop U (SC)	15

Members of the United Negro College Fund

Members of the United Negro College Fund are private, four-year institutions, founded prior to 1945, regionally accredited for at least three years, and supportive of UNCF's objectives. Date of membership follows each school.

Barber-Scotia C (NC) (1958)
Benedict C (SC) (1945)
Bennett C (NC) (1944)
Bethune-Cookman C (FL) (1944)
Claflin C (SC) (1968)
Clark Atlanta U (GA) (1989)
Dillard U (LA) (1944)
Edward Waters C (FL) (1985)
Fisk U (TN) (1944)
Florida Memorial C (1968)
Huston-Tillotson C (TX) (1952)
Interdenominational Theological Center (GA) (1960)
Jarvis Christian C (TX) (1972)
Johnson C. Smith U (NC) (1945)
Knoxville C (TN) (1944)
Lane C (TN) (1944)
LeMoyne-Owen C (TN) (1968)
Livingstone C (NC) (1944)
Miles C (AL) (1972)
Morehouse C (GA) (1944)
Morris Brown C (GA) (1944)
Morris C (SC) (1982)
Oakwood C (AL) (1965)
Paine C (GA) (1945)
Paul Quinn C (TX) (1974)
Philander Smith C (AR) (1944)
Rust C (MS) (1972)
St. Augustine's C (NC) (1950)
St. Paul's C (VA) (1958)
Shaw U (NC) (1944)
Spelman C (GA) (1944)
Stillman C (AL) (1962)
Talladega C (AL) (1945)
Texas C (1944)
Tougaloo C (MS) (1944)
Tuskegee U (AL) (1944)
Virginia Union U (1944)
Voorhees C (SC) (1969)
Wilberforce U (OH) (1968)
Wiley C (TX) (1944)
Xavier U (LA) (1946)

Colleges with a Significant Number of Asian Students

The list indicates the percentage of students with Asian heritage/ethnicity among the undergraduate population of these colleges.

	PERCENT
Amherst C (MA)	10
Art Center C of Design (CA)	15
Barnard C (NY)	25
Biola U (CA)	10
Brown U (RI)	10
Bryn Mawr C (PA)	15
California Institute of Technology	15
California State Polytechnic U, Pomona	30
California State U, Fullerton	25
California State U, Long Beach	25
California State U, Los Angeles	25
California State U, San Francisco	35
California State U, San Jose	35
California, U of, Berkeley	40
California, U of, Davis	30
California, U of, Irvine	50
California, U of, Los Angeles	35
California, U of, Riverside	35
California, U of, San Diego	30
California, U of, Santa Barbara	10
Campbell U (NC)	15
Capital C (MD)	10
Case Western Reserve U (OH)	15
Chicago, U of (IL)	15
Claremont McKenna C (CA)	20
Columbia U (NY)	10
Cooper Union (NY)	25
Cornell U (NY)	10
Divine Word C (IA)	60
Golden Gate U (CA)	10
Harvard U (MA)	10
Harvey Mudd C (CA)	20
Hawaii, U of, Hilo	50

	PERCENT
Hawaii, U of, Manoa	65
Houston, U of (TX)	20
Illinois Institute of Technology	20
Johns Hopkins U (MD)	15
Juilliard School (NY)	10
Lewis and Clark C (OR)	10
Loma Linda U (CA)	20
Mannes School of Music (NY)	15
Massachusetts Institute of Technology	25
Mills C (CA)	15
Mt. St. Mary's C (CA)	15
New Jersey Institute of Technology	20
New York, City U of, Baruch C	25
New York, State U of, Stony Brook	10
New York U	10
Northrop U (CA)	45
Northwestern U (IL)	10
Occidental C (CA)	10
Otis/Parsons School of Art and Design (CA)	20
Pacific U (OR)	10
Pacific, U of the (CA)	10
Pennsylvania, U of	10
Pitzer C (CA)	10
Polytechnic U (NY)	30
Pomona C (CA)	20
Pratt Institute (NY)	10
Rensselaer Polytechnic Institute (NY)	10
Rutgers U (NJ)	15
San Francisco, U of (CA)	10
Santa Clara U (CA)	15
Scripps C (CA)	15
Southern California, U of	25
Stanford U (CA)	20
Stevens Institute of Technology (NJ)	15
Swarthmore C (PA)	10
Tufts U (MA)	15
Washington, U of	10
Wellesley C (MA)	20
Wesleyan U (CT)	10
Yale U (CT)	10

ENROLLMENT POTPOURRI

Commuter Colleges

Many, if not most, students commute from home to class at these schools.

Alaska, U of, Anchorage
Boise State U (ID)
California State Polytechnic U, Pomona
California State U, Bakersfield
California State U, San Diego
Christopher Newport U (VA)
Cleveland State U (OH)
Eastern Utah, C of
Florida A&M U
Florida Atlantic U
Florida State U
George Mason U (VA)
Grand Canyon U (AZ)
Houston, U of (TX)
Idaho State U
Iona C (NY)
Louisiana State U, Baton Rouge
Louisville, U of (KY)
Midwestern State U (TX)
Nevada, U of, Las Vegas
Nevada, U of, Reno
New Mexico, U of, Albuquerque
New York, City U of (most campuses)
Oakland U (MI)
Prescott C (AZ)
St. John's U (NY)
Utah State U
Utah, U of
Washburn U (KS)
Wayne State U (MI)
Weber State U (UT)
Wichita State U (KS)
Wilmington C (DE)
Woodbury U (CA)
Yavapai C (AZ)
Youngstown State U (OH)

Percentages of Out-of-State Students at State-Supported Schools

The percentages listed are approximate.

	PERCENT
Alabama, U of, Tuscaloosa	35
Arizona State U	25
Arizona, U of	30
California, U of, Berkeley	15
California, U of, Los Angeles	5
Clemson U (SC)	30
Colorado, U of	35
Delaware, U of	50
Florida, U of	10
Illinois, U of, Urbana	5
Indiana U, Bloomington	30
Iowa, U of	30
Kansas, U of	30
Maine, U of, Orono	20
Maryland, U of, College Park	25
Miami U (OH)	25
Michigan, U of, Ann Arbor	30
Minnesota, U of, Twin Cities	20
Missouri, U of, Columbia	15
New Hampshire, U of	40
New York, State U of, Binghamton	5
North Carolina, U of, Chapel Hill	20
Ohio State U, Columbus	10
Ohio U, Athens	25
Oregon, U of	30
Pennsylvania State U, University Park	20
Rhode Island, U of	40
Rutgers U (NJ)	10
Texas, U of, Austin	20
Vermont, U of	50
Virginia, U of	35
Washington, U of	10
Wisconsin, U of, Madison	30

COST

EXPENSIVE/LESS EXPENSIVE

Average College Costs

These are average costs for 1997–98 at four-year schools, including tuition, fees, books, supplies, room and board, and transportation.

Resident student at private college	$21,424
Resident student at public college	10,069
Commuter student at private college	18,263
Commuter student at public college	8,133

Source: The College Board, New York, NY.

Most Expensive Colleges

The fees at these schools are often in excess of $25,000 a year for tuition and room and board.

Amherst C (MA)
Bard C (NY)
Barnard C (NY)
Bates C (ME)
Bennington C (VT)
Boston U (MA)
Bowdoin C (ME)
Brandeis U (MA)
Brown U (RI)
Bryn Mawr C (PA)
Bucknell U (PA)
Carleton C (MN)
Carnegie Mellon U (PA)
Chicago, U of (IL)
Colby C (ME)
Colgate U (NY)
Columbia U (NY)
Connecticut C
Cornell U (NY)
Dartmouth C (NH)
Dickinson C (PA)
Drew U (NJ)

Most Expensive Colleges (continued)

Duke U (NC)
Franklin and Marshall C (PA)
George Washington U (DC)
Georgetown U (DC)
Gettysburg C (PA)
Hamilton C (NY)
Hampshire C (MA)
Harvard U (MA)
Haverford C (PA)
Hobart C/William Smith C (NY)
Holy Cross, C of the (MA)
Johns Hopkins U (MD)
Lafayette C (PA)
Lehigh U (PA)
Massachusetts Institute of Technology
Miami, U of (FL)
Middlebury C (VT)
Mt. Holyoke C (MA)
New York U
Oberlin C (OH)
Pennsylvania, U of
Pepperdine U (CA)
Pitzer C (CA)
Pomona C (CA)
Princeton U (NJ)
Reed C (OR)
Rochester, U of (NY)
St. Lawrence U (NY)
Sarah Lawrence C (NY)
Scripps C (CA)
Skidmore C (NY)
Smith C (MA)
Southern California, U of
Stanford U (CA)
Swarthmore C (PA)
Trinity C (CT)
Tufts U (MA)
Tulane U (LA)
Union C (NY)
Vanderbilt U (TN)
Vassar C (NY)
Washington U (MO)
Wellesley C (MA)
Wesleyan U (CT)
Wheaton C (MA)
Williams C (MA)
Yale U (CT)

Top-Notch Low-Cost Colleges

Charges for tuition and room and board at these well-respected colleges are much lower than average.

Acadia U (Canada)
Alabama, U of, Tuscaloosa
Alaska, U of, Fairbanks
Alice Lloyd C (KY)
Alverno C (WI)
Appalachian State U (NC)
Arizona State U
Arizona, U of
Arkansas, U, Fayetteville
Auburn U (AL)
Austin C (TX)
Baylor U (TX)
Berea C (KY)
Boise State U (ID)
Brigham Young U (UT)
British Columbia, U of (Canada)
California State U, Humboldt
Calvin C (MI)
Carleton U (Canada)
Charleston, C of (SC)
Clemson U (SC)
Colorado State U
Cooper Union (NY)
Cottey C (MO)
Dallas, U of (TX)
Dayton, U of (OH)
Deep Springs C (CA)
Delaware, U of
Elon C (NC)
Evergreen State C (WA)
Flagler C (FL)
Florida International U
Florida State U
George Mason U (VA)
Georgia Institute of Technology
Georgia Southern U
Georgia, U of
Grove City C (PA)
Guilford C (NC)
Hendrix C (AR)
Houston, U of (TX)
Howard U (DC)
Idaho, U of
Illinois C
Illinois, U of, Urbana
Indiana U, Bloomington
Iowa, U of
James Madison U (VA)
Kansas, U of
Kent State U (OH)
Kentucky, U of
Maine, U of, Orono
Mary Washington C (VA)
McGill U (Canada)
Miami U (OH)
Missouri, U of, Columbia
Montana State U
Montana, U of
Moody Bible Institute (IL)
Morehouse C (GA)
Mt. Allison U (Canada)
Nebraska, U of, Lincoln
Nevada, U of, Reno
New C (FL)
New Mexico, U of
New York, City U of, City C
New York, City U of, Hunter C
New York, City U of, Queens C

Top-Notch Low-Cost Colleges (continued)

New York, State U of, Albany
New York, State U of, Binghamton
New York, State U of, Geneseo
New York, State U of, Potsdam
New York, State U of, Stony Brook
North Carolina State U
North Carolina, U of, Ashville
North Carolina, U of, Charlotte
North Carolina, U of, Greensboro
North Dakota State U
Northern Arizona U
Northwest Missouri State U
Ohio State U, Columbus
Ohio U
Oklahoma State U
Oklahoma, U of
Oregon State U
Oregon, U of
Ozarks, C of the (MO)
Presbyterian C (SC)
Prescott C (AZ)
Purdue U (IN)
Queens U (Canada)
Ramapo C (NJ)
St. John's U (MN)
St. Louis U (MO)
St. Mary's C (MD)
Shippensburg U (PA)
Simon Fraser U (Canada)
Slippery Rock U (PA)
South Carolina, U of, Columbia
South Dakota, U of
Southern Illinois U, Carbondale
Southern Vermont C
Stephen F. Austin State U (TX)
Tennessee, U of, Knoxville
Texas A&M U
Texas Christian U
Texas Tech U
Texas, U of, Austin
Toronto, U of (Canada)
Trent U (Canada)
Trenton State C (NJ)
Truman State U (MO)
U.S. Air Force Academy (CO)
U.S. Coast Guard Academy (CT)
U.S. Military Academy (NY)
U.S. Naval Academy (MD)
Washington State U
Washington, U of
Waterloo, U of (Canada)
Webb Institute of Naval Architecture (NY)
West Virginia, U of
Western Washington U
Westminster C (MO)
Wheaton C (IL)
William Jewell C (MO)
York C (PA)

States Offering Tuition Discounts to Students in Neighboring States

Residents of a state that belongs to one of the clusters listed below may be able to attend a public college in another state within the same group at a reduced tuition charge. Programs vary considerably in tuition discounts provided, colleges participating, academic programs available, and admission criteria.

ACADEMIC COMMON MARKET

Alabama
Arkansas
Florida
Georgia
Kentucky
Louisiana
Maryland
Mississippi
Oklahoma
South Carolina
Tennessee
Texas
Virginia
West Virginia

Source: Southern Regional Education Board, Atlanta, GA.

MIDWESTERN HIGHER EDUCATION COMMISSION STUDENT EXCHANGE PROGRAM

Kansas
Michigan
Minnesota
Missouri
Nebraska

Source: Midwestern Higher Education Commission, Minneapolis, MN.

NEW ENGLAND REGIONAL STUDENT PROGRAM

Connecticut
Maine
Massachusetts
New Hampshire
Rhode Island
Vermont

Source: New England Board of Higher Education, Boston, MA.

WESTERN UNDERGRADUATE EXCHANGE

Alaska	New Mexico
Colorado	North Dakota
Hawaii	Oregon
Idaho	South Dakota
Montana	Utah
Nevada	Wyoming

Source: Western Interstate Commission for Higher Education, Boulder, CO.

THE MOST BANG FOR THE BUCK

Colleges with Comprehensive Programs at a Fair Price

These schools earn high praise for their academic quality; at the same time, their costs are comparable to, or less than, colleges with similar academic strengths.

Agnes Scott C (GA)
Auburn U (AL)
Augustana C (IL)
Austin C (TX)
Baylor U (TX)
Beloit C (WI)
Bethany C (WV)
Birmingham-Southern C (AL)
Bradley U (IL)
Buena Vista U (IA)
California Institute of Technology
California State U, Sacramento
California, U of, Berkeley
California, U of, Irvine
California, U of, Los Angeles
California, U of, Riverside
California, U of, San Diego
California, U of, Santa Barbara
California, U of, Santa Cruz
Canisius C (NY)
Centenary C (LA)
Centre C (KY)
Charleston, C of (SC)
Clarkson U (NY)
Colorado School of Mines
Colorado, U of, Boulder
Cottey C (MO)
Creighton U (NE)
Dallas, U of (TX)
Davis and Elkins C (WV)
Dayton, U of (OH)
Delaware, U of
Elms C (MA)
Evergreen State C (WA)
Fisk U (TN)
Flagler C (FL)
Florida Institute of Technology
Furman U (SC)
Georgia Institute of Technology
Green Mountain C (VT)
Guilford C (NC)
Gustavus Adolphus C (MN)

Colleges with Comprehensive Programs at a Fair Price (continued)

Hanover C (IN)
Hendrix C (AR)
High Point U (NC)
Holy Cross, C of the (MA)
Illinois, U of, Urbana
James Madison U (VA)
John Carroll U (OH)
Judaism, U of (CA)
Kalamazoo C (MI)
Kentucky, U of
Knox C (IL)
Lenoir-Rhyne C (NC)
Linfield C (OR)
Loras C (IA)
Loyola U (LA)
Marquette U (WI)
Mary Washington C (VA)
Miami U (OH)
Michigan State U
Michigan, U of, Ann Arbor
Millikin U (IL)
Millsaps C (MS)
New Hampshire, U of
New Mexico Institute of Technology
New York, State U of, Binghamton
North Carolina, U of, Chapel Hill
Otterbein C (OH)
Pennsylvania State U, University Park
Pepperdine U (CA)
Puget Sound, U of (WA)
Quinnipiac C (CT)
Rhode Island, U of
Rhodes C (TN)
Rice U (TX)
Richmond, U of (VA)
Ripon C (WI)
Rutgers U (NJ)
Southwestern U (TX)
Spelman C (GA)
Spring Hill C (AL)
Stetson U (FL)
Stonehill C (MA)
Susquehanna U (PA)
Tennessee, U of, Knoxville
Texas Christian U
Texas, U of, Austin
Thomas Aquinas C (CA)
Trenton State C (NJ)
Trinity U (TX)
Truman State U (MO)
Tulsa, U of (OK)
Ursinus C (PA)
Valparaiso U (IN)
Virginia, U of
Wabash C (IN)
Wake Forest U (NC)
Wartburg C (IA)
Washington and Jefferson C (PA)
Washington C (MD)
Washington, U of
Wesley C (DE)
Western Washington U
Whitworth C (WA)
Willamette U (OR)
William and Mary, C of (VA)
Wisconsin, U of, Madison
Wofford C (SC)

The Experts' Choice: Twenty-five Colleges High in Academic Quality But Low in Cost

1. Rice U (TX)
2. Virginia, U of
3. North Carolina, U of, Chapel Hill
*4. William and Mary, C of (VA)
5. Cooper Union (NY)
*6. New York, State U of, Binghamton
7. California, U of, Berkeley
*8. California, U of, Santa Cruz
*9. Mary Washington C (VA)
10. Davidson C (NC)
*11. Miami U (OH)
*12. Wisconsin, U of, Madison
13. James Madison U (VA)
*14. Michigan, U of, Ann Arbor
*15. New College (FL)
*16. Rhodes C (TN)
*17. Texas, U of, Austin
*18. Wake Forest U (NC)
19. St. Mary's C (MD)
*20. Vermont, U of
*21. Washington and Lee U (VA)
22. Furman U (SC)
*23. Grove City C (PA)
*24. Millsaps C (MS)
*25. Tulsa, U of (OK)

*See Author's Note, p. xxv.

Best Values/Discount Prices at National Universities

U.S. News and World Report rated these schools highest in offering a high-quality education at a reasonable cost.

1. Pepperdine U (CA)
2. Rice U (TX)
3. Clarkson U (NY)
4. Rochester, U of (NY)
5. Stanford U (CA)
6. Illinois Institute of Technology
7. Northwestern U (IL)
8. Tulane U (LA)
9. Case Western Reserve U (OH)
10. Dartmouth C (NH)
11. Princeton U (NJ)
12. North Carolina, U of, Chapel Hill
13. Virginia, U of
14. Massachusetts Institute of Technology
15. Chicago, U of (IL)
16. Yale U (CT)
17. Cornell U (NY)
18. Harvard U (MA)
19. Washington U (MO)
20. Carnegie Mellon U (PA)
21. California Institute of Technology
22. Columbia U (NY)
23. Johns Hopkins U (MD)
24. Clark U (MA)
25. Emory U (GA)

Source: Copyright © 1997, *U.S. News and World Report.*

Best Values/Discount Prices at Liberal Arts Colleges

U.S. News and World Report rated these liberal arts schools highest in offering a high quality education at a reasonable cost.

1. Grinnell C (IA)
2. Wells C (NY)
3. Mt. Holyoke C (MA)
4. Knox C (IL)
5. Centre C (KY)
6. Macalester C (MN)
7. Ripon C (WI)
8. Wabash C (IN)
9. Agnes Scott C (GA)
10. Amherst C (MA)
11. Hendrix C (AR)
12. Lake Forest C (IL)
13. Lawrence U (WI)
14. Pomona C (CA)
15. Thomas Aquinas C (CA)
16. Occidental C (CA)
17. Wooster, C of (OH)
18. Claremont McKenna C (CA)
19. Colgate U (NY)
20. Middlebury C (VT)
21. St. Olaf C (MN)
22. South, U of the (TN)
23. Swarthmore C (PA)
24. Allegheny C (PA)
25. Connecticut C
26. Wellesley C (MA)

Source: Copyright © 1997, *U.S. News and World Report.*

WHERE THE MONEY IS

Colleges with Money Available for Scholars

These colleges offer generous and/or numerous financial aid awards based on merit (not necessarily on family income or assets). Many of the awards are based on academic excellence.

Adelphi U (NY)
Alabama, U of, Tuscaloosa
Albion C (MI)
American U (DC)
Arizona State U
Arkansas, U of, Fayetteville
Bard C (NY)
Beloit C (WI)
Boston U (MA)
Brandeis U (MA)
Brigham Young U (UT)
Centre C (KY)
Cincinnati, U of (OH)
Claremont McKenna C (CA)
Clark U (MA)
Colorado School of Mines
Dayton, U of (OH)
Denver, U of (CO)
DePaul U (IL)
DePauw U (IN)
Drew U (NJ)
Emory U (GA)
Florida A&M U
Florida, U of
Fordham U (NY)
Franklin and Marshall C (PA)
Furman U (SC)
George Washington U (DC)
Gonzaga U (WA)
Grinnell C (IA)
Hiram C (OH)
Hofstra U (NY)
Holy Cross, C of the (MA)
Hood C (MD)
Hope C (MI)
Ithaca C (NY)
Kalamazoo C (MI)
Kenyon C (OH)
Knox C (IL)
Lewis and Clark C (OR)
Marquette U (WI)
Miami U (OH)
Missouri, U of, Columbia
Mt. St. Clare C (IA)
Muhlenberg C (PA)
New York U
Occidental C (CA)

Ohio Wesleyan U
Puget Sound, U of (WA)
Rhodes C (TN)
Richmond, U of (VA)
Ripon C (WI)
Rochester, U of (NY)
Southern California, U of
Southern Methodist U (TX)
Tennessee, U of, Knoxville
Texas, U of, Austin
Toledo, U of (OH)
Trinity U (TX)
Tulane U (LA)
Tulsa, U of (OK)
Wagner C (NY)
Washington U (MO)
Whitman C (WA)
Wooster, C of (OH)

Number of Recipients of Student Aid Programs

The programs are followed by the number of recipients and the average amount of aid per recipient, 1995–96.

Program	Recipients	Average aid
Pell Grants	3,600,000	$1,502
Stafford Student Loans—subsidized	3,190,000	3,461
Stafford Student Loans—unsubsidized	1,697,000	3,685
State Grants and State Student Incentive Grants	1,648,000	1,210
Supplemental Educational Opportunity Grants	984,000	588
Perkins Loans	776,000	1,233
College Work-Study	709,000	864
Parent Loans for Undergraduate Students	282,000	5,819

Source: Reproduced with permission from *Trends in Student Aid: 1986 to 1996*.

WORKING WHILE STUDYING

Colleges with Large Cooperative Education Programs

Cooperative education (co-op) programs enable students to combine academic study with periods of off-campus work for pay.

Antioch C (OH)
Bowling Green State U (OH)
Brigham Young U (UT)
Cincinnati, U of (OH)
Clemson U (SC)
Cleveland State U (OH)
Concordia C (MN)
Diablo Valley C (CA)
Drexel U (PA)
Eastern Kentucky U
Georgia Institute of Technology
Hawaii Pacific U
Illinois State U
Illinois, U of, Urbana
Kettering U (MI)
Lane Community C (OR)
Long Island U, C. W. Post C (NY)
Maryland, U of, Baltimore County
Mississippi State U
New York, City U of, La Guardia Community C
New York Institute of Technology
North Carolina State U
North Texas, U of
Northeastern U (MA)
Pace U (NY)
Palomar C (CA)
Rochester Institute of Technology (NY)
St. Norbert C (WI) (Professional Practice Program)
Sinclair Community C (OH)
Sterling C (VT)
Utah State U
Utah, U of
Virginia Polytechnic Institute and State U
Waukesha County Technical C (WI)

Colleges with Large Cooperative Education Programs (continued)

Weber State U (UT)
Wentworth Institute of Technology (MA)
Wichita State U (KS)
Widener U (PA)

Colleges with Many Internship Possibilities

Internship programs allow undergraduates to explore fields of interest. Such work experiences may lead to better jobs after graduation.

American U (DC)
Bennington C (VT) (fieldwork program)
Hawaii Pacific U
Indiana U (PA)
Kalamazoo C (MI)
Keuka C (NY) (every student participates in a four-week career-exploring "field period" each year)
Lake Forest C (IL)
New York, City U of, Queens C
Pine Manor C (MA)
Trinity C (CT)
Upsala C (NJ)
Wellesley C (MA)
Wells C (NY)
Westbrook C (ME) (internships offered in every major)

Colleges Where Physical Work Is Common

These schools encourage or require students to work on campus as part of their college experience.

Alice Lloyd C (KY) (students work ten to twenty hours a week)
Berea C (KY) (students work ten to fifteen hours a week)
Berry C (GA) (85 percent of students work)
Blackburn C (IL) (students work ten to fifteen hours a week)
Deep Springs C (CA) (students work twenty hours a week)
Goddard C (VT) (students work five to ten hours a week)
Ozarks, C of the (MO) (students work fifteen hours a week)
Warren Wilson C (NC) (students work an average of fifteen hours a week)

MORSELS

THE CAMPUS

Colleges with Beautiful Campuses

Alabama, U of, Tuscaloosa
Allegheny C (PA)
Atlantic, C of the (ME)
Bentley C (MA)
Bowdoin C (ME)
British Columbia, U of (Canada)
Bryn Mawr C (PA)
Bucknell U (PA)
California, U of, Santa Cruz
Colby C (ME)
Colgate U (NY)
Colorado, U of
Cornell U (NY)
Dartmouth C (NH)
Davidson C (NC)
DePauw U (IN)
Duke U (NC)
Emory U (GA)
Furman U (SC)
Hampden-Sydney C (VA)
Hanover C (IN)
Hendrix C (AR)
Hiram C (OH)
Kenyon C (OH)
Lafayette C (PA)
Middlebury C (VT)
Montana, U of
Mt. Holyoke C (MA)
North Carolina, U of, Chapel Hill
Notre Dame, U of (IN)
Oklahoma State U
Principia C (IL)
Rhodes C (TN)
Richmond, U of (VA)
Rochester, U of (NY)
St. Bonaventure U (NY)
St. Olaf C (MN)
Santa Clara U (CA)
Smith C (MA)
Southern Methodist U (TX)
Stanford U (CA)
Vassar C (NY)
Virginia, U of
Wake Forest U (NC)
Washington C (MD)
Washington U (MO)
Washington, U of
Washington and Lee U (VA)
Wellesley C (MA)
Westmont C (CA)
Whitman C (WA)
William and Mary, C of (VA)
Wittenberg U (OH)

The Experts' Choice: Great-Looking Campuses

Babson C (MA)
Bucknell U (PA)
California, U of, Santa Cruz
Colby C (ME)
Colgate U (NY)
Colorado, U of
Cornell U (NY)
Dartmouth C (NH)
Denison U (OH)
Duke U (NC)
Kenyon C (OH)
Lewis and Clark C (OR)
Miami U (OH)
Middlebury C (VT)
Pepperdine U (CA)
Princeton U (NJ)
Richmond, U of (VA)
Rollins C (FL)
Smith C (MA)
South, U of the (TN)
Stanford U (CA)
Swarthmore C (PA)
Sweet Briar C (VA)
Virginia, U of
Wake Forest U (NC)
Washington and Lee U (VA)
Wellesley C (MA)
William and Mary, C of (VA)
Williams C (MA)

Colleges with Great Views

Alaska, U of, Fairbanks (of glaciers, rivers, Mt. McKinley, and the Alaska Range)
Brandeis U (MA) (the "Castle Overlook" provides a panoramic view of Boston)
California, U of, Santa Barbara (of the Pacific Ocean)
Colorado, U of (of the foothills of the Rocky Mountains)
Hobart C/William Smith C (NY) (of Seneca Lake)
Lewis and Clark C (OR) (of Mt. Hood)
Montana, U of (of the valley bounded by the Yellowstone and Glacier national parks)
Mt. St. Mary's C (CA) (of the panorama of Los Angeles)
Nevada, U of, Reno (of the Sierra Nevadas)
New C (FL) (of Sarasota Bay, looking toward the Gulf of Mexico)
Pepperdine U (CA) (of the Pacific Ocean, coastal islands, and the city of Los Angeles)
Sweet Briar C (VA) (of the Blue Ridge Mountains)
U.S. Air Force Academy (CO) (of the Rocky Mountains)
Utah, U of (of the Wasatch Mountains)

The Top Fifteen Colleges in Acreage

These schools have the largest land holdings. Numbers indicate size of campus in acres.

1.	Berry C (GA)	28,000
2.	U.S. Air Force Academy (CO)	18,000
3.	U.S. Military Academy (NY)	16,000
4.	Paul Smith's C (NY)	15,000
5.	Deep Springs C (CA)	10,000
*6.	South, U of the (TN)	10,000
7.	Stanford U (CA)	8,800
8.	Duke U (NC)	8,500
9.	New Mexico State U	6,000
10.	Liberty U (VA)	5,700
11.	Texas A&M U	5,142
12.	Pennsylvania State U, University Park	5,013
13.	California Polytechnic State U, San Luis Obispo	5,000
*14.	Michigan State U	5,000
*15.	Tuskegee U (AL)	5,000

*See Author's Note, p. xxv.

Source: *National College Databank* (Princeton, NJ: Peterson's Guides, 1990), 22.

Excellent Student Unions

California State U, San Diego
California, U of, Los Angeles
Colorado State U
Indiana U, Bloomington
Kansas State U
Michigan, U of, Ann Arbor
Rochester, U of (NY)
Stanford U (CA)
Texas, U of, Austin
Wisconsin, U of, Madison

Campuses Where Movies Were Filmed

The colleges below served as at least one on-site location for the films indicated.

Agnes Scott C (GA): *Scream 2,* 1998
Barnard C (NY): *Husbands and Wives,* 1992
California Institute of Technology: *Beverly Hills Cop,* 1984
California, U of, Los Angeles: *The Threesome,* 1994; *Higher Learning,* 1995; *The Nutty Professor,* 1996
Chicago, U of (IL): *When Harry Met Sally . . .*, 1989
Columbia U (NY): *Marathon Man,* 1976
Fordham U (NY): *The Verdict,* 1982
Hamilton C (NY): *The Sterile Cuckoo,* 1969
Harvard U (MA): *Love Story,* 1970
Illinois, U of, Urbana: *With Honors,* 1994
Indiana U, Bloomington: *Breaking Away,* 1979
Lake Forest C (IL): *Ordinary People,* 1980
Mississippi, U of: *Heart of Dixie,* 1989
Morehouse C (GA): *School Daze,* 1988
New York, City U of: *Reversal of Fortune,* 1990
New York U: *When Harry Met Sally . . .*, 1989; *The Freshman,* 1990
Notre Dame, U of (IN): *Rudy,* 1993
Oregon, U of: *Animal House,* 1978
Pacific, U of the (CA): *Raiders of the Lost Ark,* 1981
Pennsylvania, U of: *A Kiss Before Dying,* 1991
Smith C (MA): *Malice,* 1993
South Carolina, U of, Columbia: *The Program,* 1993
Southern California, U of: *The Graduate,* 1967; *Gross Anatomy,* 1989
Spelman C (GA): *School Daze,* 1988
Toronto, U of (Canada): *The Paper Chase,* 1973
Union C (NY): *The Way We Were,* 1973
Virginia, U of: *True Colors,* 1991
Wheaton C (MA): *Soul Man,* 1986
Wisconsin, U of, Madison: *Back to School,* 1986

COLLEGE CITIES

Great Cities in Which to Go to School

These cities have large numbers of colleges (and typically an accepting atmosphere for students), a prominent university around which city life revolves, or an unusual amount of college spirit and nightlife.

Amherst, MA
Ann Arbor, MI
Atlanta, GA
Austin, TX
Boston, MA
Boulder, CO
Burlington, VT
Chapel Hill, NC
Chicago, IL
Columbia, MO
Eugene, OR
Iowa City, IA
Ithaca, NY
Lawrence, KS
Madison, WI
New York, NY
Oneonta, NY
Provo/Orem, UT
Rochester, NY
Seattle, WA
Washington, DC

Populations of Some College Towns

Populations are approximate.

New York, NY	7,500,000	Home of dozens of colleges
Los Angeles, CA	4,000,000	Home of dozens of colleges
Boulder, CO	225,000	Home of the U of Colorado
Durham, NC	180,000	Home of Duke U
Peoria, IL	115,000	Home of Bradley U
Ann Arbor, MI	110,000	Home of U of Michigan
Walla Walla, WA	50,000	Home of Whitman C
Richmond, IN	40,000	Home of Earlham C
Northfield, MN	15,000	Home of Carleton and St. Olaf colleges
Hanover, NH	6,500	Home of Dartmouth C
Hamilton, NY	5,000	Home of Colgate U
Williamstown, MA	4,800	Home of Williams C
Gambier, OH	2,000	Home of Kenyon C
Sewanee, TN	2,000	Home of U of the South
Henniker, NH	1,700	Home of New England C

Source: Rand McNally

Twenty-five Cities Where the Highest Percentage of College-Aged People Reside

Metropolitan areas ranked by percent of their 1990 population aged eighteen to twenty-four. Some nearby colleges are listed with each city.

	PERCENT
1. Norfolk–Virginia Beach–Newport News, VA Hampton U; Norfolk U; Old Dominion U; William and Mary, C of; etc.	13.8
2. San Diego, CA California State U, San Diego; California, U of, San Diego; San Diego, U of; etc.	13.5
3. Anaheim–Santa Ana, CA Dozens of colleges and universities	12.5

		PERCENT
4.	Los Angeles–Long Beach, CA Dozens of colleges and universities	12.3
5.	Boston–Lawrence–Salem–Lowell–Brockton, MA Over sixty colleges and universities	12.0
6.	Washington, DC American U; Catholic U; Georgetown U; George Washington U; Trinity C; etc.	11.1
7.	Dallas, TX Southern Methodist U; Texas Christian U; etc.	11.0
8.	Atlanta, GA Agnes Scott C; Emory U; Georgia State U; Oglethorpe U; etc.	10.9
9.	Houston, TX Houston, U of; Rice U; etc.	10.7
*10.	Phoenix, AZ Arizona State U, etc.	10.7
11.	Chicago, IL Dozens of colleges and universities, including Chicago, U of; DePaul U; Loyola U; Northwestern U; etc.	10.5
*12.	New York, NY Over forty colleges and universities	10.5
13.	Baltimore, MD Goucher C; Johns Hopkins U; etc.	10.4
*14.	Oakland, CA California, U of, Berkeley; Mills C; etc.	10.4
*15.	Philadelphia, PA Drexel U; Pennsylvania, U of; Villanova U; etc.	10.4
*16.	Riverside–San Bernardino, CA California, U of, Riverside; etc.	10.4
17.	Nassau–Suffolk, NY Long Island U, C. W. Post C; New York, State U of, Stony Brook; etc.	10.3
18.	Minneapolis–St. Paul, MN–WI Hamline U; Macalester C; Minnesota, U of, Twin Cities; etc.	10.1
*19.	Newark, NJ New Jersey Institute of Technology; Rutgers U; Seton Hall U; etc.	10.1

Twenty-five Cities Where the Highest Percentage of College-Aged People Reside (continued)

	PERCENT
20. Detroit, MI	10.0
Detroit Mercy, U of; Wayne State U; etc.	
21. Seattle, WA	9.8
Seattle U; Seattle Pacific U; Washington, U of; etc.	
22. St. Louis, MO–IL	9.5
Fontbonne U; St. Louis U; Washington U; etc.	
23. Pittsburgh, PA	9.4
Carnegie Mellon U; Pittsburgh, U of; etc.	
24. Tampa–St. Petersburg–Clearwater, FL	8.6
Eckerd C; South Florida, U of; Tampa, U of; etc.	
25. Miami–Hialeah, FL	1.0
Barry U; Miami, U of; etc.	

*See Author's Note, p. xxv.

Source: William Dunn, "Hanging Out with American Youth," *American Demographics* (February 1992): 32. Reprinted with permission. © *American Demographics.*

College Towns with Excellent Pop Music Scenes

These are cities identified by music critic Dave Marsh as being particularly known for musical entertainment.

Ann Arbor, MI
Athens, GA
Austin, TX
Berkeley, CA
Boston/Cambridge, MA
Columbia, SC
Columbus, OH
Greenwich Village, New York, NY
Lawrence, KS
Raleigh/Durham/Chapel Hill, NC
Seattle, WA
Tampa, FL

COLLEGE NAMES

Nicknames for Colleges or Students at Particular Schools

Babson C (MA)	Babsonites
Bard C (NY)	Bardie
Bates C (ME)	Batesies
Bennington C (VT)	Bennies
Bryn Mawr C (PA)	Mawrters
California Polytechnic State U, San Luis Obispo	Cal Poly/SLO
California, U of, Berkeley	Cal
Carleton C (MN)	Carls
Clark U (MA)	Clarkies
Colgate U (NY)	'Gate
Connecticut C	Conn
Drew U (NJ)	Drewids
Duke U (NC)	Dukies
Earlham C (IN)	Earlhamites
Emory U (GA)	Emeroids
Evergreen State C (WA)	Greeners
Florida A&M U	Fam-You
Franklin and Marshall C (PA)	Fummers
Gustavus Adolphus C (MN)	Gusties
Hampden-Sydney C (VA)	Hampsders
Hartwick C (NY)	The Wick
Harvey Mudd C (CA)	Mudders
Haverford C (PA)	The Ford
Heidelberg C (OH)	The Berg
Lake Forest C (IL)	Foresters
Lewis and Clark C (OR)	LC

Massachusetts Institute of Technology	The Tute
Missouri, U of, Columbia	Mizzou
Morehouse C (GA)	The House
Muhlenberg C (PA)	The Berg
North Carolina, U of, Chapel Hill	Carolina
Oberlin C (OH)	Obie/Oberliners
Occidental C (CA)	Oxy
Pittsburgh, U of (PA)	Pitt
Pitzer C (CA)	Pitzies
Reed C (OR)	Reedies
Rhode Island School of Design	Rizdee
St. John's C (MD)	Johnnies
St. John's C (MN)	Johnnies
St. John's C (NM)	Johnnies
St. Lawrence U (NY)	Larries
St. Mary-of-the-Woods C (IN)	Woodsies
St. Michael's C (VT)	St. Mike's
St. Olaf C (MN)	Ole
Scripps C (CA)	Scrippsies
Skidmore C (NY)	Skiddies
Smith C (MA)	Smithies
South Carolina, U of, Columbia	Carolina
South, U of the (TN)	Sewanee
Swarthmore C (PA)	Swatties
U.S. Coast Guard Academy (CT)	Coasties
U.S. Military Academy (NY)	West Point
U.S. Naval Academy (MD)	Annapolis
Valparaiso U (IN)	Valpo
Vanderbilt U (TN)	Vandy
Villanova U (PA)	Nova
Wabash C (IN)	Wallies
Washington State U	Wah-sue
Washington, U of	U-Dub
Wheaton C (IL)	Wheaties
Wheaton C (MA)	Wheaties
Whitman C (WA)	Whitties
Williams C (MA)	Ephs (shortened first name of the college founder)
Wittenberg U (OH)	Witt
Worcester Polytechnic Institute (MA)	Whoopies
Yale U (CT)	Yalies/Elis (shortened first name of the college founder)

The "Don't Let the Name Fool You" List

Anna Maria C (MA): a coed institution
Boston U (MA): a private institution
California Lutheran U: the student body is about 40 percent Lutheran
California U (PA): yes, there is a college with this name in Pennsylvania
Indiana U (PA): a college with this name is in Pennsylvania
Madonna C (MI): no relation
Mary Washington C (VA): a public, coeducational college
Miami, U of (FL): in Coral Gables, not Miami
Mississippi U for Women: a coed institution
Pacific Lutheran U (WA): only 40 percent Lutheran
St. Mary's C (MD): public, not church related
Southern Methodist U (TX): the student body is only 20 percent Methodist
Temple U (PA): a public university
Texas Christian U: not church supported, not a "bible school"
Texas Woman's U: a coed institution
Transylvania U (KY): think Daniel Boone rather than Count Dracula
Western Maryland C: in eastern, not western, Maryland

Colleges with the Same or Similar Names

Allegheny C (PA) and Allegany Community C (MD)
Anderson C (SC) and Anderson U (IN)
Antioch C (OH) and Antioch U (WA)
Armstrong C (CA) and Armstrong State C (GA)
Augustana C (IL) and Augustana C (SD)
Baker C (MI) and Baker U (KS)
Barry U (FL) and Berry C (GA)
Bethany C (CA), (KS), and (WV)
Bethel C (IN), (KS), (MN), and (TN)
California State Polytechnic U and California Polytechnic State U
California, U of, San Diego; San Diego, U of (CA); and San Diego State U (CA)
Capital U (OH) and Capitol C (MD)

Carroll C (WI) and Carroll C (MT)
Central C (IA) and Central C (KS)
City U (WA) and City U of New York
Clark C (WA), Clarke C (IA), and Clark U (MA)
Columbia C (CA), (IL), (MO), (SC); and Columbia C (NY) (part of Columbia U)
Concordia C (AL), (MI), (MN), (NE), (NY), (OR); and Concordia U (CA), (IL), (WI)
Cumberland C (KY) and Cumberland U (TN)
East Central C (MO) and East Central U (OK)
Emmanuel C (GA) and Emmanuel C (MA)
Franklin C (IN) and Franklin C (KY)
Georgetown C (KY) and Georgetown U (DC)
Gordon C (GA) and Gordon C (MA)
Howard C (TX) and Howard U (DC)
Huntingdon C (AL) and Huntington C (IN)
Indiana U (IN) and Indiana U (PA)
Jacksonville C (TX) and Jacksonville U (FL)
King C (TN) and King's C (NY), (PA)
La Salle U (PA) and Lasell C (MA)
Lee C (TN), (TX) and Lees C (KY)
Lewis and Clark C (OR) and Lewis-Clark State C (ID)
Lincoln U (CA), (MO), and (PA)
Loyola C (MD) and Loyola U (IL), (LA)
Marymount C (CA), (NY); Marymount U (VA); and Marymount Manhattan C (NY)
Miami, U of (FL) and Miami U (OH)
Monmouth C (IL) and Monmouth C (NJ)
Mt. St. Mary C (NY) and Mt. St. Mary's C (CA), (MD)
National C (CO), (MN), (MO), (NM), and (SD)
Northern Illinois U and Northeastern Illinois U
Northwestern C (IA), (MN), (OH), (WI); and Northwestern U (IL)
Notre Dame C (NH), (OH); Notre Dame, C of (CA), (MD); and Notre Dame, U of (IN)
Pacific U (OR) and Pacific, U of the (CA)
Phillips C (IL) and Phillips U (OK)
Quincy C (IL) and Quincy C (MA)
Randolph-Macon C (VA) and Randolph-Macon Woman's C (VA)
Regis C (MA) and Regis U (CO)
Robert Morris C (PA) and Robert Morris C (IL)

Colleges with the Same or Similar Names (continued)

St. Augustine C (IL) and St. Augustine's C (NC)
St. Francis C (IN), (NY), and (PA)
St. John's C (MD), (NM) and St. John's U (MN), (NY)
St. Joseph's C (IN), (ME), (NY); St. Joseph C (CT); and St. Joseph's U (PA)
St. Mary C (KS); St. Mary's C (IN), (MI), (MN), (NC); and St. Mary's U (TX)
St. Thomas U (FL) and St. Thomas, U of (MN), (TX)
Shorter C (AR) and Shorter C (GA)
Simpson C (CA) and Simpson C (IA)
Southwestern C (AZ), (CA), (KS); and Southwestern U (TX)
Sterling C (KS) and Sterling C (VT)
Thomas Aquinas C (CA) and St. Thomas Aquinas C (NY)
Thomas C (GA) and Thomas C (ME)
Trinity C (CT), (DC), (IL), (VT); and Trinity U (TX)
Union C (KY), (NE), and (NY)
Washington U (MO) and Washington, U of
Wayne State C (NE) and Wayne State U (MI)
Wesley C (DE) and Wesley C (MS)
Wesleyan C (GA) and Wesleyan U (CT)
Westminster C (MO), (PA), and (UT)
Wheaton C (MA) and Wheaton C (IL)
Wilmington C (DE) and Wilmington C (OH)
Xavier U (OH) and Xavier U (LA)
York C (NE) and York C (PA)

Colleges That Have Changed Their Names

Listed are current name, former name, and date of name change.

Albertson C (ID), The College of Idaho, 1991
Audrey Cohen C (NY), College for Human Services, 1992
Barton C (NC), Atlantic Christian C, 1990
Claremont-McKenna C (CA), Claremont Men's C, 1981
Concordia U (CA), Christ C, Irvine, 1993
Duke U (NC), Trinity C, 1924
Eckerd C (FL), Florida Presbyterian C, 1972
Hardin-Simmons U (TX), Simmons C, 1930s
Kettering U (MI), GMI Engineering and Management Institute, 1997
Lewis and Clark C (OR), College of Albany, 1942
Linfield C (OR), McMinnville C, 1922
Lynn U (FL), College of Boca Raton, 1991
Memphis, U of (TN), Memphis State U, 1994
Nebraska, U of, Kearney; Kearney State C, 1991
New York, City U of, Lehman C; Hunter C Uptown, 1968
Princeton U (NJ), College of New Jersey, 1896
Rhodes C (TN), Southwestern at Memphis, 1984
Richard Stockton C (NJ), Stockton State C, 1993
Rowan C (NJ), Glassboro State C, 1992
Salem-Teikyo U (WV), Salem C, 1989
Teikyo Post U (CT), Post C, 1990
Texas A&M U, Commerce; East Texas State U, 1997
Texas, U of, El Paso; Texas Western C, 1967
Truman State U (MO), Northeast Missouri State U, 1996
U.S. International U (CA), California Western U, 1973
Western Oregon State C, Oregon College of Education, 1980

TIDBITS

Educational Attainment of Adults

	PERCENT
Eighth grade or less	10.4
Some high school, no diploma	14.4
High school diploma	30.0
Some college, no degree	18.7
Associate degree	6.2
Bachelor's degree	13.1
Graduate or professional degree	7.2

Source: U.S. Census Bureau.

Unemployment Rate by Educational Background

	PERCENT
1–3 years of high school	12.2
4 years of high school	5.8
1–3 years of college	4.2
4 or more years of college	2.4

Source: *Digest of Educational Statistics,* U.S. Department of Education.

Oldest Schools in America

1. Harvard U (MA) (1636)
2. William and Mary, C of (VA) (1693)
3. St. John's C (MD) (1696)
4. Yale U (CT) (1701)
5. Pennsylvania, U of (1740)
6. Moravian C (PA) (1742)
7. Delaware, U of (1743)
8. Princeton U (NJ) (1746)
9. Washington and Lee U (VA) (1749)
10. Columbia U (NY) (1754)
11. Brown U (RI) (1764)
12. Rutgers U (NJ) (1766)
13. Dartmouth C (NH) (1769)
14. Charleston, C of (SC) (1770)
15. Salem C (NC) (1772)
16. Dickinson C (PA) (1773)
17. Hampden-Sydney C (VA) (1776)
18. Transylvania U (KY) (1780)
19. Washington and Jefferson C (PA) (1781)
20. Washington C (MD) (1782)
21. Becker C, Leicester (MA) (1784)
22. Georgia, U of (1785)
23. Castleton State C (VT) (1787)

*24. Franklin and Marshall C (PA) (1787)
*25. Louisburg C (NC) (1787)
*26. York C (PA) (1787)

*See Author's Note, p. xxv.

Source: *National College Databank* (Princeton, NJ: Peterson's Guides, 1990): 2.

The Top College Fight Songs

These are the top college fight songs according to researcher William Studwell of Northern Illinois University. Studwell's comments are included here.

THE TOP TWENTY-FIVE

1. Notre Dame, U of (IN): "Notre Dame Victory March" ("best known and perhaps the most borrowed")
2. Michigan, U of, Ann Arbor: "The Victors" ("most rousing and stunning; very proud song")
3. Wisconsin, U of, Madison: "On Wisconsin" ("smooth and much borrowed old classic")

The Top College Fight Songs, the Top Twenty-Five (continued)

4. Yale U (CT): "Down the Field" ("another smooth and much borrowed old classic")
5. U.S. Naval Academy (MD): "Anchors Aweigh" ("very dynamic and uplifting")
6. Maine, U of, Orono: "Stein Song" ("great melody, but it's a drinking song")
7. Southern California, U of: "Fight on, USC" ("brilliant, sparkling, and innovative")
8. Georgia Institute of Technology: "Ramblin' Wreck from Georgia Tech" ("fine tune; great sense of humor")
9. Texas, U of, Austin: "The Eyes of Texas" ("tune borrowed from 'I've Been Working on the Railroad,' but has a lot of sweep and energy")
10. Ohio State U, Columbus: "Across the Field" ("smooth and active; takes you pleasantly across the field")
11. Minnesota, U of, Twin Cities: "Minnesota Rouser" ("dynamic and rousing, as the title suggests")
12. Indiana U, Bloomington: "Indiana, Our Indiana" ("tugs at the heart while causing foot tapping")
13. Illinois, U of, Urbana: "Illinois Loyalty" ("smooth, sensitive, and flowing")
14. Washington and Lee U (VA): "Washington and Lee Swing" ("very catchy and likable; well named")
15. Pennsylvania, U of: "Fight on, Pennsylvania" ("creative and different from the rest of the pack")
16. Oklahoma, U of: "Boomer Sooner" ("borrowed from 'Yale Boola,' but rocks the stadium")
17. Georgia, U of: "Glory, Glory to Old Georgia" ("uses the rouser 'Battle Hymn of the Republic' as its tune; a passing mention to the University of Colorado, which also uses the tune for its 'Glory, Glory, Colorado' ")
18. U.S. Air Force Academy (CO): "U.S. Air Force Song" ("excellent uplifting march; also used as the Air Force's song")
19. U.S. Coast Guard Academy (CT): "Semper Paratus" ("lesser known but quite stirring march; also used as the Coast Guard's song")
20. Clemson U (SC): "Clemson Fight Song" ("uses the delightful 'Tiger Rag' as its tune")

21. Tennessee, U of, Knoxville: "Down the Field" ("uses the exact same title and tune as Yale's 'Down the Field'; F for originality, but A+ for taste")
22. Kansas, U of: "Stand up and Cheer" ("reportedly a fine song that has been borrowed by others, but its recordings have so far eluded the compiler of this list")
23. Northern Illinois U: "NIU Fight Song" ("lively and distinctive; can't ignore my own university")
24. Cornell U (NY): "Far Above Cayuga's Waters" ("really an alma mater rather than a fight song, but is such a collegiate classic, how can one overlook it?; if played with a lively enough tempo, it becomes a pretty good fight song")
25. Harvard U (MA) and Rice U (TX): "Our Director March" ("these two universities both use this excellent march, but not primarily as a fight song; if the melody had a clearer institutional identity, it would be in the top fifteen")

HONORABLE MENTIONS

Alabama, U of, Tuscaloosa
Lamar U (TX)
Michigan State U
Northwestern U (IL)
Pennsylvania State U, University Park
Princeton U (NJ)
Tulane U (LA)
Washington, U of

Traditions at Colleges and Universities

Allegheny C (PA)—First-year women are not considered a coed until they are kissed by an upperclassman on the thirteenth plank of an old campus bridge. Freshmen men usually steal the thirteenth plank.

Augustana C (IL)—Sorority big sisters initiate new little sisters by having a man kiss the new pledge under the bell tower. At graduation, flags from all the states and international countries represented by students are displayed in the gymnasium and the faculty forms a reception line so students can say thank-yous and good-byes.

Bates C (ME)—On St. Patrick's Day, students cut a hole in the ice in the campus pond and jump in.

Beloit C (WI)—The Folk and Blues Festival, in the fall, incorporates outdoor music and an open microphone for spontaneous student performances.

Benedictine C (KS)—First week of school in the fall, freshmen don red and black felt beanies for the Hallowed Beanie Blessing.

Brandeis U (MA)—To prepare for the "screw your roommate" dance, students arrange a blind date for their roommate and think of creative ways for the two to meet.

Brigham Young U (UT)—At 8 A.M., as students file to class, the first four measures of "Come, Come Ye Saints" is played from the bell tower; the national anthem is played twice a day.

Bryn Mawr C (PA)—On lantern night, sophomores present lanterns to freshmen.

Bucknell U (PA)—Freshman have their first meal together with college deans, as do seniors before they graduate. On the first night of orientation, freshmen light candles and sing the alma mater. On Conference Day, the first Saturday of orientation, the faculty meets with students and speeches are given on various topics.

California Institute of Technology—On Ditch Day, in the spring, seniors lock their dorm rooms in humorous, whimsical (and sometimes electronically clever) ways and skip classes. Underclassmen must "break into" the rooms and fetch the reward.

Carleton C (MN)—During convocations, students blow bubbles as faculty members exit; this is known as the "bubble brigade."

Carnegie Mellon U (PA)—Rubbing the nose of a sculpture of CMU's first president is said to bring good luck during exams.

Chatham C (PA)—A song contest is held annually; classes compete against each other in original and traditional song categories.

Colgate U (NY)—For graduation, graduating seniors walk down the campus hill at night with torches and throw them into a fire at the bottom of the hill.

Colorado Mountain C—The Totally Tasteless and Tacky Talent Show is held annually.

Connecticut, U of—Oozeball is the name for the annual mud volleyball tournament.

DePauw U (IN)—"The Monon Bell" is a football game that has been played more than one hundred times.

Eckerd C (FL)—Since Eckerd has no football team and no homecoming, they celebrate "homely-coming," when guys dress up in women's clothing and a contest is held to select the most outrageous.

Florida, U of—Gator Growl is the pep rally before the homecoming game.

Gonzaga U (WA)—Each year students, faculty members, and administrators walk to Cataldo Mission, about ten miles from campus, to honor a different campus event or achievement.

Grinnell C (IA)—Campus screams are held twice each year during examination periods.

Hendrix C (AR)—On their birthdays, students are thrown into the campus fountain.

Hollins C (VA)—On Tinker Day, in October, bells ring, classes are cancelled, and students dress up outrageously to climb nearby Tinker Mountain. Skits are held on the top of the mountain, and the seniors serve lunch to those present.

Holy Cross, C of the (MA)—The first snowfall precipitates the "annual streak." Participants clad in boxer shorts run across campus dodging snowballs thrown by the student body.

Illinois, U of, Urbana—Chief Illiniwek performs Indian ceremonial dances at halftime of football games.

Indiana, U of, Bloomington—A "Little 500" intramural cycling race is held.

Kenyon C (OH)—At the end of student orientation, freshmen get together and sing Kenyon fight songs. The process is repeated when students complete their senior year.

Traditions at Colleges and Universities (continued)

Knox C (IL)—Flunk day is held in the spring, when classes are cancelled without warning.

Lehigh U (PA)—Turkey Trot is a race up the hill at Thanksgiving.

Lynchburg C (VA)—"Sibs and Kids Weekend" includes an outdoor picnic, trip to the zoo, and a scavenger hunt for siblings and children of faculty. Another tradition is "duckfest," a meal of roast duck, clams, and shrimp followed by entertainment.

Massachusetts Institute of Technology—Nighttime invasion of off-limit areas, such as airshafts and steam tunnels.

Massachusetts, U of, Amherst—Students stand throughout each home basketball game.

Michigan, U of, Ann Arbor—During Nude Run, students move, *au naturel,* from one side of the campus to the other on the last day of exams.

Middlebury C (VT)—Winter carnival, a three-day event held the last weekend in February, includes ski and cross-country races, student-sponsored events, snow sculptures, and ice show. Also, all February grads ski or snowboard down a trail at the college's ski area to the base for a graduation photo.

Mt. Holyoke C (MA)—On Mountain Day, bells ring, classes are cancelled, and students go to the mountains.

New York, State U of, Buffalo—The university sponsors a knee-deep mud volleyball competition.

Northwestern U (IL)—Painting "the rock" is a long-standing tradition. Students paint the rock in the common square with dorm names, student council candidates' names, art, etc. Another tradition is marshmallow tossing at football games.

Oberlin C Conservatory of Music (OH)—"Mock Students" is an impious annual variety show.

Ohio State U, Columbus—Medieval and Renaissance Festival is held the first week in May.

Ohio Wesleyan U—"Monnett Weekend" is held in April for parents and siblings. Siblings stay in dorms and go to class with their brothers and sisters.

Pacific, U of the (CA)—During the annual Band Frolic, Greek and residence halls compete in skits.

Pennsylvania, U of—On Hey Day, college juniors celebrate "rite of passage." Students wear Styrofoam hats, carry canes, dress in red and blue, and march around the campus. They are addressed by the school president on what it means to be a senior.

Pepperdine U (CA)—Midnight Yell, during exam week, is a time when students scream each night.

Princeton U (NJ)—To celebrate the first snowfall, naked sophomores do calisthenics in a campus courtyard and run through town at midnight. This is called the Nude Olympics.

Randolph-Macon Woman's C (VA)—"Odd/Even Rivalry," begun in the early 1900s, identifies students by graduation year and promotes class unity through song competitions, the wearing of different colored shirts on special occasions, and the use of separate staircases in the administration building.

Reed C (OR)—Seniors parade with their completed theses in hand.

Rhode Island, U of—The newspaper is called *The Good 5-Cent Cigar*.

Rochester, U of (NY)—Classes end at noon on Wednesday afternoons.

Rollins C (FL)—Fox Day is an unscheduled day when school is called off.

St. Lawrence U (NY)—As part of Peak Weekend, students set out to climb all forty-six peaks of the Adirondack Mountains. The goal is for at least one student to be on each summit at the same time.

Simmons C (MA)—Afternoon tea is held on Friday.

South, U of the (TN)—Professors and honor students wear academic gowns to class. The more tattered and worn the gown, the more it's valued. If the gown is handed down, initials of those who wore it are placed on the shoulder. Dresses and coats and ties are worn by other students.

Spalding U (KY)—Running of the Rodents is held the week before the Kentucky Derby, at which time student-trained rats run around a miniature version of Churchill Downs.

Swarthmore C (PA)—Students build boats for the Crum Regatta and race in Crum Creek. This event is held on Parents Weekend.

Syracuse U (NY)—During Animation Festival, held midyear, students watch hours of cartoons and animated feature films.

Texas A&M U—Silver Taps, held the first Tuesday of every month, memorializes deceased A&M students with a twenty-one-gun salute and honor guard.

Traditions at Colleges and Universities (continued)

Ursinus C (PA)—Bells ring hourly each day from 9 A.M. to 6 P.M. Also, Lorelei, a semiformal dance, is held every spring (since 1926) to which the women invite the men.

Valparaiso U (IN)—A big popcorn celebration is held each year. (Valparaiso, Indiana, is the home of Orville Redenbacher.) People come from all over the state for a parade with floats. The theme of the parade relates to popcorn.

Vanderbilt U (TN)—The Rites of Spring festival is a week-long event with food, crafts, entertainment, and T-shirt sales.

Vermont, U of—Winterfest includes student-sponsored activities, snow sculptures, and ski races.

Wabash C (IN)—At "Chapel Sing," fraternity pledges link arms on the steps of the school chapel and try to outbellow each other in singing the Wabash fight song.

Wellesley C (MA)—Flower Sunday is held the first Sunday of the academic year, when big sisters and little sisters go to church and brunch, and big sisters give little sisters a flower. Another tradition is Wednesday afternoon tea.

Wells C (NY)—On graduation day, seniors travel to their commencement ceremony in a restored Wells Fargo stagecoach.

Westminster C (PA)—A three-day mock political convention is held every four years.

William and Mary, C of (VA)—At Yule Log, held in December, students gather to hear the president read a holiday tale and then burn a yule log.

Alma Maters of Actors and Actresses

Ed Asner, Chicago, U of (IL)
Annette Benning, California State U, San Francisco
Albert Brooks, Carnegie Mellon U (PA)
Betty Buckley, Texas Christian U
Sandra Bullock, East Carolina U (NC)
Dean Cain, Princeton U (NJ)
Carrottop (Scott Thompson), Florida Atlantic U
Richard Chamberlain, Pomona C (CA)
Chevy Chase, Bard C (NY)
George Clooney, Northern Kentucky U

Glenn Close, William and Mary, C of (VA)
Kevin Costner, California State U, Fullerton
Geena Davis, New England C (NH)
Colleen Dewhurst, Lawrence U (WI)
Harrison Ford, Ripon C (WI)
Jodie Foster, Yale U (CT)
Brendan Fraser, Cornish C of the Arts (WA)
Sara Gilbert, Yale U (CT)
Hugh Grant, Oxford U (UK)
Woody Harrelson, Hanover C (IN)
Ethan Hawke, Carnegie Mellon U (PA)
Katherine Hepburn, Bryn Mawr C (PA)
Hal Holbrook, Denison U (OH)
James Earl Jones, Michigan, U of, Ann Arbor
Tommy Lee Jones, Harvard U (MA)
Michael Keaton, Kent State U (OH)
Greg Kinnear, Arizona, U of
Kris Kristofferson, Pomona C (CA)
Tony Kushner, Columbia U (NY)
Joey Lawrence, Southern California, U of
Shelley Long, Northwestern U (IL)
Kyle MacLachlan, Washington, U of
John Malkovich, Illinois State U
Kelly Martin, Yale U (CT)
Martin Mull, Rhode Island School of Design
Paul Newman, Kenyon C (OH)
Carroll O'Conner, Montana, U of
Jamison Parker, Beloit C (WI)
Mary-Louise Parker, North Carolina School of the Arts
Brad Pitt, Missouri, U of, Columbia
Phylicia Rashad, Howard U (DC)
Christopher Reeve, Cornell U (NY)
Adam Sandler, New York U
Fred Savage, Stanford U (CA)
Roy Schneider, Franklin and Marshall C (PA)
Arnold Schwarzenegger, Wisconsin, U of, Superior
Craig Sheffer, East Stroudsburg U (PA)
Andrew Shue, Dartmouth C (NH)
Sinbad, Denver, U of (CO)
Sylvester Stallone, Miami, U of (FL)
Meryl Streep, Vassar C (NY)

Alma Maters of Actors and Actresses (continued)

Spencer Tracy, Ripon C (WI)
Denzel Washington, Fordham U (NY)
Scott Wolf, George Washington U (DC)
Joanne Woodward, Sarah Lawrence C (NY)
Steven Wright, Emerson C (MA)

Alma Maters of Artists, Musicians, and Filmmakers

Kathleen Battle, musician, Cincinnati, U of (OH)
Jim Berry, cartoonist, Ohio Wesleyan U
Ken Burns, filmmaker *(The Civil War)*, Hampshire C (MA)
Tracy Chapman, musician, Colby C (ME)
Natalie Cole, musician, Massachusetts, U of, Amherst
Francis Ford Coppola, filmmaker, Hofstra U (NY)
Evan Dando, musician, Skidmore C (NY)
Roberta Flack, musician, Howard U (DC)
Matt Groening, cartoonist, Evergreen State C (WA)
Francis Scott Key, composer, St. Johns C (MD)
Gary Larson, cartoonist, Washington State U
Spike Lee, filmmaker, Morehouse C (GA)
Roy Lichtenstein, artist, Ohio State U, Columbus
Lorin Maazel, musician, Pittsburgh, U of (PA)
Johnny Mathis, musician, California State U, San Francisco
Meatloaf, musician, Amherst C (MA)
Arthur Miller, playwright, Michigan, U of, Ann Arbor
Jim Morrison, musician, California, U of, Los Angeles
Martin Scorcese, filmmaker, New York U
John Singleton, filmmaker, Southern California, U of
Stephen Sondheim, composer, Williams C (MA)
Steven Spielberg, filmmaker, California State U, Long Beach
Oliver Stone, filmmaker, New York U
John Tesh, musician, North Carolina State U
Bill Watterson, cartoonist, Kenyon C (OH)
John Williams, composer, California, U of, Los Angeles

Alma Maters of Sports Personalities

Kareem Abdul-Jabar, California, U of, Los Angeles
Chris Berman, Brown U (RI)
Larry Bird, Indiana State U
Wilt Chamberlain, Kansas, U of
Bob Cousey, Holy Cross, C of the (MA)
John Elway, Stanford U (CA)
Bob Gibson, Creighton U (NE)
Greg Gumbel, Loras C (IA)
Magic Johnson, Michigan State U
Michael Jordan, North Carolina, U of, Chapel Hill
Nancy Kerrigan, Emmanuel C (MA)
Sandy Koufax, Cincinnati, U of (OH)
Steve Largent, Tulsa, U of (OK)
Vince Lombardi, Fordham U (NY)
Nancy Lopez, Tulsa, U of (OK)
John Madden, California Polytechnic State U, San Luis Obispo
Dan Marino, Pittsburgh, U of (PA)
Joe Montana, Notre Dame, U of (IN)
Jack Nicklaus, Ohio State U, Columbus
Arnold Palmer, Wake Forest U (NC)
Dan Patrick, Dayton, U of (OH)
Walter Payton, Jackson State U (MS)
Jackie Robinson, California, U of, Los Angeles
Bill Russell, San Francisco, U of (CA)
Don Shula, John Carroll U (OH)
Dave Winfield, Minnesota, U of, Twin Cities
Carl Yastrzemski, Merrimack C (MA)

Alma Maters of Politicians and Lawyers

Corazon Aquino, Mt. St. Vincent, C of (NY)
Chester A. Arthur, Union C (NY)
Hugo Black, Alabama, U of
Bill Clinton, Georgetown U (DC)
Hillary Clinton, Wellesley C (MA)
Calvin Coolidge, Amherst C (MA)
Clarence Darrow, Allegheny C (PA)

Alma Maters of Politicians and Lawyers (continued)

David Dinkins, Howard U (DC)
Napoleon Duarte, Notre Dame, U of (IN)
James Garfield, Hiram C (OH)
Alexander Hamilton, Columbia U (NY)
Herbert Hoover, Stanford U (CA)
Jesse Jackson, North Carolina A&T State U
Thomas Jefferson, William and Mary, C of (VA)
Jack Kemp, Occidental C (CA)
John F. Kennedy, Jr., Brown U (RI)
Thurgood Marshall, Howard U (DC)
Daniel Patrick Moynihan, Tufts U (MA)
Richard Nixon, Whittier C (CA)
Sam Nunn, Emory U (GA)
James K. Polk, North Carolina, U of
Dan Quayle, DePauw U (IN)
Louis Sullivan, Morehouse C (GA)
Clarence Thomas, Holy Cross, C of the (MA)
Byron "Whizzer" White, Colorado, U of, Boulder

Alma Maters of Television Personalities

Willow Bay, Pennsylvania, U of
Steven Bochco, Carnegie Mellon U (PA)
Tom Brokaw, South Dakota, U of
Montgomery Burns, Yale U (CT)
Johnny Carson, Nebraska, U of
Katie Couric, Virginia, U of
Phil Donahue, Notre Dame, U of (IN)
Al Franken, Harvard U (MA)
Kathie Lee Gifford, Oral Roberts U (OK)
Bryant Gumbel, Bates C (ME)
Arsenio Hall, Kent State U (OH)
Lisa Kudrow, Vassar C (NY)
Ricki Lake, Ithaca C (NY)
Jay Leno, Emerson C (MA)
David Letterman, Ball State U (IN)
Rue McClanahan, Tulsa, U of (OK)
Ed McMahon, Catholic U (DC)

Bill Moyers, North Texas, U of
Bob Newhart, Loyola C (IL)
Deborah Norville, Georgia, U of
Conan O'Brien, Harvard U (MA)
Jane Pauley, Indiana U
Regis Philbin, Notre Dame, U of (IN)
Stone Phillips, Yale U (CT)
Joan Rivers, Barnard C (NY)
Fred Rogers (Mr. Rogers), Rollins C (FL)
Tim Russert, John Carroll U (OH)
Diane Sawyer, Wellesley C (MA)
David Schwimmer, Northwestern U (IL)
Willard Scott, American U (DC)
Jerry Seinfeld, New York, City U of, Queens C
Harry Smith, Central C (IA)
Jerry Springer, Tulane U (LA)
Jon Stewart, William and Mary, C of (VA)
Alex Trebek, Ottawa, U of (Canada)
Chris Wallace, Harvard U (MA)
Mike Wallace, Michigan, U of, Ann Arbor
Paula Zahn, Stephens C (MO)

Alma Maters of Writers and Journalists

Dave Barry, author, Haverford C (PA)
Peg Bracken, author, Antioch C (OH)
Helen Gurley Brown, publisher, Woodbury U (CA)
Leo Buscaglia, author, Southern California, U of
Jim Carroll, author, Wagner C (NY)
Julia Child, author, Smith C (MA)
Tom Clancy, author, Loyola U (MD)
Ann Compton, journalist, Hollins C (VA)
Annie Dillard, author, Hollins C (VA)
Roger Ebert, film critic, Illinois, U of, Urbana
John Gardner, author, Washington U (MO)
Theodore Geisel (Dr. Seuss), author, Dartmouth C (NH)
Nikki Giovanni, poet, Fisk U (TN)
John Grisham, author, Mississippi State U
Nathaniel Hawthorne, author, Bowdoin C (ME)

Alma Maters of Writers and Journalists (continued)

S. E. Hinton, author, Tulsa, U of (OK)
John Irving, author, New Hampshire, U of
Erica Jong, author, Barnard C (NY)
Garrison Keillor, author, Minnesota, U of, Twin Cities
Stephen King, author, Maine, U of, Orono
Henry Wadsworth Longfellow, poet, Bowdoin C (ME)
Janet Maslin, journalist, Rochester, U of (NY)
James Michener, author, Swarthmore C (PA)
P. J. O'Rourke, journalist, Miami U (OH)
Liz Phair, author, Oberlin C (OH)
Cokie Roberts, journalist, Wellesley C (MA)
Betty Rollin, author, Sarah Lawrence U (NY)
Lawrence Sanders, author, Wabash C (IN)
Matt Stone, author, Colorado, U of
Arthur O. Sulzberger, Jr., journalist, Tufts U (MA)
Alice Walker, author, Sarah Lawrence C (NY)
Robert Penn Warren, author, Vanderbilt U (TN)
Linda Wertheimer, journalist, Wellesley C (MA)
George Will, author, Trinity C (CT)
Tennessee Williams, author, Washington U (MO)
Tom Wolfe, author, Washington and Lee U (VA)

Alma Maters of Other Well-Known Individuals

Barbara Bush, first lady, Smith C (MA)
Johnnetta Cole, educator, Oberlin C (OH)
Peter Coors, businessman, Denver, U of (CO)
John Dewey, educator, Vermont, U of
Michael Eisner, businessman, Denison U (OH)
Joycelyn Elders, surgeon general, Philander Smith C (AR)
Milton Friedman, economist, Rutgers U (NJ)
Alan Greenspan, economist, New York U
Hugh Hefner, *Playboy* founder, Illinois, U of
E. Howard Hunt, Watergate coconspirator, Brown U (RI)
Lee Iacocca, businessman, Lehigh U (PA)
Robert Jarvik, scientist, Syracuse U (NY)

Steve Jobs, Apple Computer, Reed C (OR)
Vernon Jordan, civil rights activist, DePauw U (IN)
Brian "Kato" Kaelin, O. J. Simpson residence caretaker, Wisconsin, U of, Eau Claire
Martin Luther King, Jr., civil rights activist, Morehouse C (GA)
Calvin Klein, clothier and businessman, Fashion Institute of Technology (NY)
Eugene Lang, philanthropist, Swarthmore C (PA)
Murray Lender, bagels, Quinnipiac C (CT)
Monica Lewinsky, Clinton scandal, Lewis and Clark C (OR)
Rush Limbaugh, Southeast Missouri State U
Lyle Menendez, Princeton U (NJ)
Michael Milken, junk bond king, Pennsylvania, U of
Jacqueline Kennedy Onassis, editor, George Washington U (DC)
I. M. Pei, architect, Massachusetts Institute of Technology
Carl Sagan, astronomer, Chicago, U of (IL)
Phyllis Schlafly, conservative activist, Washington U (MO)
B. F. Skinner, psychologist, Hamilton C (NY)
Howard Stern, radio personality, Boston U (MA)
Donald Trump, businessman, Pennsylvania, U of

Myths about Colleges

These represent *untrue* perceptions about the colleges named.

American U (DC): only for political science/international affairs majors
Brandeis U (MA): only for Jewish students
Carnegie Mellon U (PA): just for scientists
Case Western Reserve U (OH): associated with the military
Colgate U (NY): only for jocks
Colorado, U of: everyone skis
Chicago, U of (IL): little social life
Dallas, U of (TX): a public, nonreligious school
George Washington U (DC): only for political science/international affairs majors
Georgia Institute of Technology: a private school
Johns Hopkins U (MD): little social life/all premeds
Kansas, U of: flat and physically unappealing campus

Myths about Colleges (continued)

Oklahoma City U: a public, nonreligious school
Pepperdine U (CA): unbelievably religious
Rice U (TX): only for science/engineering students
Rutgers U (NJ): a private university
Skidmore C (NY): primarily for artists
Southern California, U of: in the middle of South Central or Watts section of Los Angeles
Stanford U (CA): all the students are from California
Trenton State C (NJ): in downtown Trenton
Vassar C (NY): a women's school
Virginia Polytechnic Institute and State U: "just" an engineering school
Washington U (MO): in Washington state

The Best New Student Orientation Programs

Adelphi U (NY)
Arizona State U
Arizona, U of
Babson C (MA)
Bard C (NY)
Beloit C (WI)
Bethany C (WV)
Brandeis U (MA)
Colby C (ME)
Colgate U (NY)
Cornell U (NY)
Dartmouth C (NH)
Davidson C (NC)
Dayton, U of (OH)
DePauw U (IN)
Earlham C (IN)
Eckerd C (FL) (a three-week orientation; students take one class)
Elmira C (NY)
Emory U (GA)
Franklin and Marshall C (PA)
Georgetown U (DC)
Green Mountain C (VT)
Hartwick C (NY) (Awakening, an Outward Bound–type orientation program)
Hiram C (OH) (freshman institute)
Iowa State U
James Madison U (VA)
Kalamazoo C (MI)
Louisville, U of (KY)
Middlebury C (VT)
Millsaps C (MS) (Perspectives is a semester-long orientation with weekly discussion groups)
Mt. St. Mary's C (MD)
North Carolina, U of, Wilmington
Otterbein C (OH)
Pacific, U of the (CA)
Pennsylvania, U of

Pratt Institute (NY)
Prescott C (AZ) (three-week wilderness orientation)
Princeton U (NJ)
Puget Sound, U of (WA) (Preludes and Passages combines on-campus activities with a hiking experience)
South Carolina, U of, Columbia (orientation is a semester-long course called University 101)
Susquehanna U (PA)
Villanova C (PA) (a four-day comprehensive orientation program)
Wesleyan U (CT)
Xavier U (OH)

The Students' View: Most Important Issues Facing the Country

1. AIDS
2. Crime
3. Drugs
4. Quality of education
5. Cost of health care
6. Moral values
7. Race relations
8. Budget deficit
9. Damage to the environment
10. Poverty

Source: College Track™. Based on March 1996 survey of undergraduates at Creighton U (NE).

The Students' Choice: Leading Spring Break Destinations

Breckenridge, CO
Cabo San Lucas, Mexico
Cancun, Mexico
Daytona Beach, FL
Fort Lauderdale, FL
Jamaica
Lake Havasu, AZ
Las Vegas, NV
Mazatlan, Mexico
Rocky Point, Mexico
South Padre Island, TX

Options for Students Who Want to Wait Before Entering College

Not all students go directly from high school to college. Some plan for, and benefit from, unique and interesting experiences. Below, David Denman, an educational consultant, provides a sampling of these precollege opportunities.

EXTRAORDINARY STUDY/TRAVEL

Audubon Expedition Institute, Belfast, ME: semester and yearlong environmentally oriented bus/camping trips throughout the United States

International Honors Program of Bard C, Boston, MA: worldwide semester or academic year-long environmental study tour with college credit

Study Travel Program of Eastern Michigan U: semester-long European or Asian cultural history tour

Up With People, Tucson, AZ: a year-long "road show" with community service as an integral part of the program at every stop

INTERNSHIPS

Dynamy, Worcester, MA: semester and year-long urban internships, apartment living, and community involvement

National Society for Internships and Experiential Education, Raleigh, NC: offers many internship opportunities

OUTDOOR/WILDERNESS PROGRAMS

Colorado Mountain C: "Outdoor Semester in the Rockies" for college credit

National Outdoor Leadership School, Lander, WY: semester-long outdoor courses in the United States, Mexico, Kenya, India, and Argentina

Yamnuska, Alberta, Canada: semester and semisemester programs in mountaineering skills and leadership

UNCONVENTIONAL STUDY PROGRAMS (SOME OFFER COLLEGE CREDIT)

Aegean Center for the Fine Arts, Paros, Cyclades, Greece: twelve-week mentored studio sessions in English and eight-week fall program in Italy

Alliance Française: a foreign language school with centers in major cities internationally

Goethe Institute: a foreign language school with centers in major cities internationally

Hallmark Institute of Photography, Turners Falls, MA: ten-month program covering the artistic, technical, and business aspects of photography

Instituto Allende, San Miguel de Allende, Guanajuato, Mexico: an international school of the arts and crafts, offering intensive Spanish in the "Montmartre" of Mexico

Ithaka, Chania, Crete, Greece: semester-long cultural immersion and study program

La Sabranenque, St. Victor Lacoste, France: indigenous semester-long French language and cultural immersion program in a historic French village

Marchutz School, Aix-en-Provence, France: small group summer and semester-long painting classes in Cézanne country for college credit

Penland Art School, Penland, NC: offers a broad range of studio courses; also available are two-month "concentration" sessions and a two-year professional studio program

School for Field Study, Beverly, MA: short- and semester-length opportunities available worldwide

Sea Education Association, Woods Hole, MA: semester-length programs combine marine study on land and at sea

Sierra Institute, Santa Cruz, CA: academic quarter-length environmental field courses

STUDENT EXCHANGE PROGRAMS

AFS Intercultural Programs, New York, NY: semester- and year-long homestay and school opportunities

Youth for Understanding, Washington, DC: international exchange offering semester- and year-long homestay and school opportunities

Options for Students Who Want to Wait Before Entering College (continued)

VOLUNTEER/SOCIAL SERVICE

American Hiking Society, Washington, DC: offers internships on America's public lands
City Year, Boston, MA: a privately funded VISTA-type program
Community Service Volunteers, London, England: this national charitable organization places young people in full-time voluntary service positions
International Christian Youth Exchange, New York, NY: community service and high school homestay opportunities in Europe and Africa
Kibbutz Aliya Desk, New York, NY: a conduit for extended volunteer opportunities in Israel
Raleigh International, London, England: physically challenging humanitarian and conservation expeditions worldwide
VISTA, Washington, DC: the domestic, urban Peace Corps
Youth Conservation Association, Charlestown, NH: twelve-week outdoor conservation work in national and state parks
Youth Service International, Raleigh, NC: provides conservation and humanitarian aid projects in adventurous settings abroad and in Alaska

POSTGRADUATE ACADEMIC PROGRAMS

American and international boarding schools: approximately half the major American boarding schools, and some schools abroad, admit students for a thirteenth year
Bridgton Academy, North Bridgton, ME: exclusively a postgraduate boarding school
Oxford Advanced Studies Program, England: programs provide the equivalent of the first year of college work in America

WORK ABROAD

Alliances Abroad, San Francisco, CA: opportunities to work abroad—in resorts, as a language tutor, or as an au pair
Au Pair/Homestay Abroad, Washington, DC: language and cultural immersion as a working member of a European family
YMCA International Camp Counselor Program, New York, NY: camp counselor positions internationally

Source: David Denman, specialist in enrichment opportunities for teens, TIME OUT, Sausalito, CA.

RESOURCES FOR COLLEGE PLANNING

The Application Process

Antonoff, Steven R., and Marie A. Friedemann. *College Match: A Blueprint for Choosing the Best School for You!* Alexandria, Virginia: Octameron Associates, Inc. Published every two years.

Berger, Sandra L. *College Planning for Gifted Students.* Reston, Virginia: ERIC/Council for Exceptional Children, 1998.

The Best College for You. New York: Time and The Princeton Review. Published annually.

Davidson, Wilma, and Susan McCloskey. *Writing a Winning College Application Essay.* Princeton, New Jersey: Peterson's Guides, 1996.

Fiske, Edward B. *The Fiske Guide to Getting into the Right College.* New York: Times Books/Random House, 1997.

Greene, Howard, and Robert Minton. *Scaling the Ivy Wall in the '90s.* Boston, Massachusetts: Little, Brown, and Company, 1994.

Hayden, Thomas C. *Handbook for College Admissions.* Princeton, New Jersey: Peterson's Guides. Published every few years.

How to Get into College. New York: Newsweek and Kaplan. Published annually.

McGinty, Sarah Myers. *Writing Your College Application Essay.* New York: College Board Publications, 1991.

Pope, Loren. *Colleges That Change Lives.* New York: Penguin Books, 1996.

Pope, Loren. *Looking Beyond the Ivy League.* New York: Penguin Books, 1995.

Spencer, Janet, and Sandra Maleson. *The Complete Guide to College Visits.* New York: Princeton Review Publishing, 1997.

Wall, Edward B. *Behind the Scenes: An Inside Look at the Selective College Admission Process.* Alexandria, Virginia: Octameron Associates. Published every two years.

College Costs

Barron's Best Buys in College Education. Hauppauge, New York: Barron's Educational Series, Inc. Published every few years.

Cassidy, Daniel. *The Scholarship Book.* Englewood Cliffs, New Jersey: Prentice Hall. Published every few years.

The College Cost Book. New York: College Board Publications. Published annually.

Keeslar, Oreon, and Judy Kesslar Santamaria. *Financial Aids for Higher Education.* Dubuque, Iowa: Brown and Benchmark Publishers. Published every few years.

Leider, Robert, and Anna Leider. *Don't Miss Out: The Ambitious Student's Guide to Scholarships and Loans.* Alexandria, Virginia; Octameron Associates. Published annually.

Renz, Loren, ed. *Foundation Grants to Individuals.* New York: The Foundation Center. Published every few years.

Schimke, Ann. *The A's and B's of Academic Scholarships.* Alexandria, Virginia: Octameron Associates. Published annually.

Scholarships. New York: Kaplan Educational Centers/Simon and Schuster. Published annually.

Schwartz, John. *College Scholarships and Financial Aid.* New York: Arco/Macmillan, 1997.

Sullivan, Robert. *Ivy League Programs at State School Prices.* New York: Arco/ Macmillan, 1994.

Vuturo, Chris. *The Scholarship Advisor.* New York: Princeton Review Publishing. Published annually.

Graduate School Guidebooks

Association of American Medical Colleges. *Medical School Admission Requirements.* Washington, DC. Published annually.

The College Board. *Index of Majors and Graduate Degrees.* New York: College Entrance Examination Board. Published annually.

Doughty, Harold R. *Guide to American Graduate Schools.* New York: Penguin Books. Published every few years.

Graduate & Professional Programs: An Overview. Princeton, New Jersey: Peterson's Guides. Published annually. (Note: Peterson's Guides also publishes specific guidebooks to graduate schools in most academic/professional fields.)

Law School Admission Council. *The Official Guide to U.S. Law Schools.* New York: Broadway Books. Published annually.

Guidebooks

America's Best Colleges. Washington, DC.: *U.S. News & World Report.* Published annually.

Barron's Profiles of American Colleges. Hauppauge, New York: Barron's Educational Series, Inc. Published annually.

Boehm, Klaus, and Jenny Lee-Spalding. *The Student Book.* London: Macmillan Press. Published annually. (Note: This is a guidebook about UK colleges.)

Bowman, J. Wilson. *America's Black and Tribal Colleges.* South Pasadena, California: Sandcastle Publishing, 1992.

Cass-Liepmann, Julia, ed. *Cass and Birnbaum's Guide to American Colleges.* New York: HarperCollins. Published annually.

Cernea, Ruth. *Hillel Guide to Jewish Life on Campus.* New York: Princeton Review Publishing. Published annually.

Choose a Christian College. Princeton: Peterson's Guides. Published every few years.

The College Board. *The College Handbook.* New York: College Entrance Examination Board. Published annually.

The College Board. *Index of Majors and Graduate Degrees.* New York: College Entrance Examination Board. Published annually.

Custard, Edward. *The Best Colleges.* New York: Princeton Review Publishing. Published annually.

Custard, Edward, ed. *The Complete Book of Colleges.* New York: Princeton Review Publishing. Published annually.

Fiske, Edward B. *The Fiske Guide to Colleges.* New York: Times Books/Random House. Published annually.

Four-Year Colleges. Princeton, New Jersey: Peterson's Guides. Published annually.

Killpatrick, Frances, and James Killpatrick. *The Winning Edge: The Student-Athlete's Guide to College Sports.* Alexandria, Virginia: Octameron Press. Published every two years.

Mitchell, Robert. *The Multicultural Student's Guide to Colleges.* New York: Noonday Press, 1996.

National Directory of College Athletics (Men's Edition). Cleveland, Ohio: Collegiate Directories, Inc. Published annually.

National Directory of College Athletics (Women's Edition). Cleveland, Ohio: Collegiate Directories, Inc. Published annually.

Paul, Kevin. *The Complete Guide to Canadian Universities.* North Vancouver, British Columbia: Self-Counsel Reference Series. Published every few years.

Stedman, Caitlin, and Ruth Stultz, eds. *College Admissions Data Handbook.* Itasca, Illinois: Riverside/Wintergreen-Orchard House. Published annually.

Straughn, Charles T., II, and Barbarasue Lovejoy Straughn, eds. *Lovejoy's College Guide.* New York: Macmillan. Published every few years.

Sykes, Charles, and Brad Miner, eds. *The National Review College Guide.* New York: Fireside/Simon and Schuster, 1993.

Weinstein, Miriam, ed. *Making a Difference College Guide.* New York: Princeton Review Publishers, 1997.

The Yale Daily News Staff. *The Insider's Guide to the Colleges.* New York: St. Martin's Press. Published annually.

Learning Disabilities

Kravets, Marybeth, and Imy F. Wax. *The K&W Guide to Colleges for the Learning Disabled.* New York: Princeton Review Publishing, 1997.

Lipkin, Midge. *Colleges with Programs or Services for Students with Learning Disabilities.* Belmont, Massachusetts: Schoolsearch, 1993.

Mangrum, C. T., and Stephen Strichart, eds. *Colleges with*

Programs for Students with Learning Disabilities. Princeton, New Jersey: Peterson's Guides, 1997.

Straughn, Charles T. *College Guide for the Learning Disabled.* New York: Macmillan/Lovejoy's Guides. Published every few years.

Majors and Programs

Charles, Jill, ed. *Directory of Theatre Training Programs.* Dorset, Vermont: American Theatre Works. Published every few years.

Dow Jones Newspaper Fund. *The Journalist's Road to Success.* Princeton, New Jersey: Dow Jones Newspaper Fund, 1996.

Everett, Carole J. *The Performing Arts Major's College Guide.* New York: Macmillan, 1994.

Fenza, D. W., and Beth Jarock, eds. *The Associated Writing Program's Official Guide to Writing Programs.* Paradise, California: Dustbooks. Published every few years.

Horrigan, William, ed. *The American Film Institute Guide to College Courses in Film and Television.* New York: Prentice Hall, 1990.

Kelly, Karin, and Tom Edgar. *Film Schools Confidential: The Insider's Guide to Film Schools.* Berkeley, California: Berkeley, 1997.

Pintoff, Ernest. *Complete Guide to American Film Schools.* New York: Penguin Books, 1994.

Rugg, Frederick E. *Rugg's Recommendations on the Colleges.* Haydenville, Massachusetts: Rugg's Recommendations. Published annually.

Parents' Guidebooks

Boyer, Ernest L., and Paul Boyer. *Smart Parents Guide to College.* Princeton, New Jersey: Peterson's Guides, 1996.

Coburn, Karen Levin, and Madge Lawrence Treeger. *Letting Go: A Parent's Guide to Today's College Experience.* Bethesda, Maryland: Adler and Adler, 1992.

Pasick, Patricia. *Almost Grown: Launching Your Child from High School to College.* New York City: W. W. Norton, 1998.
Shields, Charles J. *The College Guide for Parents.* New York: College Board Publications, 1995.

SUBJECT INDEX

COLLEGE INDEX

© Mark Guenther

ABOUT THE AUTHOR

STEVEN R. ANTONOFF, Ph.D., is a nationally recognized educational consultant. For over twenty-five years, he has been a part of the world of education. Antonoff Associates, Inc., was founded in 1981 and serves the needs of students and families seeking counseling in finding appropriate undergraduate and graduate colleges, boarding schools, therapeutic and speical needs programs, and other schooling and transitional options. Dr. Antonoff has worked with over 2,500 students in educational planning and has visited hundreds of schools and colleges. Earlier in his career, Antonoff spent eleven years in college administration, serving as dean of admissions and financial aid, executive director of admissions and student affairs, and dean of students at the University of Denver. He holds a Ph.D. in human communication studies from the University of Denver, an M.A. in education from the University of Denver, and a B.S. in psychology from Colorado State University.

Dr. Antonoff chairs the Commission on Credentialing of the American Institute of Certified Educational Planners. The Institute is authorized to grant professional certificates to qualified educational consultants nationwide. He has served as president of the Independent Educational Consultant Association (the largest organization of professional educational consultants). In the same organization he has served on the board of directors, and as chairperson of the college relations committee. Other professional involvements include: National Association for College Admission Counseling, American Association for Counseling and Development, and the Secondary School Admission Testing Board.

He is also the coauthor of *College Match: A Blueprint for Choosing the Best School for You.*